T0369475

A Line Out the Door

Strategies and Lessons to Maximize Sales, Profits, and Customer Service

RICHARD L. GORDON

iUniverse, Inc.
Bloomington

A Line Out the Door
Strategies and Lessons to Maximize Sales, Profits, and
Customer Service

Copyright © 2010 by Richard L. Gordon

All rights reserved. No part of this book may be used or reproduced by any means, graphic, electronic, or mechanical, including photocopying, recording, taping or by any information storage retrieval system without the written permission of the publisher except in the case of brief quotations embodied in critical articles and reviews.

iUniverse books may be ordered through booksellers or by contacting:

iUniverse
1663 Liberty Drive
Bloomington, IN 47403
www.iuniverse.com
1-800-Authors (1-800-288-4677)

Because of the dynamic nature of the Internet, any Web addresses or links contained in this book may have changed since publication and may no longer be valid. The views expressed in this work are solely those of the author and do not necessarily reflect the views of the publisher, and the publisher hereby disclaims any responsibility for them.

ISBN: 978-1-4502-7006-9 (sc)
ISBN: 978-1-4502-7008-3 (ebook)
ISBN: 978-1-4502-7007-6 (dj)

Library of Congress Control Number: 2010916850

Printed in the United States of America

iUniverse rev. date: 12/30/2010

Acknowledgments

My deep appreciation and love go to my wife Ellen, who encouraged me and believed in this project. Thanks are extended to my daughter Lindsey and son Weston for their love, and interest in this book. My love and fondest regards go out to my mom and dad who both recently passed away. They were always interested and supportive of my business, even though they thought I was crazy for going into business. A salute goes out to my father in-law who told me he'd only read the book if it was published. His comments truly motivated me and I'm looking forward to seeing that he puts on his reading glasses. My gratitude to the Glazer-Kennedy Insider's Circle group in St. Louis for their knowledge, collective support and encouragement. Credit and thanks must also go to Mary Baker and Amanda Lansche for their invaluable contributions to this book. Last but not least, I'd like to express my appreciation to my old Basset Hound, "Franklin," who slept at my feet on most days as I wrote this book.

Table of Contents

IV Service Beyond Mediocrity

V Marketing Beyond Mediocrity

VI The People in Your Business

Rich would be delighted to speak at your next meeting, convention or conference. For more information on consultations or events, you can contact Rich at Retail Redefined, 636-928-2336 or richlgordon@ retailrichez.com , or visit his website at retailrichez.com.

Why This Book?

I consider myself an experienced small business person, having worked in many different areas over the course of my career. Considering my experience and my observations of others over the years, I have insights from many different perspectives that the average entrepreneur may never come to know. While my education did not come entirely from the classroom, I have experienced and benefited from the Fortune 500 world. I have also risked it all, as many of you have, as a small business owner starting with only a handful of employees. Certainly my being out there in the trenches and making a small business work and survive, coupled with my corporate background, has given me an education that no academic institution could ever provide.

There are strengths and weaknesses in corporate America, the academic world, and the world of small business ownership. For instance, my experience has been that the large majority of folks in the corporate world do not have the imagination, chutzpa, street smarts, and loyalty to their people that is found in America's small businesses. They are often focused on protecting their own hides at the expense of their people. I have watched small entrepreneurs who never worked in or benefited from the expertise one can gain in the corporate world try to move their business ahead without the corporate world's acumen and standard practices that could have made their labors so much more effective and straightforward. I've often thought, "If only they had the awareness of the many viewpoints, policies and practices that are taken for granted in the corporate world, they would benefit greatly."

The academic world also cannot possibly replace the real world of experience and skills that take time to develop—especially people skills, which are critical. Many of the academics out there, who are telling new minds how to operate a business, have not spent one day in the real world, dealing with real business problems and creating REAL profits. And in corporate America, many of these same theories and philosophies coupled with a lack of ethics have cluttered the minds of many of today's managers, unfortunately to the detriment of their employees and stockholders.

I love small business and especially the retail specialty store business. Small business owners work very hard, just like their Fortune 500 counterparts do; however, small business owners lay it all on the line everyday and literally put their money where their mouth is. They don't go nuts when their paycheck is not available to cash "on the button" on Friday afternoons, and they quite often pay others first, only hoping there will be enough to pay themselves. Many of them have succeeded as a result of very hard work, street savvy, intelligence, common sense and love for what they do. Some fail due to poor planning or perhaps one bad decision. Many of them succeed amazingly in spite of themselves. I have watched someone I considered an absolutely brilliant marketing and sales person size up the market and see years ahead of his time, and at the same time, watched him recklessly spend money like a drunken sailor.

Though I've made my share of mistakes, I have worked very hard, just like millions of other small business owners do every single day. More than anything else, I've learned my lessons. And as I strive every day to put my solutions into practice, I still look back and wish I had been this informed years ago.

Throughout my career, I have worked with professionals in sales and retail management at the store level and at the corporate level. I have worked with what I consider to be one of the best loss prevention experts in the country and have worked within the walls of one of the best human resource organizations in the country. I have sold computers, computer supplies, monitors, custom homes, pre-owned homes, health insurance, life insurance, Medicare supplements, PEO services, mortgage loans, barter memberships, paintings, spas, portable buildings, gourmet popcorn, chocolates, ice cream, piranhas, parrots and hamsters. I have worked in management for a major mass merchandiser, starting from a department manager to making presentations to senior management of a billion dollar plus corporation on a monthly basis. I have managed loss prevention teams over a corporate office and two 500,000 sq. ft. distribution centers. I have sold to and called on such names as Macy's, Wal-Mart, May Company, McDonnell Douglas, Southwestern Bell and an array of other retail dealers and shop owners. I helped introduce the Macintosh and Apple IIC computers to the world. I have started and built my own small specialty retail and wholesale business taking it from five employees up to about 63 employees. I've obtained a small business loan from the Small Business Administration. I have sold to many of the areas largest corporations and leading citizens, and won sales contests selling insurance, and yet I gave up and sold off my own business when I grew tired of the fight with the banks for a line of credit (one of my mistakes).

This book is not an academic study or a manual of formulas, projections or even expensive ideas or concepts. This book represents an important part of what I learned by doing, observing, experiencing, listening, succeeding and, yes, failing. Its purpose is to enlighten, inspire, educate, confirm, remind and provoke thought in a straight, to-the-point manner regarding topics that are important and sometimes critical to starting and building a business. Many entrepreneurs are detailed and deliberate people, but the majority have little or no patience for long, drawn-out, self-serving explanations of minute information that someone else thinks is important for them to know. This book is meant to be a quick reference and a thought provoking guide to implement some critical strategies to take your sales to the next level. It is about real, solid, tested strategies and ideas in specific, short and easy-to-read chapters that will make a real difference in your store(s). I believe it will benefit anyone who reads it in some way. I hope you'll take your passion and imagination and follow through and research an area further to educate yourself in more detail once you find a good idea or are exposed to an intriguing concept.

What I've found from writing and assembling this book is that even things we all "know we know" need to be reviewed and run through the brain from time to time. Do I have all of the answers? No. But I CAN give you some very solid advice to increase your profits and greatly improve your odds of success in the retail business world. If you get only one good idea or money saving concept out of this book, then it will be a worthwhile endeavor. But, I'm confident you will find many more ideas than that.

Last but not least, this book is about opening up your mind to things that you may have never given enough thought or attention. Since there are too many important issues to address in one book, I have zeroed in on the areas I think have the power to elevate and give you a much improved shot at "A Line Out the Door."

About the Author . . .

Rich Gordon is a consultant and former retailer who not only understands retail, but also welcomes its challenges and creative opportunities. He is a respected, successful and creative manager with close to 40 years of sales, and retail management experience and over 24 years of direct retail experience. His experiences have taken him through a variety of retail management, merchandising, design, training and buying roles working in the Fortune 500 world, consulting with retail stores and the creation and building of his own retail business.

He truly has been in the trenches and worked with everyone from small business owners, friends, relatives, and students to senior corporate management, through times of great pride, tears, fears, panic and yes, a great deal of fun and personal satisfaction.

In 1974, Gordon left the University of Missouri to accept an entry-level management position with Venture Stores, a former division of May Company (St. Louis, MO). At the age of 21, he was chosen to start an experimental department for the major mid-west mass merchandiser. After success at the first experimental store, his department was expanded into other stores, where his departments soon became the leader in the local market. Gordon also served in management at the store level and later at the corporate office. While at the corporate office, Gordon made regular presentations to the executive committee of the company where he presented his research on profit challenged departments and made recommendations for corrective action.

After almost 10 years with Venture Stores, Gordon found himself accepting a very attractive offer to leave Venture and work for one of the original Apple computer rep organizations who served as Apple's marketing and sales arm during the company's early years. In his four plus-state territory, Gordon was available to all of the Apple retailers to improve merchandising and other retail issues including advertising, co-op money, training and store design. While serving in this capacity, Gordon helped introduce the original Macintosh and Apple 2C computers to dealers.

Gordon also started his own specialty store operation, retailing and manufacturing gourmet popcorn, along with fine candies and high-quality ice cream. His stores became the dominant retailer in his market, and catered to major area corporations including McDonnell Douglas, Southwestern Bell, Tubular Steel, Turley Martin, the Fox Theatre, Schnucks, Dierbergs, and many others. His products became a popular gift item for area celebrities and business owners.

The rest of Gordon's career became devoted to sales, consulting, painting and photography; however, his heart remains in the world of retailing and marketing. Gordon lives in the St. Louis, Missouri area, and has been married for over 25 years to his wife Ellen. He has two children, Lindsey who is a Nuclear Pharmacist and Weston who is a student at St. Louis University.

Introduction

A Store With "A Line Out The Door"

It's every retailer's dream, a store with so many customers they are literally lined out the door waiting to get in. One event comes to mind as a result of my relentless pursuit to build a serious retail business and a recognizable name. It came one day after my Christmas season was over and I'll probably never forget it.

I had met the buyer for Famous Barr (one of May Company's department store divisions based in St. Louis). I had spent almost two hours with the buyer of the gourmet foods department. This department also had produced their own chocolates at the main store in downtown St. Louis for decades. They were very popular with customers, but sales in this area, as well as the rest of the gourmet foods area, had been trailing downward for years. I had considered the appointment a success because the buyer had been positive and he had, after all, spent a considerable amount of time with me, even if he did spend most of that time talking about himself. He was a young guy and a bit arrogant, but he was nice to me so I was happy. After the appointment when I called to follow up, he would never return my calls and I never seemed to be able to get through. Three months of trying brought me no results, and I subsequently became preoccupied with preparations for my all-important Christmas holiday sales. Like most retailers, Christmas was my "make-it or break-it" season.

After getting through the Christmas season, I had a little room to breathe, and I needed to relax. I was stressed out from loading trailers out of the back of my main store. This was in addition to shipping out 200-300 cartons a day via U.P.S. and handling my own store's very heavy walk-in traffic. One walk-in customer might come in and order anywhere from one (1) tin to 100 tins. Some of them ordered in advance and some expected to walk out with large orders without notice. We tried to take care of them all. One morning as I was taking a breath and beginning to relax I received a call. It was the buyer from Famous Barr that had never, returned or taken my calls. What did he want all of a sudden?

The conversation started out like I was his best buddy. "How was your Christmas season?" he asked. After the niceties, I cut to the chase. "What can I do for you?" He got serious. "Have you ever heard of the name "Richard Battram"? he asked. I said, "Sure, he is the vice chairman of all of May Company." He pressed on, "Do you know him?" "No I don't know him. Why do you ask?" as I began to wonder what was going on. "Well," he said, "he knows who YOU are!" I responded, a bit in disbelief, "Well that's news to me! What's going on?" He pressed on further with the questions. "Is he a relative of yours?" he asked. "No", I said, "I've never even met the man. I only know who he is because I used to work for May Company." Now, I was starting to get a little irritated with the 3rd degree and no answers. "Well," he said, "I got a call from Mr. Battram this morning. He evidently at least knows who you are. Do you know how unusual it is for a buyer at Famous Barr to get a call from the Vice Chairman of May Company"? "Yes," I replied, "I can imagine." He went on, "Mr. Battram requested, correction, demanded that I get in touch with you and that we meet. Are you sure you don't know him?" he asked again. "No," I said, emphatically. He followed up without hesitation, "When can we get together?" I was excited, but tired. I was also sure if they wanted my gourmet popcorn tins, they wouldn't be wanting them until some holiday period. There was plenty of time and this conversation was sounding a bit flaky. I responded, "How about next week?" He came back without hesitation, "No, how about tomorrow?" Now I was really paying attention. I thought to myself, this guy is feeling some pressure. "OK," I said "tomorrow is fine." We made our arrangements and I hung up feeling a bit important, but guarded.

The next day when I showed up at the buying offices in Famous Barr, I was not only greeted enthusiastically by the buyer, but the buyer's merchandise manager, who also was there waiting for me. Just as I thought we were going to sit down, I was informed that we were going up to the executive offices to see a senior vice president of Famous Barr. Unfortunately, I can't remember any of their names any longer. They were all very nice, and we engaged in some casual conversation and then we got down to business, as I asked, "What can I do for you gentlemen?"

They went over the story again as to how Mr. Battram had wanted them to talk to me. He even suggested that they do some business with me. I was feeling better. More importantly for them, Mr. Battram had told them he wanted them to find out why Famous Barr's business was on such a downward trend and why my business was going like gangbusters. Mr. Battram, they explained, had driven by one or two of my stores over the weekend and had observed people lined outside of my store(s) waiting to get in. He also observed a regular parade of customers out of my store with purchases in hand and sometimes they had help from store employees. The three (3) Famous Barr executives began firing questions at me as fast as I could answer them and all three of them were taking notes on about everything that came out of my mouth. I was beginning to feel pretty important—like some sort of genius. I laughed to myself, "If I had still been with May Company, no one here would probably give a rip about what I thought!" All I could think of was, "I have arrived"!

Customers were really lined outside of my stores. I was running huge increases. Large companies were calling us for orders, and I actually had some respect from my peers in retailing. Not too bad! I went on to make some fairly bold comments about their products and their gourmet foods area. One of my observations was that they were selling a very mediocre brand of popcorn filled tins (the same brand found in Wal-Mart). However, they were retailing it at a ridiculously high margin. I pointed out to them that customers expected to find high quality products at Famous Barr and were usually willing to pay the higher price. In this case, they were selling an inferior product at a higher gourmet price. I further stated that surely they knew that customers might be fooled for a while, but in the scheme of things, the consumer knew what real value was about. As the conversation went on and observations were traded, for over an hour, I sensed they really did respect what I had to say.

The end result was that we did do business, after I warned them that I would need to be paid on time and that I was aware that May Company used their accounts payable as a profit center. I received a promise from the Senior V.P. that they would take care of me. The truth is, he kept his word, until the day I sold my business.

I drove back to my main store feeling pretty good about myself. I was proud, but in small business, good things can change fast. Upon arriving at the back door of my store, my ever-reliable right hand associate, Ann, shouts out to me, "Would you take a look at the toilet? It keeps running!" With a simple request, I was back down to reality with my own problems once again. However, at least I still had "A Line Out The Door," and people were taking notice.

 Traditional Retail Will Be Around,
But It's Changing And You Must Too!

1

I do understand. The world of retailing continues to evolve while the economy has further squeezed profit margins and created greater pressure than ever on lower prices. While customers haven't stopped spending, their habits have certainly changed. Customers are also becoming more discriminating and savvy about how they do spend their hard earned dollars. Many smart retailers have correctly built their businesses around quality, service, education and fashion, rather than price and yet, still the sales are frustrating.

To make matters worse, internet sales have grown at a stunning rate in the last decade. In fact estimates are that 154 million people bought something on line in 2009. If you plan on being a retailer, you also need to react and deal with online advertising, website traffic, and now, social media or social networking. Even though retail sales are still dominated by traditional brick and mortar stores, you should have no skepticism about the growing influence of the internet on traditional retail. It is a fact of life you can no longer ignore. However, it should be somewhat reassuring that it still only represents a relatively small portion of total retail sales activity. In fact, e-commerce sales represent a miniscule 6% of all retail sales.

The Internet & Traditional Retail
Only a few years back, even traditional retailers who were profitable didn't seem to be very interesting or even viable to some, when compared with their online brothers and sisters. The traditional brick and mortar stores were considered old fashioned and heavily tied down by the entire overhead typically associated with physical retail stores. Internet retailing has been the fresh newborn attraction with all of the possibilities and potential, while old, traditional retailing has been looked on at times like a troublesome stepchild.

But things are changing again. Old traditional brick and mortar retailers have not been written off; however, the stores where mom and grandma shopped have gone the way of saving stamps and elevator operators.

Today's traditional retailers are rapidly changing the way they have done almost everything, and I believe they will continue to be viable and popular with consumers for the foreseeable future. Why am I so convinced? Because, prophets of the demise of brick and mortar retailing lost sight of one thing, customers will always prefer holding, handling, smelling, touching and feeling what they are about to buy, to looking at it on a color screen. Nothing beats reality and having it now as opposed to waiting for delivery. It's as simple as realizing that we would all rather be with our friends in person than to see and talk to them on a computer monitor. Better yet, there are still successful retailers running impressive sales gains out there and some of them even have "A Line Out The Door." That's the good news.

There Is No Room for Mediocre.
The sobering truth now is that if you want to own and operate a traditional retail shop and you want to do more than just exist, you will need to step up your game. You will need to become more innovative, more aware of trends, more interesting and possibly even more entertaining, not to mention the obvious basics such as great merchandising, interesting and current product assortments and yes, excellent customer service. But I won't be talking in this book about the traditional lip service that is given to customer service by most retailers. I'm talking about sensational "over the top" customer service. No matter what you think about your customer service, read the chapters in the book dealing with customer service.

The fact is that shoppers have more exciting and attractive stores than ever to choose from while retail space has dramatically increased over the past couple of decades. While internet retailing will continue to grow, other retailers are evolving and giving birth to whole fun ideas and unique experiences. You too will need to be working in that direction. I can't emphasize enough that there is less and less room for just another run of the mill retailer as there are just too many good concepts and imaginative retailers out there running after too few dollars. It becomes brutally apparent when you look at the way larger retailers have merged or disappeared over the past years. Gone are May Department Stores, Montgomery Ward, S. S. Kresges, Woolworths, H. Q., Katz Drug Stores, T.G. & Y, Linens & Things and Circuit City. It is becoming harder and harder to operate as you always have and expect to survive, as former employees from these giants will tell you. These retailers went for decades without fundamentally changing, and now most all of them are gone. As retailing becomes more specialized and targeted in going after "their" specific customers, many other familiar names will also disappear.

Great Opportunities, But New Tactics

Nevertheless, there remain enormous opportunities for energized, innovative retailers to go after those specialized product niches that the big box retailers avoid. As an owner/operator, you will need to put increased emphasis on those areas that make you unique and special. If you become desperate like many, by adopting a price-driven strategy, you are buying a ticket to failure. Your approach must be less about price and large advertising expenses, and more about emphasizing what should be your greatest asset—your people and your stores relationship with its customers. You will also need to assess your competition, and then compare them with your own business's strengths and weaknesses.

Information

The world has been turned upside down now as the customer may be more informed than the seller, with instantly accessed prices and information out the whazooo (from their computers, blogs, and smart phones.) Going after "your" customers will mean identifying and knowing your customers while collecting information on customer buying habits in any number of ways. You will also need to use information and buyer preferences to appeal to a focused customer base that is more selective, savvy and sophisticated than ever before.

As a retailer, you can no longer make it your store's mission to go after a typical female shopper. There is no typical female shopper. This is a stereotypical memory from the past, and you can't market to stereotypes. Targeting and finding YOUR customer now means knowing much more about shoppers than whether they're male or female. A general broad appeal will no longer suffice. Knowing that you want a female shopper's business will most likely not be enough. You will need to meet very specific needs or tastes and truly stand for something special. You will also need to know your female shopper's age and whether or not she's a businesswoman. If you are truly going to know your customer, you will need to know if she's an ethnic minority, if she's into gourmet cooking, if she's a plus size, a running enthusiast, or a soccer mom. You will need to know if she's into decorating, antiques, scrap-booking, knitting or flower arranging too. It is more important than ever that you correctly learn her needs, and more importantly, her current wants.

ompetition is too strong, today's buyers are too selective and there are too many choices out there for a small specialty retailer to apply a broad brush when trying to catch their eye and appeal to them. Think about it: even an auto manufacturer can no longer market a car for a typical female buyer. Is she a soccer mom with an SUV or a "going green mother?" Is she a sports car buyer—upscale or on a budget? Your customers will shop you because you know and appeal to their tastes to a tee. You will need to know why they come to your store, and more importantly, how to get them back in. Stereotypes such as female shopping trips to the mall with the girls while hubby brings home the bacon, are no longer the norm.

Are You A Serious Retailer?
You may be saying to yourself at this point; "Wait, I've just got a little specialty shop here. I'm not trying to take over the marketplace." And if you just want to exist, bide your time, and possibly watch business erode over a period of years, maybe you don't need to hear all of this. But if you want to be taken seriously as a retailer that intends to be fully engaged in the marketplace and you want to build something, then I would definitely read on.

Good Ideas & A Sense of Urgency

Assuming you are a serious retailer and you are working to build a name and brand, not to mention increasing sales, you will need to have a sense of urgency as well. Considering how the market and the way we all communicate is changing at break neck speed, ideas, especially good ideas, travel around the world almost instantaneously thanks to satellites, the media, the internet and now smart phones.

Assuming you do manage to create and develop a great new concept, or prototype, you've got to get it together fast, as you have even less time than ever before to refine and perfect your idea before some other entrepreneur or large retailer with deep pockets comes along, copies the idea, develops it and rolls it out. Even if you don't create the latest "Build-A-Bear" or "Anthropologie," the need to experiment and change are becoming more important than ever to stay in business and ahead of the competition. You cannot become complacent! A significant percentage of those retailers who can't or won't make serious efforts to change, innovate and improve, will most likely be forced out of business because they were never able to find that distinctive niche or "unique selling proposition" in the marketplace and stand for something in the customer's mind! You will also need to be aware of trends and changing technology by becoming a student of retailing, so that you can react by knowing your own strengths as well as weaknesses.

Innovate And Distinguish

Yes, you will need to live and prosper with the likes of Walmart and Home Depot. As a result, you will need to do it by finding a way to be unique, better, faster, more fun, or first. . . something that makes the experience better and different from the big box store down the street.

What if you could do all of this, but you still failed because you were not able to give serious attention to customer service, or possibly tried to implement a great idea with poor standards or people skills? I believe the coming chapters of this book will make a difference, not only in finding that great concept, but also in implementing it with your people.

The Basics Plus

There is one thing that has not changed. You've always had to combine your own unique appeal and special marketing approach with the ability to do it in adequate sales volume to make your store viable. But how do you do a great job of merchandising and selling your products and services while giving customers over the top service or a memorable or entertaining experience? One aspect of this book is learning to be a retailer who can form a connection and bond between his store, his people and the customer. If you can achieve this, you will have engendered a more superior form of customer loyalty and advocacy, that very few retailers are familiar with. The result is that selling price and advertising become much less important and margins stabilize or increase.

Now what all are we talking about here? We've got the importance of staying on top of trends, reacting to changing markets and the internet, improving customer service, knowing your customers and making use of customer information you collect to help you create a line of customers out the door of your store.

Sounds like fun, doesn't it?

"The future will be determined in part by happenings that it is impossible to foresee; it will also be influenced by trends that are now existent and observable."

Emily G. Balch
(writer, Nobel Peace Prize Recipient)

"You don't skate to where the puck has been, you skate to where the puck will be."

Wayne Gretzky

"I don't set trends. I just find out what they are and exploit them."

Dick Clark

 Watching Trends And
Learning From Other Retailers

2

Any retailer who sincerely wants to be successful needs to be a very observant student of trends, as well as of other retailers. In looking for new opportunities, a prime example of watching for new trends comes in the form of the book Trading Up by authors Michael J. Silverstein and Neil Fiske. This book is a great read for entrepreneurs or anyone who wants to understand and capitalize on just how trends might make a difference in creativity and inspiration, as it does a remarkable job of explaining how new consumer trends in the late 80's and 90's changed and went more upscale while creating whole new concepts as a result of changes in demographics and other conditions. Their book does a great job of explaining how and why these new ideas and concepts worked in the marketplace. A few of the American trends cited by the authors of Trading Up are as follows:

♦ The advent of "New Luxury" goods has meant that manufacturers and retailers have positioned these products to be better quality while determining an optimal availability level so that these goods don't become too available or common. This capitalistic version of self expression allows consumers to say in a variety of ways, I'm intelligent, sophisticated or possibly a trendsetter. For sophisticated and discriminating spenders, New Luxury goods have been providing more upscale and varied methods to set our personalities, sense of style and small successes apart from the masses without uttering a syllable. When this type of merchandise or services look like they are somewhat limited in availability and not commonly available to the masses, they become easier to garner a premium price.

- "For example "Old Luxury" goods such as a Rolls Royce were about exclusivity and priced to ensure that only the top earning 1–2 percent of consumers could afford. Where New Luxury goods such as a Lexus or a Volvo are always priced at a premium to conventional middle market products, yet still priced within the financial reach of 40 percent of American households."

- Another example of "Old Luxury" may have been a few of the fanciest 5 star restaurants in a given city while a chain or a restaurant like the Cheese Cake Factory might represent "new luxury." "New Luxury" goods tend to be introduced to the marketplace by retailers like Crate & Barrel, Sharper Image, Williams Sonoma, Whole Foods, etc.,

- Shoppers are going to the mall less. They are becoming weary of the time and energy required to get around mega-malls and mega stores to find one (1) or two (2) items. As a result, terms like "quick shopping" or "precision shopping" have been coined, and are entering the retailing vocabulary. Even Walmart began experimenting years ago with a 40,000 square foot "Neighborhood Market" concept or "Small-Mart" as it has been nicknamed.

- Brand name stores are on the increase such as Tommy Hilfiger, Apple, Fossil, IKEA and American Eagle just to mention a few.

- "The growth in single-person households has been a major driver in the rise of away-from-home eating, because singles don't want to bother cooking for themselves." They point out that "middle-market" consumers prefer to eat away from home because these people feel they have less time to shop than before and because they have been exposed to better and more diverse cooking in their travels and through the media." Silverstein and Fiske state that all of this points out opportunities for restaurants and fast, casual food places such as Panera Bread and Chipotle Grill. These trends also create opportunities for those marketing store-bought prepared foods, which are more upscale gourmet in nature.

♦ "Ethnic groups in the United States are growing faster than the general population as a whole. Thirty percent of the U.S. population is now classified as black, Asian or Hispanic, and we are beginning to see significant ethnic influences on the foods we eat, as well as the music we listen to, and the clothes we wear."

The reason I point these well-stated observations and trends from the book *Trading Up* is not necessarily because they will be valid tomorrow or next year, but because I believe YOU should be watching and reacting to these types of trends. This is the way you need to observe the world and adjust your own retail concepts accordingly. You must become a student of trends, changing demographics and new ideas. You can no longer say, "I like bagels so I'm going to open a bagel store." There are too many demographic and social factors that play into your stores objectives and strategies. As a result, retailers who know their customers and want to take advantage of trends must adapt, and react to many of these changes, if they truly want to build something special.

Other trends and considerations might include the following:
♦ Increasing influence and competition for shoppers on the internet.

♦ Shoppers are looking to be impressed and entertained, thus there is a trend toward what some are calling the "entertainmentization" of retailing. Even the old shopping malls that we have come to know over the past decades are trying to re-invent themselves as they move to more of an entertainment theme. Now we are seeing the introduction of outdoor theatre areas, piano bars and high-end restaurant experiences such as

The Cheesecake Factory. What can you do to possibly increase the entertainment factor in *your* store?

- A large obvious shift in demographics has been mostly effected by the aging baby boomers of which I am one. The boomers who are already very experienced consumers, are shifting into new phases of their lives. As a result, their needs and wants are changing, including the fact they have more disposable income. Many of the hotter home oriented stores such as Restoration Hardware coupled with catalog concepts such as Coldwater Creek and J. Jill are all about catering to the needs of the boomers.

- Large screen televisions, increased use of high-end fountains, and entertainment-oriented lighting are being used more effectively in what is being termed "lifestyle malls." Lifestyle malls (sometimes called boutique malls), are generally shopping centers that combine the traditional retail activities of a shopping mall with leisure-oriented features aimed more towards upscale consumers. The bottom line is that shoppers are being lured by activities and attractions that would have never been considered years ago.

- Growing terrorism and concerns over the economy has caused many consumers to long for things from the past that make them feel a little more warm and fuzzy, like the Main Street of old. How might you and *your* store react accordingly to warm and fuzzy?

- Since the recession of 2008, more cautious consumers seem to be moving away from more ostentatious brands. While this seems to fly in the face of what I have described over the last couple of pages, it may only be a temporary trend based on the economic woes of the more recent recession. At any rate, companies like McDonalds's are trying to make inroads on a more upscale brand like Starbucks by offering a better product than previously offered, but with a more down to earth price. This is the exact opposite of what has been going on, however it is working.

There are many more trends out there than I have elaborated on. The point of all of this? Be observant of the big picture and apply the lessons learned to *your* store(s).

Observing & Learning from Other Retailers

I strongly believe that a lot of what I have learned comes from constantly walking through other retail stores and being an ongoing student of retail through observation. This has been a great supplemental education when combined with the knowledge and experience gained as a retailer. Anyone who owns a retail store should be constantly watching all types of retailers to learn what to do, what works and what's hot. But you can also learn a lot by observing below-average retailers and asking yourself if you see your store displaying those same worn out traditional approaches, substandard housekeeping, outdated displays and poor customer service.

Today's cutting edge retailers zero-in with imagination on very unique niche markets and then react and move aggressively. They have an unbelievable grasp of their customers' demographics, tastes and wants, all while very successfully riding the current trends—and sometimes—even helping to create them. However, as you begin to observe others, you need to ensure your understanding of what your own store is and is not about. Let's take a look at a number of different perspectives, issues and strategies you need to consider and study as a retailer who is committed to stepping your own store performance up a few notches.

Customer Service

What is the customer service experience at your store, and what type of genuine customer attention is necessary to be successful? Do your customers easily find real help in your store, or do they wander around looking for a body, only to be told that they need to talk to someone else who's busy or not here right now? Take a look at Apple's Genius Bar. Clearly defined and easily found. You can't miss it. It is a focal point of the store! My son came in with a friend's iPod a couple of years ago. It had gotten wet and was gone. The Apple® store rep took it from my son, checked it out to see if it was the battery and then excused himself for about two minutes. He returned with an identical iPod, presented it to my son and said, "Here you go." There were no questions, no examination or analysis of the receipt or warranty. Just, "Here you go!" Oh, and "Sorry for your trouble." They never asked for a receipt. What kind of an act of congress does it take for your customers to get really first rate care?

Store Aesthetics
Look at aesthetics. In many stores you can't see the forest for the trees. Does you store create a pleasant environment to be in, that makes you want to stay, or is it closer to "Joe's Bargain Barn"? Does your store feel cluttered? Visit an Apple computer or a Crate & Barrel store if you'd like a good example of well thought out retail displays. Those stores feel open, spacious and clean from the moment you walk in. At Apple, large solid, spacious and uncluttered tables display and encourage customers to play with the state-of-the-art merchandise. The stores are very open, modern and visually dramatic, yet they still create a very welcoming feeling by putting products out there for people to play with, use and even get on the internet. The stores are generally packed with people playing with equipment. And yet there is very little if any sales pressure. They know what they are selling and they make sure you see it and experience it.

Try striving to create a retail environment that sets your store apart, where your brand/image is emphasized and reinforced throughout. If possible, try and make use of most, if not all, of a customer's senses. Make sure that wherever your customers look in your store, the image you want is reflected. Have music that is appropriate for your store's target demographics. Create displays that tempt and encourage your customers to touch and hold the merchandise. If your store is food oriented, find a way to keep mouthwatering smells throughout the store. Yes, there is a cost to all of this, but there is a real cost to ignoring these tools as well, and you don't know what that cost is.

The Experience
Kitchen tools and cookware were sold like hammers, screwdrivers and buckets in the past. Think of the house wares stores and departments you've seen for decades. Products were just stacked up or hung on a wall with a price. Williams Sonoma has taken almost every product in their stores and uniquely presented them with a special purpose, story and culture. They seem to make almost anything they sell feel important and special. For example, here is a paragraph written for a kitchen tool called a "Molcajete":

> *Our molcajete (mohl-kah-the) is a classic cooks' tool with ancient credentials. There's nothing like the texture of volcanic rock for grinding spices or blending fresh tomatoes, avocados and chilies into a perfectly textured guacamole. Watch our video demonstration.*

They try to make sure the customer understands the purpose for virtually every product in the store. Their products are presented with imagination and often demonstrated in a semi-complete kitchen in the center of the store. Specialty seasonings and food items are often highlighted and sampled to supplement the cookware and tools sales, as well as to provide one more way to satisfy the senses and create the experience. Again, what are you doing in your store that is unique, memorable and provides an experience?

Showrooms at Ikea stores do so much more than display furniture and housewares. They create a feeling and an atmosphere that make the customer want to live the Ikea lifestyle. They create the picture for their customers and spark their imaginations so that shoppers see themselves using and living with the merchandise. In addition, they help attract and keep customers in the store by offering breakfast, lunch and dinner. As a result Ikea's customers eventually make a connection with the store, its merchandise and ultimately—the store's brand.

Sephora, a French cosmetics concept, has re-invented the department store perfume and cosmetics buying experience. Right away, customers are totally in awe of a store design that is a feast for the eyes as it makes it clear to customers that they are in for a unique experience. A major distinction is that their products are grouped alphabetically while brand categories are eliminated. The products are not behind glass counters. Everything is out and available to sample, and there is an overwhelming array of perfumes and cosmetics to choose from. The top ten perfumes are always listed like an iTunes top ten play list, and the customer feels much less intimidated and much more in control of the sampling and buying process. In fact, the customer can reduce the time spent in going through the cosmetics buying experience if they choose or, they can have a very knowledgeable sales staff wait on them in a more traditional manner. The key is the choice, the control and *the experience* for the customer.

If you've ever visited Disney World, you should know that the customer experience is never left to chance. Every detail was designed to give the parks guests a pleasant and positive experience.

Trader Joe's has also carefully fashioned more of a store "experience." The employees are called "crew members" and are dressed in Hawaiian shirts. You'll find that these crew members are not only knowledgeable about their numerous products, but also often busy cooking up samples or offering tastes of Trader Joe's foods. The store's mission is to constantly surprise customers and create a sense of adventure through unusual foods, tastes, smells and fun experiences.

Entertainment & The Build-A-Bear Experience
I knew Maxine Clark, founder and CEO of Build-A-Bear, back when she was just a very sharp, very driven senior vice president of a major mass marketer for May Company. She has created a retail store that is truly a magical place for it's targeted customers (young children.) In addition, her execution of the idea is nothing short of spectacular. And believe me, she knows who her customers are, and she listens to them via an advisory board of children.

In case you're not familiar, the stores allow children to choose, build and create their own cute stuffed and furry friends to take home with them. First the children (her target customers, along with their parents) need to choose what type of stuffed animal they want to create. They can pick an animal or bear skin from 20 varieties or more of regularly changing creatures. It might be a bear, a dog, a bunny, etc. The children then take it to a filling station to watch it get stuffed. The very friendly and enthusiastic sales staff caters to each of the children, helping them along the way.

Once they have created their friend, the child is able to choose from a variety of clothes and accessories to outfit their new friend. They can even add a heart. There are even clothes which can be bought so that both child and furry friend have matching outfits. But this isn't the end. Birth certificates are issued, adoption papers can be filled out and the animals are taken home in a special (traveling case) box. Visiting this store is an experience in itself, as it involves kids and parents throughout the creation and purchase process. It is definitely not just about the purchase or the buying decision. It is about the imagination process. They have even extended this process to their Internet site.

What have you done to give your guest a positive experience? Try to find some way to give your guests *customers* some entertainment or an experience they can't get anywhere else. Yes, that will require some thought and imagination, but it doesn't always have to be expensive.

Signage

What are the best retailers doing with signage? Is your signage professional in appearance? Do you use signs to your advantage, or is the customer at the mercy of waiting to find a salesperson? Again, take a look at the signs in an Apple computer store or even a Trader Joe's. They educate you and make you want the product. Signage is much more useful than just displaying a "Sale" sign. In addition, if you're trying to minimize payroll and become less dependent on sales help, then you need to at least make sure your store is signed and categorized much better than average, not to mention laid out in a customer-friendly manner.

Take A Lesson From Grocery Stores And Discounters.
Are you stocking an array of higher margin impulse items near the checkout, gift-wrap area or any place where shoppers have a brief time to pause? We're talking about small inexpensive items that customers often purchase at the last minute. Look at Borders Book Stores. Even they sell chocolates at their registers.

The Purchase Or Customer Buying Process
How easy is the actual buying process in your store once the customer has made a decision? Do customers need to wait in a line? Do they have to look for help? Do they have to wait for the cashier to decide if the items they are purchasing are on sale or what the correct price is? Is the cashier fumbling around looking for a pen or a bag? Look at the bologna someone has to go through to buy a computer at Best Buy, and then look at the simplicity and speed of an Apple computer store.

Once again I mention Apple. They are making checkout lines a dinosaur from the past. In fact, they may be making the traditional "point of sale" obsolete. Do you like checkout lines? Then why have them at your own store? I hate standing in line at Sam's Club. I have even walked out of the store and left behind a whole flatbed of merchandise after watching the lines back up 10 deep while other registers sit empty. Apple's employees walk around with little modified "I-Phones" in their hands and can check you out right on the spot without making you go through the torture. The last time I purchased a computer, my receipt and warranty papers were emailed to me. Apple is, in effect, making the payment piece of the process more of an after-thought. In other words, don't worry about the paying part. It's insignificant compared to what you are getting here—great service and product! Are these people using computers to practice what they preach or what?

How Well Do You Know The Customer You're Going After?
Do you know your target customer better than your competition does? Wouldn't this be a key part of winning the wars with your competitors? Hot Topic actually encourages its own employees to report on trends. Hot Topic's strategy is, very simply, a complete and constant effort to really listen to its customers. Everything it does to improve is based on consumer input. Their CEO reads extensive customer "report cards" from the stores. The report card or comment card is placed into every shopper's bag. Hot Topic pays great attention to the resulting emails it encourages its customers to send on these cards. What a way to stay in touch and know what's going on in your customer's mind. Do their managers make changes and adjustments to the merchandise assortment based on this information? You bet they do. Do you think music is important and influential with teen customers? These stores and their fashions are really tied to the music scene. The Hot Topic stores also sell CDs and monitor concert halls to be aware of the hot bands and fashions at the time. In addition, their website offers a "community" link with discussion forums and a chance to provide feedback on all kinds of issues. All of this automatically results in a more close customer-employee-management relationship that speeds up reaction time to its customers. Hot Topic knows their target customer in a way that most of us could only dream. dELiA*s does the same thing as it goes after pre-teen and teenage girls. They are making sure that they know and cater to their customer through a very information packed website and a highly successful catalog along with their emerging chain of retail stores. The store's design, music and sales help are all tuned in to their target customers.

Walmart and now Sears also recognize they need to know their customers better, as they have become diligent in finding ways to register customers online. In order to generate customer leads and gather shopper preferences, in exchange for shopper preferences, Walmart promises to give their customers advance notice of the best deals at nearby stores. The deals that show up on the customers e-mail are only those that will appeal to specific customers based on information collected. The detail being collected will be very important for Walmart because as the future moves forward, knowing our customers will become even more imperative.

Change *With* Your Customer.
When Crate & Barrel first began, it catered more to apartment tenants and first-time homeowners with less expensive, trend setting and stylish merchandise. However, as their customers grew older and became more successful, the company also positioned themselves with more upscale and higher priced merchandise. They also added new product categories, like furniture. In other words, it chose to mature with its baby boomers, evolving to meet their needs and more upscale demands. This approach left a void as well as an opportunity for a new format like CB2, which tries to be younger, hipper and less expensive once again than the original stores have become.

Now Pottery Barn has gone another step further as it changes with its customers by creating Pottery Barn Kids. What's old is new again as some concepts aren't really new at all. In the case of Crate & Barrel's CB2, it seems to be coming full circle although I'm sure there will be some serious tweaking and testing as they continue to finesse the concept.

Make Customers Feel Like They've Found Something Special!
What are you doing that makes your store feel like a unique "find" for the customer who walks in? In this book, I talk about the importance of separating yourself from the competition. One of the best ways to distinguish your store(s) from the competition is to target a specific consumer so that when they do find you, they feel like they feel like the mother ship has landed. This is what Anthropologie stores do. They stay on top of their customers' tastes and affect them emotionally by appealing to all of the senses, by doing everything from playing French music to burning aromatic candles throughout their stores. Anthropologie has become a specialty store that isn't totally specialized, other than that it builds an assortment of unusual and diverse merchandise around a theme. This includes clothing, jewelry, books, special soaps, luxurious sheets and pillows and even patio furniture. In fact, the last time I was in one of their stores, I

found colorful birdhouses merchandised above a variety of colorful spring dresses. The stores go after the upscale 30–40 plus crowd who want to be unique and stand out from the crowd while on a budget. They know their customers want something that shows they're on top of the latest trends whether it's in fashion or an eye-catching conversation piece in their home..

With Anthropologie's wide range of merchandise, their buyers travel constantly throughout Europe and the Far East to find distinctive and unusual items that are limited in production or even one-of-a-kind. What other store would you find colorful birdhouses above spring dresses? They may go to flea markets, antique stores or out-of-the-way small towns looking for something different. Prices can range from under $10 to thousands of dollars. This strategy builds a very distinctive, yet interesting retail concept with a very different atmosphere. This retailer even sells some of the unique props that really make the store feel unusual and special. It all comes down to making customers feel they have found something unique.

What About "Lifestyle Oriented" Stores?
Remember, customers need ideas too! It's one of the reasons many people like to shop. And it's your job to do just that! By focusing on the lifestyle, instead of the products, try to create your own imaginative groupings of specially selected merchandise built around a lifestyle or theme. Pottery Barn is a great example of a retailer that has filled its stores with an assortment of products, descriptions and interesting stories about specific products to create an impression of upscale style and quality while positioning their merchandise as affordable too. Consider different types of groupings throughout the store, along with a few borrowed or rented props. Grouping different themed items together can often cause customers to buy exactly what they see. Crate & Barrel is also another great example for creating a lifestyle store experience. These people treat merchandising as a true art (which it is). Their store layout, like that of Apple stores, is clean, clear and easy to get around. Merchandise is grouped in various and logical ways where the products also complement each other. This is not about merchandising all the glassware together and

all the chairs together. It is about creating a picture and lifestyle that the customer wants to see them as a part of. Read an excerpt from a recent customer review found on the Internet:

> "There also always seems to be a bunch of items on sale at any given time. From cookbooks to small kitchen gadgets, I can always find something that I really want on the cheap. The furniture is beautiful as well, and they have a great layout upstairs for exploring that aspect of their business. The open spaces and nice furniture might even allow you to forget you're in the middle of Manhattan."

Go Upscale (A High-End Version Of A Store Like "7-Eleven"?)
Here is a retailer that once again is watching and trying to adapt to their customers' everyday needs. They really seem to want to develop their "connection" with the customer. And maybe they've learned that it is possible for almost anything to go upscale! A while back, Harrods department store in London, England opened their version of a luxury convenience store. It is called Harrods 102 and it's just like a 7-Eleven, but with some significant differences. Yes, it sells gas, groceries, wine and even Krispy Kreme doughnuts, but that seems to be where the similarities end. This particular luxury/convenience store also features a sushi bar, florist, pharmacist, drycleaner and oxygen bar. They also offer a concierge service that will deliver merchandise to local customers. As a luxury version of a 7-Eleven, the interior is also upscale, with dark woods, stainless steel and natural stone with a very impressive and modern look. So far, it's a tremendous success and it's probably only a matter of time before consumers (who are becoming increasingly sophisticated) will be buying from stores like this in more and more urban locations. And yes, you guessed it. It's open from 7 am to 11 pm.

Appeal To The Warm & Fuzzy Trend.
If you've been in a department store in recent history, you may have noticed an increase in amount of space allocated to candles. On top of that, there is now a whole myriad of specialty stores in malls aimed strictly at candles. Names include Wicks & Sticks, Illuminations,

Yankee Candle Company, Candle Makers and a number of others. What is so hot about candles? The same all consuming baby boomers with their increasing disposable incomes are now paying more attention and spending more money on decorating and outfitting their homes. And part of decorating and outfitting your home is looking at new trendy and warm things to accessorize it. This is what Crate & Barrel, Restoration Hardware and even the growth of Home Depot and Lowe's is all about. But candles are an obviously inexpensive way to warm up and beautify a home without major expense. Illuminations really stands out in the malls as it conjures up an intriguing aura with its dark stores primarily lit by candles. The unique appearance of the store creates a warmth and atmosphere that is hard for many customers to pass up. But the quality and price of these candles will make it apparent to you that these are not the candles found years ago at grandmas. They have created distinctive quality designs and combined them with a unique presentation to update an old retail approach to candles. Another related strategy for a new concept is to find a way to create a new need out of an old product.

Take Advantage Of One Feature You Already Have.
Take advantage of the one thing I know you have going for you right now. You are not currently a gigantic national or global retailer. If you think about it, you never want to feel like a huge global superstore. Make your store feel like an intimate, with-it, specialized, service-oriented store with a friendly and knowledgeable owner/manager who values the customer's business and who will take care of them no matter what. At the same time, keep in mind that looking small and intimate doesn't mean looking like the small town five and dime with clutter from front to back. Be local, be fresh, be friendly and give your customer a special experience. You don't have to be big to do that!

Give Free Samples.
Chick-fil-let and Cinnabon may offer free sample tastes, but many other retailers can offer samples as well. Dunkin' Donuts™ actually has a "Sampling Van" that is driving around the Chicago area. Sam's

Club™ and Costco™ constantly offer free samples of the foods they sell. It is not unusual to find 5–10 sample stations at one of their stores. A lawn and garden dealer might offer free soil sample tests to entice customers to their store. A unique and interesting gift shop called "The Porch" in the Soulard area of St. Louis offers up wine tastings to its customers to spur wine sales.

What Would Disney Do?

One of the things that help make the Disney experience special is their attention to the little things to which others might only give average attention. Disney is constantly cleaning and hiding the background things you're not supposed to see. What about the environment you create on a day-to-day basis? Is trash taken care of throughout the day or just at the end of the day when things are overflowing? How about the build up of clutter around the register or just outside of stockrooms? Can people see into your back areas? What does the bathroom look like? Does it reflect the class of your store? Customers have remarked online that Crate & Barrels restrooms are the cleanest in New York!

Are your store's aisles cluttered, or is it easy to move and navigate around? And then there are your employees. Look at Disney employees. Do your employees reflect the image and brand you want? Can you tell the employees from the customers? Have you considered polo shirts, possibly with an embroidered logo? Do they smile and communicate well, or do they avoid eye contact and reveal a tongue piercing when they smile? All of these details add up to a place your customers want to go and feel comfortable in as well!

Combine Food & High Tech Or "Docking & Shopping"

A couple of companies from Stockholm, Sweden have introduced what they call an "iFood Terminal." This shopping concept allows customers to hook up their iPod and download audio recipes and then be able to purchase all the necessary items from a color-coded deli area. Their purchase process translates into English as follows:

Plug in – Download – Purchase – Listen – Cook

Customers choose from a wide range of recipes and then download audio instructions to their iPod or other mp3 player before they look for the actual ingredients. They are trying to further engage customers by offering more than just a deli operation. iFood may also eventually include an online food community to encourage members to share and collect recipes and cooking tips. Think about it . . . the idea allows customers who are already carrying and using a very popular state-of-the-art device to plug into their shopping experience and get even more out of it. It's a very clever and unique way to get closer and more personal with your customers and their lifestyle. Will this work? Who knows. . . . But at least they're trying to innovate!

Overwhelm Them

Jungle Jim's International Market in Fairfield, Ohio provides a feast for the eyes as well for the stomach. Even though there are thousands of food stores around the country, there isn't another food store anywhere quite like Jungle Jim's. While most supermarkets are 40,000–60,000 square feet in size, Jungle Jim's is "gi-normous" (really big). It is about 300,000 square feet. That's about three times the size of your average discount store.

With size hopefully comes variety, right? And they succeed in every category. They have over 1,200 imported and domestic beers for you beer lovers, and if you like your foods hot with those beers, they have 1,400 kinds of hot sauce alone. There are also 1,600 types of cheese along with a tremendous variety of foods from all parts of the world, including 32 different kinds of rice in bags up to 50 pounds. But they don't stop with just having a broad selection. They also make it very interesting and appealing by being about the most visually exciting and energetic stores of their type. The hot sauces are a great example. They have a full-sized fire truck on top of the hot sauce display! There's also a forty-foot boat in the fish department and an authentic rickshaw near the Chinese foods. There's even a horse-drawn carriage in the meat department. I could go on, but you get the idea.

In Conclusion:

What today's retailers do well is create an identity and niche of their own by developing and fine-tuning merchandise mixes and lifestyle categories. Many combine these with special, imaginative and somewhat interactive shopping experiences. By observing today's trends and connecting with the emotions of their customers, retailers are ultimately very successful at getting customers to surrender substantial amounts of their disposable income. The bottom line is that good retailers change and experiment. And while change and experimentation don't always guarantee success, just doing it the way it has always been done is probably a ticket to failure. There will always be trends to watch and changes will continue to transform retailing again and again!

While following the latest consumer trends is not always easy, just remember that you must continue to experiment and try new ideas. The ideas and niches are all around us. We simply need to find a way to tap into them. If you do it because of your own imaginative instincts, great. If it is by trying, failing and stumbling on to something, great, that's fine too. It doesn't really matter. The fact is that you must experiment. It is a necessary effort to keep pace with changing habits, needs, behaviors and tastes and thus necessary to survival. Remember, if your efforts are not failing efforts at least some of the time, then you must not be experimenting at all.

 Living And Thriving
With Walmart

3

How did Walmart become the force of nature they are today? They went after common retailing and business issues with a relentless emphasis on cost-control as well as a willingness and ability to execute down in the trenches at the front lines where millions of shoppers live with them day-in and day-out. In fact Walmart is more successful because of its ability to actually follow through and execute its company mission and goals, rather than the actual strategies themselves.

The secret to surviving with retailers like Walmart isn't about fighting Walmart on its terms. It's about setting some new and different rules for your business and then working around Walmart. Retailers actually can live with Walmart in a way that allows them to survive and thrive. Just don't try to beat Walmart at their game. Competing on price is not the answer. You will most likely lose if this is your only game plan. Hopefully you already recognize this fact. The truth is that Walmart does an excellent job at what they do.

"Your job is NOT to sell what Walmart sells."

Walmart does a great job of providing value to the American consumer by tenaciously and systematically holding down costs and constantly working to increase efficiency. Walmart separates itself from its competitors by distributing high volume basic items more efficiently than any entity has ever done in history. In fact, they are undeniably unparalleled in their ability to distribute merchandise at minimal cost around the globe. But Walmart offers a low cost variety of basic merchandise in a variety of categories, and that is the limit.

Generally, they will not win anywhere else. Remember that. So the question becomes, "What can you be unparalleled at?"

Walmart is NOT The Villain.
It seems to me that in the minds of many small retailers, there has always been a big bad villain out there. Today it seems to be Walmart. But they are not the big bad villain they're made out to be. I'm told that in the 1940's (before my time), the upcoming 'supermarket' was deemed the big bad villain. The supermarket was ruining things for all the thousands of 'mom and pop' family grocery stores. They said no one could compete with the supermarkets. During the 1960's, the shopping mall came along and scared the daylights out of strip centers and downtown shopping areas. Also from the 60's into the 70's came the tremendous growth of the discounters. Names like Shoppers Fair, G.E.M, W.T. Grants, E. J. Korvette, Spartan, K-Mart, Woolco, Walmart, Arlans, Venture, Caldor and Zayre came along. During the 1980's, mail order came on stronger than ever with the introduction of names like Sharper Image, Talbots, Lillian Vernon and Land's End. Later, out of the discount store playbook, came a new kind of store called the "category killer," or "big box" stores, like Drug Emporium, Best Buy, Lowe's, PetSmart and even Borders.

Now it's Walmart's turn, as they have replaced most of the large discounters, and in doing so, have become the largest retailer in the world. No one seemed to complain about them before they became dominant. Yet, now they are considered evil, and they are doing the same thing they have always done. . . drive costs and prices down by doing a more efficient job than any company has ever done.

The reality is that retailing evolves and changes, and retail will continue to change. Remember S. S. Kresge's? They were incorporated in 1912 and by 1966 had 753 stores in North America. They too met their demise due to the discount stores, but not before spawning K-Mart. The fact is that buying habits and companies change. Even Walmart will need to change. If I had told you 40 years ago that Woolworth's, Kresge's and Montgomery Ward would be gone or that K-mart and Sears (both formerly the worlds largest retailers) would have to merge, you would have asked me what I was smoking. I probably wouldn't have believed it myself.

Change has already affected the large CD retailers and booksellers like Borders. Look what Amazon.com and iTunes have done to their business. But things do change in this world, and each time the latest version of retailing comes along, those small retailers who forget what retailing is truly all about attack and cry and scream that the sky is falling. Retailing at its most basic level is buying what the customers want and then selling it to them at a price the customer is willing to pay. There is no one on the planet who does a better job of that than Walmart. Remember, they started out themselves with one rather amateurish store in 1962. Their buying power and clout were no different than any small retailer. But, Sam Walton had a vision, worked doggedly on his dream and certainly understood what retailing was all about. The rest is history.

"Find out what people want, then sell it to them."
—Sam Walton

While I'm no Sam Walton, I would add; "Display it effectively and put it in an environment that makes them want it!"

For every 10 customers out there who are in love with Walmart, I can show you at least a few dozen others who are waiting for someone to give them a better or different retail experience and to fill their needs and wants in other ways!

The good news is many customers don't care about saving money. Some don't like buying imports from China. Others want to be shown how it works. Some people want a pleasant or unique shopping experience and still others want to be waited on, hand and foot. Many customers want quality and are willing to pay for it. You must be focused on everything else you can do besides offering the lowest price. If a good longtime customer tells you he or she may buy from Walmart because they have a better price, consider matching the price if you can, to avoid losing the customer. But for every merchant that loses a customer to the big bad Walmart, I can show you a merchant that to some extent, lost sight of exactly who they were and what their job was, as a specialty retailer.

The sad fact is that most of the small retail shops out there who have been finished off by Wal-Mart, never really understood what retailing was truly all about. Many of these retailers would have been run out of business if ANY other competition had come along. It's a lot easier to place blame on the big mean mega store than to look at our own faults.

If your prices were high to begin with, and your store was the same old unexciting uninteresting place for decades, you were not a true retailer. If your merchandise assortment changed at the pace of a snail, or your idea of customer service was taking the customers money at the register, you were going to pay a price no matter who opened up across the street. Yes, Wal-Mart may have been guilty of hastening the demise. I have worked with many small business owners over the years and I love small business, but there is some old misguided idea out there that small business owners are blameless and this is not always the case. Why is it that everyone thinks they can operate a small retail shop?

The simple fact is that if Walmart or any another retailer out there can do it better than you, you're going to lose business. That's the way it's supposed to work in a capitalist society.

You have the option of doing your category so well that customers will feel they should shop your store before making any purchase decision. In other words, shoppers should actually feel they are missing out on variety, quality, knowledge and service in the category they are shopping if they buy at Walmart instead of your store. Shoppers that are only looking at price were never your customers anyway.

While the common wisdom may be that Wal-Mart's competitors sweat bullets when the huge "smiley faced" gorilla says we're coming into town. The fact is you can either hitch up the wagon and try to move where there will never be a Wal-Mart (good luck with that), you can close your doors, or you can fight back by playing by *your* rules.

Believe it or not, there are retailers that love the fact that they have a Wal-Mart to generate traffic for them. Despite many new stories to the contrary, many are doing better than before the big box stores arrived. As a result they seek out locations as close to Wal-Mart as possible. In retailing, the whole name of the game is to feed off your competitors' traffic. Isn't that what shopping malls were all about? Well, Wal-Mart is the biggest traffic generator around. It gets over 160 million customers a week, so why not get a piece of that? Believe it or not, there are all kinds of retailers who are succeeding and even thriving in the same world as Wal-Mart because they focus not just on sales but also on becoming the best in their arena of competition.

Yes, shadowing Wal-Mart will not work for every store. It will only work if your business offers something that is truly different or unique from Wal-Mart. Your strategy will need to be in selection, service, higher quality products or even convenience. Many shoppers, such as my daughter, don't even like walking into a Wal-Mart. She is not at all impressed with their assortments, product quality and often very limited customer service. That means opportunity for any other retailer, since there are plenty of customers just like her, out there looking for better alternatives.

Opportunities in the Fight With Walmart and the Big Box Stores

Just look at all of the opportunities below to beat Walmart. Take a look at the list and determine what you can emphasize in your store to better separate your store from the big box stores.

Walmart Strengths
- Efficiency in Buying and Distributing Merchandise (Low Prices)

30

- Great Customer Return Policy
- Gigantic Ad Budget
- Convenient Hours

Your Potential Strengths

- Depth in Any Given Merchandise Category (Walmart's depth in any one merchandise category is minimal at best.)
- Variety of Merchandise in Your Specialty Field (you need to be in cutting edge products or a variety of products that Walmart cannot begin to touch.
- Educated and Knowledgeable Sales Staff ("How-To" Help for Customers)
- Unique and Memorable Customer Experience
- Highest Quality Merchandise
- "Over the Top" Customer Service
- Easy to Tailor and React to Customer Needs & Wants
- Unique, Hard-to-Find Merchandise
- Latest and State-of-the-Art Merchandise
- Pleasant, Low-Stress Environment
- Convenient to Get In and Out Quickly
- Upscale Experience
- Gift Wrapping Services
- Tailoring
- Knowing the Customer's Name
- Seminars and Classes (Training for the Customer)
- Design Services
- Installation Services
- Lay-A-Way Service
- Drive-up Services

It may be selection, service, expertise or even atmosphere. It may be something some call the WOW factor. Be impressive at whatever you do. There are plenty of examples out there of retailers who thrive and succeed with Walmart.

Build-A-Bear has done it.
Hobby Lobby has done it.
PetSmart has done it
Radio Shack has done it.
Bass Pro has done it.
Anthropologie has done it.
Restoration Hardware has done it.
Any gift shop is doing it.
A good lawn mower store is doing it.
A health food store is doing it.
A framing store does it.
Any Mexican grocery store is doing it.

Best Buy has done it.
Crate and Barrel has done it.
Trader Joe's has done it.
Office Depot has done it.
Casual Male has done it.
The Limited has done it.
Williams Sonoma has done it.
Any local nursery is doing it.
Any local chocolate /candy store is doing it.
An ink refill store does it
Your basic Hallmark store does it.

These stores are all finding a niche and doing a better job within their niche than Walmart. While I'm sure that some of you will point out that there are a handful of "big box" retailers on this list, the point is that they took a merchandise category, went after it aggressively, and did it better than Walmart—and you can too. There really is room for you, Walmart and the other big box retailers. Remember, even if Walmart takes 30 percent or so of any regional market that it enters, that still leaves approximately 70 percent of the market for others to capture.

Real Proven Strategies for Beating the Big Box Stores

While I'm not suggesting that all of these should be implemented for your store, I advise that you take a hard look at each of the following to determine where you could benefit most.

1. Go Upscale
Turn to higher end items that go above and beyond where the big box stores leave off. This might be in tools, barbecue grills, clothing, art, giftware, etc. Stores that turn to big-ticket items such as high-end

appliances and accessories that appeal to a higher income clientele will generally do better.

2. Deepen Your Merchandise Selection

Many customers believe that because of their sheer size, the big box stores have almost everything. But in reality the big stores generally cherry pick a more limited assortment of the most popular items for the large majority of buyers. For instance, a big hardware store might not carry the more specialized or high end hand tools. Often the big box stores also have a very poor selection of replacement items and refills, such as special batteries or replacement reels for string trimmers. I have never been able to find the replacement spool for my string trimmer since I bought it at my local big box store. Stocking replacement parts (where applicable) for all brands and/ or older models is another opportunity to provide more for your customers. While Walmart sets some very low unbeatable prices to draw customers, they're also counting on many customers to step up to a higher priced item of the same type where Walmart can find a higher profit margin. In fact, higher priced items are quite often priced no better at Walmart than a smaller retail shop. If you're going to advertise, you should be emphasizing and running ads encouraging customers to buy the best items in the manufacturers assortment, not the cheapest.

3. Focus On Core Merchandise First

Concentrate on basic core merchandise that consumers expect to find in your type of store. Look for items and brands that the big guys don't stock. Obviously you should try to buy from manufacturers who offer an alternative line of merchandise or who do not sell to big box retailers at all.

4. Find Other Niche Categories

What are you missing? Review your marketing plan and re-evaluate your target market. Is there a niche group of customers that you've overlooked? Are there customers out there that you are not marketing to? Can the products or services you provide be adapted to another market or group of markets? Go after niche categories that big box stores either neglect or do poorly. Wal-Mart has never even attempted true men' s dress shoes. In a hardware store, it might be a whole specialty mailbox department. Walmart also doesn't sell much in the way of educational toys—they cherry pick the highest volume and most profitable ones. In a fashion store, it may be a special selection of local handmade jewelry or insect repelling shirts. Yes, I said insect repelling shirts. (I'm not kidding!)

5. Fighting Low Prices

This is a tough tactic and not one of the strategies I recommend being concerned with. But if you insist, read on. There is a significant perception by customers that big stores will always be cheaper, which is not always true. One of the best ways to fight this perception is for you to know the prices of your big box competition. Notice I said "perception." It really is all about perception. Walmart works very hard to maintain the perception that they are always low even when they're not. Remember that. Make competitive shopping part of your regular activities. You must also know your customers well enough to know what items about which they are price sensitive and price aware. And then you must react to those items, if you're going to play the price/comparison game. When I competed with Walmart during my Venture days, I would shop them monthly. Often when I went back to their stores, I'd find that they had shopped *me* and under-cut my price by one penny.

If you are hell-bent on getting into this game, make regular use of some loss leaders to help bring people into your store and further help the perception that your prices are competitive. If price is really critical in your case, one way to battle this perception is by actually listing a number of items each week on a large board or sign that show your price and the big box store's price on the same item. You can also prominently place signs throughout your store that you will match or beat any advertised item from a big box store.

Stores that do well against the big box retailers know their customers—what they need and what they can afford to buy. They also know their competitors—what they stock and how they price. They use this information to make adjustments around their 800 lb. gorilla competitors. Personally I don't like to spend my efforts to build the perception that I offer competitive pricing, especially if doing so means a reduction in gross profits. In general, retailers should pursue the other strategies listed in this chapter and throughout this book.

6. Offer "The Experience"
I talk about "the experience" quite a bit in this book. "The experience" is about giving the customer something beyond "find-the-merchandise-and-buy-it." It can be educational, entertaining, sensory, or simply memorable, but it is always a unique, buying experience that a customer will not generally find elsewhere. Build-A-Bear provides the experience. Disney provides it. The Whole Foods Market and Trader Joe's provides it. Keep in mind that, depending on what you sell, just watching a product being created can be a unique experience. "The experience" can also be provided by unusual, "over the top" customer service not found anywhere else. We'll talk about achieving "the experience" later in this book.

7. Training
Focus more effort on an ongoing training program so that your employees can answer questions and know the products they are selling. It should be obvious, if you want an important selling advantage over the big box stores, your employees should be knowledgeable about what they're selling. The real problem is that it is generally ignored as most owners want an easy, short-term solution to their problems.

8. Flexibility
Stay open past official posted hours for someone in need. Make an emergency delivery for someone. Special situations like these are remembered over the years.

9. Participate In Community Organizations
Participating in local organizations and activities allows you to know the people who are your customers and to talk more personally to

customers who will most likely be more honest with you about their observations.

10. Special Services
Offer the ability to place special orders without a deposit. Offer a layaway service, as well as the ability to hold merchandise as long as necessary for pick-up. Consider local deliveries. These services are highly valued and make you more customer-friendly. Depending on what you sell, consider Offering services such as cleaning, repair, design rentals or installations. These types of special services aimed at supporting and meeting unique customer needs can also set you apart.

11. Customer Relations
Pay attention to customer service and customer relations. Three (3) big areas that will help you compete with the big box guys are:

- Actually having sales help available on the sales floor.
- Personal relationships are very rare in big box stores. Greet your customers by name and work to develop relationships where possible.
- Asking questions and having professional salespeople who will take time with customers to really determine what they need.

12. Learn How To Motivate Your Employees
Most Walmart employees feel as though they are a part of a special mission. Do your employees feel that way? Walmart employees have also benefited to the tune of hundreds of millions of dollars as a result of Walmart's profit sharing. Employees are called "associates" and not "clerks" or "stockers" and Wal-Mart also welcomes employee input and reacts to good ideas. Employees feel valued as a result.

13. Store Policies To Keep Customers Happy
Offer and promote "hassle-free," satisfaction guaranteed, return policies. Take a look at my sub-chapter titled "Offer a Bold Guarantee."

In Conclusion:
Research the big box stores strengths and combat them by fitting into the niches they can't satisfy. There are a lot of things the big boxes can't or don't do well. Be aware of what products the big stores sell and what retail prices they charge. One way or the other, you must know your customers "wants" and communicate with them whenever possible. Customers will let you know what they observe about your store as well as the big box guys, IF you get to know them.

Do You Get the Idea? If you don't get it now, you may end up calling Walmart the devil all the way until you close your doors. In 2007, independent research from Global Insight showed that, through lowering prices and putting pressure on the competition, Walmart saved American families $2,500 each year (even those who don't shop at Walmart.) **We know what Walmart is doing for their customer! What are you doing for yours?**

"The secret of successful retailing is to give your customers what they want. And really if you think about it from your point of view as a customer you want everything."

Sam Walton, Founder, Chairman--Walmart (1918-1992)

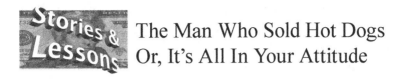

The Man Who Sold Hot Dogs
Or, It's All In Your Attitude

(An old story that's been passed around for years)

There once was a man who lived by the side of the road and sold hot dogs. He was hard of hearing, so he had no radio. He had trouble seeing so he didn't watch any television and really couldn't see well enough to read the newspapers. So he focused on his hot dog business. He had a fabulous hot dog stand and quite a large clientele. He sold very high quality hot dogs. He had different kinds of mustard, fresh onions, three (3) different kinds of relish and freshly baked hot dog buns. He put up signs on the side of the highway advertising how good they were. He stood by the side of the road and cried, "Buy a hot dog, mister, they're the best for miles and miles around." And people bought, and bought often. He was a very personable old guy. It was quite a business with quite a following. He bought a bigger stand with a larger stove to handle the increasing business. And he increased his meat orders and his bun orders. His suppliers were amazed at how much he continually ordered. He even increased the size and the number of signs he had on the road for miles. Life was great. The only thing that bothered him was that his son (the business major) had been gone for four (4) years to college, and he missed his son and wanted him to share in his good fortune. Now, after a number of pleas from his old dad, his son finally was coming home to help out.

One day, upon arriving home to help his dad, the son made some observations and voiced his concerns. The son said, "Dad, haven't you been listening to the radio? There has been a huge downturn in the economy. The price of gas is horrible and we're in a severe recession. The European situation is terrible. The domestic situation is even worse!" People are cutting back. You can't keep operating like this. You've got a big investment here and a lot at risk."

The old man thought for a while. Well, I guess my son's right. He's been to college, he reads the newspapers, watches the news on television and listens to the radio. He ought to know. So the old man cut back on his meat and bun orders. He cut back to one kind of mustard and one kind of relish, when he stocked it at all. Sales started falling off and he cut back to a cheaper mix of meat to increase profits. In very short order he noticed that his son was right. Sales were falling off even more. So he cut back on his signs and even went to a cheaper bun to cut expenses. Fewer and fewer people came by. And, in time, the old man no longer bothered to stand out on the roadside to holler out to people. There just didn't seem to be much point, the way business was dropping off. Some days he just used the buns that were left over from the day before.

His hot dog sales continued to drop. It was amazing how fast sales were falling off. There just wasn't any business. "No one even comes by anymore!" he said. Finally one day, the old man said to his son as he shut down the hot dog stand, "You're right son, we certainly are in the middle of a major recession. Thanks for warning me."

Note: I believe that son went on to sell shoes for a major shoe company. He was sent over to Africa to expand his company's business. Within hours of arriving and assessing his new market, he noticed that no one was wearing shoes. He emailed back to his boss immediately, "Returning on the next flight. Waste of time and effort. They don't wear shoes here." Another company about the same time had sent their more optimistic shoe salesman over to Africa. After assessing his market, he emailed back to his employer immediately too. The message read, "Start shipping shoes of all sizes and styles immediately. The market is wide open and there is no competition!"

 # You Have An Image

Is It by Design or by Accident?

4

What Is Your Business's Image?
This is an area in which too many businesses give little or no thought, yet this fact is the one area that has a real influence on customer perceptions even before you make the sale. Having once sold custom homes, I have watched too many homebuilders undermine themselves with an unpolished image and poor marketing savvy. They put out quality homes, but the image doesn't match. The builders who grow the largest in a given metropolitan area are not necessarily the ones that build the best houses, but rather the ones who market more effectively and create a polished environment and image. A first-class image dulls the inclination of many customers to look at how it's built or what's under the hood. This chapter will leave the marketing side of things for later on, but will focus instead on image, identity and whether or not your marketing is in line with these considerations. What's under the hood will come later.

Consider Your Corporate Image and Identity.
Unless your business is brand new, your business already has an image. The real question is, do you know what is, and is it something you've been working on to positively effect? Whether it's a first class image or it's less than stellar, your image is the brand, your look, your personality, the quality of your employees' performance and actions and how you're perceived by your customers. If it were me, I'd rather my image be by design and have some control over that image. Your image (the perception held by your customers) is very important to everything you attempt to do as a retailer. You certainly can't command an upscale price if your image is more like that of a mediocre store! Whatever your image is, it has already effected what customers will pay for products in your store and what they believe about your quality and reputation. I would want to know what my

image is before I go making changes. We'll get into the marketing aspect of this later.

What Are You?
Even if your store is small, it must stand for something, and you need to know or understand just what that is. If you don't know what you're supposed to be, how can anyone else (especially your employees) understand what you are trying to achieve? Think about it. If your store isn't strongly identified with any particular strengths or traits, then why should customers bother coming to you at all? You must give them good, persuasive and compelling reasons to come in your store. The image you want must be realistic, clear, convincing and consistent if it is to be effective.

Is Your Store Name Appropriate For Your Image?
Your name should always keep in mind your market, your customer and your style (cutting edge, classy, fun). Try to increase the odds in your favor by having a positive or memorable name. An easy to pronounce name or something that is easy or memorable to spell might be a good start. A memorable name would certainly be an asset for internet purposes. In addition, a somewhat descriptive name—like Build-A-Bear Workshop—could be a real asset to building an image of what your company is all about. You can't get a whole lot more descriptive than that.

Merchandise
Are you the place to go for the latest products on the market, or does your store remain a bit stale and predictable? Change is a must. Are you seen as a bit behind in what's going on out there? Your goal should be to give customers continuing and persuasive reasons to revisit your store. There is no room for another ordinary retailer. Presentation is also key. Is your merchandise presented in a logical, and organized fashion that is interesting and attractive to your target customer? Is it presented in a way that fits the image you are trying to project? Poor or inappropriate merchandise choices can also confuse customers as to just what you are supposed to be about.

Your Brand And Image Are Reflected In Everything You Do!
Once you know what you want your name, logo and company values are, they need to be reinforced and reestablished in everything you do. A brand is your stamp of identity to the rest of the marketplace and the world. So wouldn't you want your image and your marketing efforts to go together? Everything from advertising, merchandising, store appearance, service and product assortment should tie together and make sense to the customer in terms of what you are all about.

Consider this scenario: If you were a high-end menswear store, you wouldn't offer any merchandise that could be found at Walmart or J.C. Penney or any other store that doesn't claim to have the highest quality products to be found. Likewise, your employees wouldn't be dressed like a Walmart clerk and your store fixtures wouldn't look like they were from Joe's Bargain Barn. Your dressing rooms would look the part for an upscale menswear store, and you might offer comfortable, cushy, well-upholstered chairs throughout the store for customers to sit. Your store fixtures would look more like fine furniture than pieces picked up at a resale shop. Everything would be clean, crisp and accented with nice wall coverings and something other than fluorescent shop lights. You would offer tailoring and other convenience services not found elsewhere. You might make fresh bottled water, coffee or other drinks available to your customers. Your employees would talk like people who know how to converse intelligently with senior executives and other successful people. I could go on and on, but hopefully you get the picture.

If you were this retailer, where might you be off track in creating an image? If the restrooms are filthy or look like they belong in an old gas station, this would be inconsistent with the image that you are trying to project. If you put coupons for a cross promotion with Denny's in your customers' shopping bags or you had Metallica posters on you dressing room walls, you would be sending a confusing message. Your advertising would also NOT feature a special weekend appearance of "Max" the tattoo artist at your store. You wouldn't have painters working during store hours with their shirts off, blaring grunge music on their portable radios. You also might not want your store seamstress to be parking her rusted out 1974 Monte Carlo with the rear bumper missing in front of your store. While I may be giving some seemingly extreme examples to make my point, retailers must be protective of the image they are trying to create. Even surrounding tenants can have a negative effect on a store's image.

A retailer who wants to have *a line of customers out the door* must keep in mind that you do it by realizing and addressing your image in everything you do, from company letterheads, merchandising, atmosphere, product presentation, packaging, labels, brochures, business cards, signage, music, employee appearance, store or business appearance, sales literature, advertising, to the atmosphere and corporate culture you carry forward everyday. If you were a sales representative of a high-end product, even a cheap folder or a poor copy made on an office supply copy machine can affect your image. Direct mail or sales literature that is delivered in a high quality envelope leaves an impression on the person opening the envelope. If you're thinking about buying a new home, think about what your initial impression might be of a builder who has his floor plans and literature on cheap 20lb. copies out of a copy machine? Does he look likes he's into quality? These are all things that can easily help or hurt your efforts to help you build an image and a brand. Think about the best of the retailers and other large corporations out there. When you think of Disney, what do you think? When you think of Apple, what do you think? What about Tiffany's, Neiman Marcus, Nordstrom or Macy's? What do you want people to think and feel about your business as you carry on day in and day out?

In her book *The Bear Necessities*, founder and CEO of Build-A-Bear Maxine Clark says, "Brands, like countries, have their own unique cultures and language. We think of ourselves as a country with our language, rituals, and traditions. . ."

More than anything, though, "brand" is another name for a company's soul. Being a brand means intentionally exposing the outside world to your image and to the culture of your business. Of course, this involves much more than lip service. You aren't going to be able to tell the world what you are; you're going to have to demonstrate it by your actions. Creating a real and a successful brand is what separates the pros from the average mom and pop store on the street. Once you decide you're going to build a brand, and that you no longer want to be the average retail business, you begin creating a foundation and an outline for how everything will be done from now on.

"THINK OF YOUR BRAND AS A PROMISE YOUR COMPANY MAKES AND FULFILLS EVERY DAY."

Maxine Clark
Founder & Chief Executive,
Build-A-Bear Workshops

People Impressions
If you think about it, one of the first impressions many customers have of you is affected by the way the phone is answered. It should be answered clearly with your company's name as well as the name of the person answering the phone. It shouldn't be rattled off so fast that the caller isn't sure what or where they called. I've also heard phones answered by employees who sounded like they were aggravated about being interrupted. While having a real human answer the phone is always preferable to a recording, if you do use a message, be sure it is positive, pleasant, short, easy to understand and professional.

Another first impression is the look of your store from the parking lot all the way up to the first look at your store inside the door. We'll talk more about this later, but you only have one chance to make a first impression, and that impression can stick, good or bad. Once in the store, are you seen as a customer friendly store with top-notch service or does it depend on who's there at the time? Your focus has to be on YOUR customers and how to best satisfy them. (There will be much more on this later.)

Your Website

Every aspect of your website should be reviewed from graphics and colors to the message, attitude, images and photos. Your website is an extension of your store and its image. Colors, sounds, and overall feel should all work together to reinforce your brand. Also, think about the feel of your website. Do dark colors present the image you want or do you want to create something more fun and carefree? Do you want your website to feel high tech, or do you want it to feel warm and fuzzy? Should it be family oriented or should it be attractive to teens? If your funds are extremely limited, use your own photographs or those provided by a supplier, as long as they're good, and fit in with your identity. Read the chapter on "Internet Tips."

Logos

A logo can do a lot to help build a visual image for your business. The best logos not only establish this visual image of your company, but they also capture your attitude or company culture. A tagline with the logo can help support or clarify your message, especially if the business name doesn't exactly convey any message of any kind. In addition, if you are serious about building your business and name for the long-term, you will need to trademark your logo and name, especially *before* you start building a reputation.

Advertising

Do NOT use your meager and very limited advertising dollars for the exclusive purpose of building your brand or name. See the chapter on "Considerations Before You Advertise." This is for the big boys with budgets to match. You need to focus on getting sales now as efficiently as possible. If you happen to develop some brand recognition by accident through your advertising over a period of years, I'm sure you won't have a problem with that!

In Conclusion:

The problem for many businesses is that they create a mediocre or poor image by default when they give little or no conscious attention to building an image. Any lack of attention and focus on your image is much worse than anything you could probably do to create a positive image. If you think about it, cluttered sales counters, dirty windows, ceiling tiles and sales floors, loud poorly chosen music in the background, dirty hair and body piercings on employees all create an image you probably don't want. LOSE THESE —as well as the employee who is carrying on a private conversation with a friend at a sales counter. Cheap interior store signage and lighted exterior signs with unlit sections all add up to create an image you'd never consider doing on purpose. It is usually a handful of details and impressions over time. If you're trying to be more than a mom and pop store, a cheap handwritten sign doesn't do one thing to help your image. If a handwritten sign fits the image you are going for, then a handwritten sign might be perfect.

Remember that having and controlling your image are not about creating some false facade. It must be truly about who you are and what your reputation, purpose and promise is to everyone who sees you and does business with you. Just make sure your marketing efforts, your brand and the customer's perception of your business are all in alignment, or no one will understand what you're about!

Forging An Image
And A Mission Statement
For A Business With A Soul

5

You can't have an image built on a facade. A facade with no soul or with a fake image will eventually catch up with your business. So if you are going to be a good retailer and a good leader of the people in your business, this chapter is as important, if not more so, than any other in this book. Do not treat it lightly.

What Do You Believe?

Remember that no one knows what's in your head when you are trying to build a business. No one truly sees your intentions or the background, experiences and influences that have lead you to where you are today, only you! You need to understand first and foremost what your beliefs are about and how and why you believe the way you do. For instance, know what has shaped your way of doing business and whether or not your feelings are conducive and appropriate for your business.

What Is Your Business About?
What All Are You Trying To Accomplish?

Why are you and your business here? What are those compelling reasons for even existing? What are you trying to do better? What are you trying to change? If you don't have a clear purpose for being here or a clear idea of just what your business is all about and it's mission, how can you guide your people to understand what all you are trying to do? . . . Think about it. What business are you really in? If you sell warm cookies, are you in the cookie production business, or are you really in the gourmet foods and warm fuzzy feeling business? Are you a unique gift business that offers cookies too?

Are You Just Here To Make Money?

If you are just here to make money and sell as many cookies, shirts, widgets, as you can, however you can, you are much more likely to limit your ability to succeed on a significant scale. Your people will not be able to get very excited about a retail store that has no other purpose other than to make money. A store that is there just for the cash is not setting itself apart from anything. Employees also find it much easier to get behind a business that has a mission to be the best at something. It's much harder to get behind anyone that just wants to open another mediocre store, offering the same unimproved "sameness" as everyone else. Hopefully you originally believed you could do something better when you started your store. If you want to be among the best at what you do, you need to reexamine what originally inspired you to start your business, and then you must convey and transfer that inspiration to your employees. I would rather have an employee I can inspire, even if he or she is not quite as gifted or experienced as someone who just wants a paycheck. I want employees who love what they do and believe whole-heartedly in what I'm trying to do. They will go the extra mile and serve your customers better in the long run.

Have Unshakeable Beliefs That Guide Your Mission, Ethics and Decisions.

Consider issues such as integrity, relationships with customers and employees, company culture, and try hard to define what success is to you, and what it should look like. Will your beliefs and values come at the expense of customers or employees . . . or family? What if some of your values conflict with each other? For instance, would you be conflicted about honesty and integrity from an employee vs. exceptional sales abilities or management skills from the same employee? Your beliefs, values and over all ethics will effect your daily decisions and objectives!

Do Your People Understand What You're Really Looking For?

If you are going to manage your people and truly lead them, then they need to understand your values and what is important to you and your business. It's always a lot easier for anyone to please the boss and do the right thing (if they care at all) if they truly know what you want and what your values are. Remember, it can be very frustrating for employees if they really care about you or your business and yet they still don't have a clue about your motives or priorities.

Ultimately, It All Comes Down To "Do What You Say And Say What You Do!" Know what is important and practice what you said was important from the beginning. Then make sure you let everyone know what it is you want to do, and then do it. Are you a living, breathing everyday example of the beliefs and values you espouse? Or, are you a hypocrite? You will see more of what you want in your own employees if they see you practice what you preach. Employees will be the first ones to see through a fraud and lose respect for the mission if it just a verbal facade. Customers too will eventually see that you are not what you say you are.

You Really Do Need a Mission Statement

I'm guessing when it comes to mission statements, your eyes are glazing over about now. But not having a really well thought out mission statement is about the same as a military leader announcing to his troops, "Join my army because we're going to war, but don't worry about who we're fighting or why we're fighting, and don't worry about how we're going to fight. Just do what I tell you and trust me—it's all in my head."

The real question is how will you know that you've achieved your mission if you don't know what the mission is, either day by day or over the long haul? And, don't you want your people to understand your mission? Think about it. . . if your day-to-day decision and activities are not in line with some type of ultimate goal or mission, then in many cases shouldn't you question what it is you're doing or why you're doing it at all?

Most mission statements I have read are more complicated to understand than my wife, and about as inspiring as a doorknob. They're usually created solely by the boss, however in larger companies they're often created by a group that has been secluded away in a hotel room or on a special retreat for a day, where many words are written up on a gigantic pad setting on an easel in front of a room of these well-meaning company people. In the end, some monumental statements are sent out and passed on throughout the corporate landscape like the Ten Commandments. They may even be engraved on a special plaque and placed on a wall in a lobby somewhere. But often they are uninspiring because they dance around the real meat and heart of the business. My bet is that many of you think a mission statement is a worthless and meaningless exercise. I once thought so too! Besides dancing around the real meat and heart of the business, the management people who create these puffy fluffy statements never really find a way to relate the goals to the real world daily work of their employees (especially those on the front lines.) As a result, no one really gets much out of most mission statements and they become irrelevant. But that is NOT the way it should be if you want to be better than the rest of the pack.

Could a mission statement that was inspirational, special, and really relevant make a real difference? I believe it can! Just imagine, what would happen if really good employees who cared were inspired by giving them a real purpose and mission that they could be excited about or proud of? Employees can get behind an exciting goal or a call to action that gives the company a special purpose (sort of a reason for being). Your mission statement should give you some kind of BIG HONKIN' BODACIOUS GOAL that you're proud of and that tells everyone why you're here and why your business exists!

Some Questions & Tips To Help In Creating A Relevant Mission Statement

Humor me here. . . can you remember back when you first began thinking about starting your business? Hopefully you were very excited. Your mission statement should be a written reminder of what you wanted to go after and what you were trying to accomplish from the very beginning. Think about the following:

What was it that originally got you so excited about starting this business?

What were you really trying to accomplish with this business?

Why was this business above others, going to be different or better? How will your store make a difference?

How do you want customers to feel while they're in your store or how do you want them to feel after they've been there?

Was there a special code of ethics or conduct that was important to you?

Was there another company or company culture that you were trying to emulate?

What is your business about at its most basic level? Think about it initially in terms of one or two words.

What are the major goals of your business?

What kind of people you want working at your business?

Think about what kinds of services or products you want your business to provide.

How will you know when your business is operating successfully (aside from sales and profit figures)?

Make sure you actually believe in what you're writing . . . if you don't believe it, you don't have a chance of living it or working it, and your customers and your employees will see the lie and the insincerity.

Work From Emotion
Why do customers pay a premium for a Build-A-Bear toy, or an Apple computer or a Hallmark card? One of the big reasons is because it

makes them feel a certain way. Buying is about *emotion* (just in case you haven't heard that one before.) Hallmark commercials seem to understand it's about emotion. Apple computers seem to command a loyalty that is unsurpassed. Many feel like they are a part of a special club or movement. Maybe the word is "special." These words and the emotions they conjure up can be very powerful. If you're goal is to really provide something special for your customers, then work to put into words something powerful that communicates these emotions.

For example, keep in mind that a teddy bear toy company isn't in the business of making teddy bears or toys; it is in the business of providing love, friends and entertainment for small children. Creating or tapping into the more expressive and emotional purpose of your business and what you are really selling inspires and communicates the big picture more effectively for your employees. If you can't put into words a mission statement that can generate a more emotional feeling in company employees to truly inspire them, try to find someone who can. It will all be worth it! If you can create a mission statement with your employees' help, you will be miles ahead of your competition and most businesses! Think about it. . . if your employees have a hand in the mission statement they may be more likely to look at your mission statement on an ongoing basis and determine if your business is living the mission statement on a day-to-day basis. They may be reminding you that you're off track!

Inspire Your People To Feel They're A Part Of Something Special!
If you're sitting back right now and thinking, "the only thing that really motivates my employees is money," then maybe there's another problem. If you honestly believe that you need more money to inspire employees, think again! No matter how much you pay to coax employees into being enthusiastic, more money will only work for a while. The extra money becomes routine after a while and without any special reason for doing anything, nothing changes.

If your personal mission for your business is just to make money, and that's it, your own people will most likely NOT feel very inspired or very good about their purpose within your business. After all, what employee can feel a real sense of purpose in making YOU money? Most employees have a strong sense of pride if they're working for a company that has a good reputation and is doing something special. It's funny how those businesses with uninspired employees never seem to deliver the service and excellence that translates into "over the top" service. I can get excited about making money for myself, but the same feeling isn't quite there if all I'm doing is helping someone else line their pockets with no other special mission or purpose. People (your employees) want to feel like they are part of something special. They want and need to feel important and most people want to believe they are making a difference. This is where your mission statement comes into play. If YOU aren't passionate about your business, or you can't create some emotion regarding your own business, how can you expect anyone else to be passionate about it? If your employees don't feel or understand this, then you just have a retail store with some paid help that is going through the motions and nothing more. Your employees need to feel that, in some small sense, you're all out to change the world (or at least city or town) through what you do.

Remember, It's Not A Top Secret Document.
If you have already created a great mission statement, it's worthless if no one knows about it or has bought into it. This is not something to file away in a folder labeled "old mission statements". Whether or not you've worked with your people to create the mission statement, everyone needs to be extremely aware of the mission, goals and purpose of your business. Run your mission statement by the employees you value most. Do they find it clear and easy to understand? Your employees should all understand it and be able to explain it as well. If you have employees who believe in you and enthusiastically embrace the mission, you have employees who actually understand the big picture and they are also aware of their own importance within the big picture. I don't think I need to convince you that it is much more inspiring and exciting to share a common goal that everyone shares than to just show up at work and collect a paycheck.

**Try to Connect Specific Employees With
Aspects Of Your Mission.**

To take this one step further, try to connect your business's mission to each of your employee's talents and strengths. Work with them to help figure out in what special way they can make a real contribution or difference in achieving the company's goals. If you can connect with an employee's talents or strengths, you've got something special going for your business. Now, if you can multiply this idea times each employee, just think of the possibilities. Once I realized I had an employee who was fantastic at merchandising, I had one less job to worry about!

 **One more attribute of a successful business is:** The business seems to have a heart, and its people have a clear succinct "vision" that came from a mission statement that was used to guide, inspire and clearly communicate the mission to all of the employees.

Some Other Mission Statements

Reading the mission statements of other companies may give you some ideas, but you've got to create one that is uniquely yours. It should reflect *your* beliefs, *your* ideals, *your* company culture and *your* purpose for existing. Even if you're a one-store operation with two (2) employees, you should still have a mission statement to serve as a daily guidepost that governs where time and effort are spent. If it isn't reflected in the mission, then it may not be helping you get where you want to go.

 Make sure you actually believe in what you're writing . . . if you don't believe it, you won't live it, and your customers and employees will see the lie and the hypocrisy.

Keep it short. The best mission statements are three (3) to five (5) simple sentences. They are not confusing and they are not self serving and loaded with B. S. like the following mission statement from our fictional friends at Goobers R' Us Inc:

"Our goal is to energetically and enthusiastically engage our patrons with state-of-the-art solutions to empower, entertain and encourage leisure-oriented pursuits through such means and methods that enhance and complement our customers' performance as well as their personal panache by enveloping them in state-of-the-art facilities that are alluring and edifying."

Goober R' Us Inc..

What???

Some Mission Statement Excerpts

"To make, distribute & sell the finest quality all natural ice cream & euphoric concoctions with a continued commitment to incorporating wholesome, natural ingredients and promoting business practices that respect the Earth and the Environment."

Ben & Jerry's Ice Cream

The mission of eBay "is to provide a global trading platform where practically anyone can trade practically anything."

eBay

"Provide freedom and independence to people with limited mobility."

Scooter Store

"The mission of The Walt Disney Company is to be one of the world's leading producers and providers of entertainment and information. Using our portfolio of brands to differentiate our content, services and consumer products, we seek to develop the most creative, innovative and profitable entertainment experiences and related products in the world."

The Walt Disney Company

"The Coca-Cola Company exists to benefit and refresh everyone it touches. Our mission is to create a growth strategy that allows us to bring good to the world—by refreshing people every day and inspiring them with optimism through our brands and our actions."

Coca-Cola

"FedEx is committed to our People-Service-Profit Philosophy. We will produce outstanding financial returns by providing totally reliable, competitively superior, global, air-ground transportation of high-priority goods and documents that require rapid, time-certain delivery."

Federal Express

"Gap Inc. was founded in 1969 on the principle of conducting business in a responsible, honest and ethical manner. Today, Gap Inc. remains committed to meeting the highest standards of business conduct. Nothing less will do. We make this commitment to our shareholders, customers, neighbors and each other not only out of legal obligation, but because it's the right thing to do. Gap Inc.'s success depends on a reputation for integrity and quality in everything we do. We all make an important contribution to the Company's reputation. As we look to the future, each of us is responsible for helping ensure that we continue to meet the standards that have made Gap Inc. a leader."

The Gap Inc.

"Our goal is to be a retailer with the ability to see opportunity on the horizon and have a clear path for capitalizing on it. To do so, we are moving faster than ever before, employing more technology and concentrating our resources on those elements most important to our core customers."

Macy's

"Our mission is to bring the teddy bear to life."

Build-A-BearWorkshop Inc.

Meaningful work is an important issue to people who are truly motivated and inspired at a given job. Good employees want to feel they have a meaningful role in the success of anything they're involved in. Your mission statement is an important tool to inspire your people to perform at their best!

In Conclusion:

A really great mission statement should not need to be revised very often. It exists to remind you of your vision, goals and direction for your business for a number of years. If or when it becomes no longer appropriate or relevant, you can always create a new one.

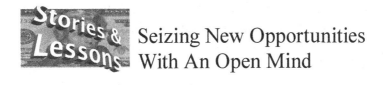

Seizing New Opportunities With An Open Mind

While this story has absolutely nothing to do with making you a better retailer, it has everything to do with becoming successful in ways not exactly anticipated. It's about allowing yourself to be more successful in your current store or even in a whole new business.

One of the great benefits of having your own business is the fact that, for various reasons, business owners seem to find themselves in front of more opportunities than the average person. It's certainly not because of some dark, sinister conspiracy out there created for the businessman. It's because business owners talk to more business owners, tend to be open to more ideas, and maybe are even presented more problems. When you own a business, there is a certain degree of respect that comes from other business owners. They have more empathy for your problems and can also see that you took action on your dream. Most other people just talk, plan or even complain about the system, or the job, or the boss or the hand that life dealt them. The entrepreneur has actually taken action and stuck his/her neck out. Doesn't that make the entrepreneur more of a person who is proactive, takes chances and is—above all—self-motivated? That's someone I want to be around. It is also someone with whom I'm more likely to brainstorm and suggest ideas. After all, most other people only see why it won't work or why they can't participate, or they'll continue to talk about it and never act on it. Isn't anyone more likely to present an opportunity to an entrepreneur?

I think you can understand what the reaction might have been from many of my family members and friends when I told them I was going to make a living selling popcorn. Doesn't sound too impressive, does it? It certainly doesn't carry the cache of being a builder or owning a software design firm, right? It's popcorn and, worse yet, it's retailing! But the point was that I got out there in the arena of businesses, bills, leases, sales taxes and payrolls and profits. In doing so, I was presented with many problems and opportunities that the average person doesn't see or become aware of because they're not there slugging through it all on a day-by-day basis.

As a result of being in a business (popcorn specifically) and having a somewhat open mind, I discovered two distinct opportunities that I would never have otherwise seen or known about. In fact, either one of them had the power to totally re-direct my business goals and even allow me to totally forget about the retail part of my business, which was the opportunity I went after initially.

Opportunity I
Through my efforts to build my brand as well as my sales, I became a fairly well-known name around the metropolitan area. My products were perceived as quality, upscale merchandise with high quality packaging, and it began to pay off. I advertised regularly by mail, print and radio, and I picked up well-known customers, including nationally known names. As a result, I began getting inquiries and orders from some of the area's and the country's largest corporations for gifts and incentives. In addition, the largest grocery store chain in this part of the country (Schnucks) actually approached me about putting my product on their grocery shelves. My product also ended up in the dominant department store chain in the area (owned by May Co.) as well as at other grocers and specialty stores. At Christmas time I would ship large orders of thousands of tins out to area corporations. Three (3) years in a row, I shipped out over 4,200 tins to the employees of a large area retailer for Christmas gifts. In fact, before I expanded my first retail store, I was handling all kinds of business out of a back room that was never designed to handle the volume we were doing. UPS dropped off a trailer for us to fill for our large orders and our small orders were picked up daily with anywhere between 150–300 cartons going out at a time. Often another truck would have to come by later because the first truck didn't have enough space. This wholesale business would eventually become larger than

the retail portion, and the investors who later bought my company decided to get out of retail to focus strictly on wholesale. As it turned out, the entire wholesale business was an obvious opportunity for my product that I hadn't fully appreciated.

Opportunity II
In my efforts to build popcorn tin sales, I was constantly frustrated by the type and quality of the artwork the two (2) major tin manufacturers were putting on their popcorn tins. Much of it seemed out of date or made use of unattractive designs and colors. Very little of the artwork used on popcorn tins seemed suitable for a business gift. My first decision to do something about this was clearly going to be geared toward the Christmas season. I decided to create a tin custom-made for my business that would have a St. Louis theme for area corporations and small businesses. After meeting with a customer, who happened to be a very talented artist, I learned just how good she really was. She had done postage stamps for something like 38 foreign countries as well as numerous designs for national greeting card companies. That's when I made up my mind to take advantage of an opportunity and make use of her talents. I told her I couldn't afford to pay her outright for her artwork, but if she would work with me, I'd pay her a .25 cent royalty on every tin I sold. She accepted, and we were off.

We worked well together when exchanging ideas. She had a great eye for design and detail, and I knew the look that I wanted for my business customers. Even after completing the design and ordering my first shipment of tins, I will admit I was a bit uneasy. I had put thousands and thousands of dollars into one design, and it couldn't even be sold year round. I placed all my bets on the Christmas season. It was a very disconcerting feeling the first time a 40 foot tractor trailer pulled up to the rear of my little store and the driver told me the whole truck was full of just my one tin design. Since we had no loading dock and no pallet jack (not even room for a pallet jack), we had to break down every pallet on the truck and pull the nested tins off one stack at a time. I'm sure the truck driver was not happy. As it turned out, my tin was a major hit and actually sold out much faster than I ever imagined. My artist received more money on my tin design than she had ever made on any piece of artwork, so we were all happy! The next year's design (with the same artist) was even better and got my brand into a number of other new business relationships.

At this point, I decided to take the opportunity another couple of steps further. I decided that, between her talent and my ideas, we would make a great team to help to solve my dissatisfaction with the tin manufacturers.

We created our own line of tins, and called the business "Cancrafters." My idea was to license out the design rights and receive royalties on our designs, rather than taking the risk upon myself to order, stock and try to sell thousands of tins. In a relatively short time, I had an agreement for a line of tins with a major manufacturer. In fact, my first check afforded me the ability to finish the entire basement in my relatively new home! It was the easiest money I ever made and actually caused me to wonder why I was even fooling around with the retail popcorn business.

While the other manufacturer wasn't interested in a line of tins, I did talk them into testing one new Christmas design. The problem came when I told them I wasn't interested in selling the artwork. My artist and I wanted a royalty for every tin they sold. We were extremely confident that we had a design better than anything in their entire catalogue. However, they responded that the only company to which they paid royalties for artwork was Coca-Cola. Since I was full of confidence at the time, I didn't balk at their comments. Instead, I stuck to my guns. And it turned out that we got our royalty, and the tin became their best seller during the Christmas season.

My point with all of this is that had I not been in business for myself, neither one of these opportunities would have presented themselves. I know, without a doubt, that I never would have awakened one morning and decided to go into the popcorn tin design business. I never would have called on the tin manufacturers to sell them on my ideas and designs. In fact, because I was in the business, I became more aware of a niche and an opportunity and had better access to key people than others, to sell the idea.

The bottom line is that we all need to be more aware of the opportunities we may be ignoring or neglecting within our business every day. In fact, I would say that most of the time these opportunities look—at first—like problems or inconveniences.

"Don't wait for extraordinary opportunities. Seize common occasions and make them great . . . weak men wait for opportunities, strong men make them."

Orson Swett Marden
(writer & founder of Success Magazine, 1897)

Each problem has hidden in it an opportunity so powerful that it literally dwarfs the problem. The greatest success stories were created by people who recognized a problem and turned it into an opportunity.

Joseph Sugarman
(direct marketing expert)

"Customers don't always know what they want. The decline in coffee drinking was due to the fact that most of the coffee people bought was stale and they weren't enjoying it. Once they tasted ours and experienced what we call "the third place". . . a gathering place between home and work where they were treated with respect . . . they found we were filling a need they didn't know they had."

Howard Schultz
Chairman and CEO of Starbucks

"I am the world's worst salesman, therefore, I must make it easy for people to buy."

F.W. Woolworth

"You now have to decide what 'image' you want for your brand. Image means personality. Products, like people, have personalities, and they can make or break them in the market place."

David Ogilvy
Advertising Executive, "The Father of Advertising."

 What Are Your Base Strategies?

6

(Get at the Core of What You Are All About First)

I am absolutely amazed at the retailers I've talked to who are concerned about dwindling sales in their store(s) but don't seem to have any plan, or any real interest for that matter, in setting a new direction, rethinking their basic purpose or just doing something different to turn sales around. Yes, I realize that no retail storeowner likes dwindling sales, but there are many who seem willing to just wait or hope for things to turn around. Yes, maybe it is the economy or a temporary downturn. But what if it isn't? Even if it is, do you ever really want to be satisfied with the status quo of any business (much less retailing)?

**Start by Getting At The Foundation Of
What Your Store Is About**
Retail stores usually fit into one of four (4) categories.

1. Stores that compete on price: Competing on price means working with profit margins that are very low. This is where the Walmart, Sam's, Target and Costco stores of the world are king, a fairly obvious category to stay away from.

2. Stores that compete by specializing: If I can assume that you're NOT going to compete on price, then you better be unique or special at something. We're talking about a true focus here. Work on finding one specialized group of customers, and then zero in on them like a laser guided

missile, and work tenaciously to make them extremely happy. This is a more viable approach as opposed to trying to appeal to everyone possible and only pleasing some of them in an average sort of way. Can you become the best place to buy _(widgets)_? Are you the store with the best variety of _(widgets)_? Are you the one place in town where you can always count on finding _(widgets)_? Do you have the best quality _(widgets)_ to pick from? Are you the store where some degree of service, education or installation is involved? For instance, if you're a hardware specialty store, you'd better have a variety in tools for customers to choose. If you offer only one drill, why would you be the place to shop for drills? In other words, the more focused you are in terms of targeting a particular group of customers, the more likely you are to truly satisfy that group of people.

3. Stores that offer a unique shopping or entertaining experience: If you're going to be special in some other way, it had better be a unique retail experience, possibly involving some bit of entertainment, atmosphere, theatrics, education or a very special presentation. Stores like this would include Whole Foods, Disney, Williams Sonoma and Build-A-Bear Workshop. These stores provide more than just a browsing or specialty shopping experience. Often they involve some level of interaction.

4. Stores that retail their own products: The only other area not mentioned above is one in which you retail your own products such as in a cupcake store or a bakery. Apple, Old Navy, Harry & David, Godiva Chocolates, American Eagle Outfitters, Sony and Bose all do this. Or you may manufacture a substantial percentage of products exclusively for your stores. Obviously this makes you unique and special assuming your product is unique or special.

Competing on price is the toughest route you could pick for your retail business. While competing on price has always been extremely difficult, the Internet is making things even more difficult when it comes to competing by price. Customers can now easily check and compare prices on everything. They can walk into your store and pull out their iPhone or some other smart phone with internet access and look up your competitors' prices on almost anything. Again, in my mind, if you are not competing on price, you are competing on some basis involving one or all of the other areas mentioned above.

YOU MUST STAND FOR SOMETHING!

To be really effective in your market, you must be dominant in at least one (1) or two (2) of the following basic strategies. These strategies are, in large part, at the foundation of what you will be about as a retailer.

Which Of These Basic Strategies Are You About?
Assuming you will not be competing by price, the following summarize the other basic approaches that a retailer can use to succeed and thrive in his marketplace. While virtually no one can excel at all of these, any retailer expecting to become a serious and dominant player in his market should be extremely strong in at least a couple of these areas!

1. Provide over-the-top customer service to appeal to customers who want you to take care of their needs and be treated in a highly service-oriented fashion. These customers are willing to pay for excellent service such as at Nordstrom.

2. Become upscale by offering strictly high quality-merchandise and being a premier brand name. You're working to appeal to status and image conscious customers with your merchandise as well as your atmosphere and employees.

3. Be totally dominant in your assortment of merchandise as a truly specialized retailer with an unbeatable selection and have employees who are knowledgeable in your

specific market area, such as at Bed Bath and Beyond or Radio Shack.

4. Provide a unique environment to sell your own manufactured product where there is little to no competition for your specific merchandise, such as at Apple. A gourmet cheesecake store that bakes all of its own product is another example.

5. Be totally convenience oriented with ease of purchase, easy to find, and easy to get in and out of, to make life easier and less time-consuming for customers, such as at Walgreens or McDonalds.

6. Provide an entertainment or educational experience that is totally unique when compared to the competition. Provide an experience in which the barrier to enter your arena of competition or service is high and hard to duplicate, such as Build-A-Bear.

Find something at which you can be the best, whether it is having the best warranties, best selection, best store hours, best delivery policy, etc.

Questions to Help You Determine and Focus on Your Strategies
If you are going to get off on the right track to turn your store around, the following 21 questions are critical.

1. Who are our target customers?

   How old are they?

   What income bracket are they likely to be in?

   How do they spend their spare time?

   What do they need or want that they may not be finding?

   Where do they shop now, and why do they shop there?

Who do they interact with and how?

Where can we go to find and get to know our core customer better?

2. What services can we provide our customers that are above and beyond the norm they will expect?

3. What might our customer dislike about the retailers where they currently shop?

4. What brands and what kinds of merchandise can we offer that will separate us from the competition in satisfying our target customers?

5. What do our targeted customers like to do in their leisure time, and where we can make a real difference for them?

6. What will we need to do to impress this customer with choices and expertise?

7. What can we do that will attract my target customers to visit here for the first time?

8. What could we do to make our target customers feel comfortable here?

9. How can we work to connect with customers' senses with sights, music, smell, taste or touch?

10. What could we do to make our target customer feel like the mother ship has arrived when they first walk in the store?

11. What would customers enjoy doing or seeing here for fun? What would they find entertaining?

12. What would make customers stay in the store longer?

13. What kind of conveniences would customers appreciate that we don't have now?

14. What can we do to educate them (if appropriate)?

15. Who might they bring with them to our store, and why?

16. Are we losing sales to Internet retailers? Get at the heart of why. It's always more than just prices.

17. What can we do that will make our target customer return again and again?

18. What can we do to help create the lifestyle or the picture they find attractive?

19. What can we do to tie our marketing efforts and image to our target customer?

20. Where will our target customers find our name and message via marketing?

21. What will interest our target customer and how can we arouse their curiosity?

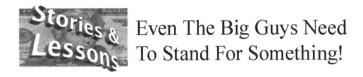 Even The Big Guys Need
To Stand For Something!

A Mass Merchandiser Was Born Of Good Retail Heritage
In 1974, I was hired to start an experimental department for the discount division of May Company. They were called Venture Stores. At their peak they had 10,000 employees and 114 stores throughout the Midwest. Venture Stores had come on strong in the early 1970's and there was great speculation as to just how big and dominant Venture Stores could become. They were backed by May Company, so it seemed as though nothing could stop them. The Venture Stores division was started for May Company by John Geisse (a true genius and legend in retailing) who had co-founded Target Stores for Dayton Hudson in 1962. In fact, Mr. Geisse originated the concept of an upscale better- quality discount store.

The chain grew rapidly and was considered a classier, upscale discounter over other chains at the time such as K-Mart, WoolCo and many others. Initially, they were laid out almost identically to a Target store; however, in their home turf in St. Louis, MO, they totally dominated Target. Venture really wasn't afraid of anyone and was very successful at dominating in the major cities where they competed with other major discounters.

A First-Rate Mass Merchandiser
Their stores at that time had a gas station, auto department, auto service and a self-standing building on the lot for lawn and garden sales. Commissioned sales staff sold Good Year tires in the auto department. The stores had a bakery where fresh donuts and cakes were baked daily along with a full service snack bar and mini

restaurant in the rear called the "Venture Inn" where one could have roast beef, mashed potatoes and pie for dinner. Venture had a shoe department with a shoe salesman to measure your feet. A cosmetician could be found in the cosmetics area along with a full-line pharmacy. The sporting goods department sold rifles and handguns. At the front of the stores, a floral department offered fresh tropical plants. Each of these areas was staffed with a professional manager who usually had a background in his area. There was specialized management for some of these departments, such as a district floral coordinator and auto service coordinator. All of the usual departments could also be found at Venture, including toys, house wares, domestics, a full-line record department (remember those) and ready-to-wear fashions for women. A men's department and a very nice jewelry department that stocked diamonds and pearls, were also available. My experimental department was a full-line pet department. It was originally stocked with 80 15-gallon tanks and four (4) 55-gallon tanks of tropical fish as well as a bird and animal room for everything from hamsters to parrots, domestic canaries, macaws, rabbits, tarantulas, iguanas and snakes were also sold. The only things really missing were dogs and cats.

A Prophetic And Wise Statement

I list all of these departments in detail because Venture really was a pretty special mass merchandiser back then. Each of these departments helped elevate and separate Venture from the rest of the pack at the time. One day, David Farrell, the chairman of all of May Company toured the stores in Kansas City where my pet departments were being tested. After grilling me and closely scrutinizing my department, he turned to the rest of the entourage that was with him and said something that certainly impressed me. He said, "This is the type of department that Venture needs more of to better separate itself from its competition."

I thought the statement rather profound at the time; however, I was a bit biased where my department was concerned. In the end, that statement became rather ironic. Within a year of that visit, the president of Venture and I agreed in a one-on-one meeting that we should close the pet departments permanently. The president told me that Venture was becoming more of a self-service store, while my departments were very service-oriented. Leading up to that point, and for years after, I observed Venture make some very disappointing and concerning changes to re-orient to a more self-service retailing approach. As it turned out, May Company eventually divested itself of Venture in 1990. I believe May Company really didn't know what to do with the discounter anymore, and ultimately abandoned their support as they saw the writing on the wall.

Compromise Begins

Over the years while working for Venture, I watched as they cut back on payroll and customer service in many of these departments. As each became more of a hassle and less profitable, payroll would be cut first. Quite often, the department would be eliminated entirely. It always seemed that the departments began to fail and disappoint management after the payroll had been cut. Hmmmm!

First the lawn and garden department went. It was too much trouble, and we couldn't seem to make any real money at it. The commissioned sales employees were eliminated from the tire department, and Good Year Tires ended up telling Venture Stores to take a hike. Good Year didn't seem to like the new compromises in our sales approach. The cosmeticians were eliminated when they became too expensive. Payroll was cut in the jewelry and shoes, so we generally ended up with inexperienced sales staff who knew very little about these departments, if anything at all. Venture closed the floral department and then removed the guns from sporting goods when they became too much of a hassle (because of all those pesky firearms regulations.) Auto service was closed. It was complicated, and we couldn't seem to make enough money at that either. The bakeries closed. The Venture Inn closed at a later date. The gas stations closed. Gas was a hassle too.

What Did They Stand For?

Now all of these departments were not cut at one time. They were just gradually eliminated over a period of 8–10 years as supposedly sharper management people came to the conclusion that fashion merchandise was the place to be with those higher profit margins. And I'm sure that they were correct to an extent. Fashion merchandise does have higher profit margins and doesn't require nearly the level of service that many of these other categories required. But somewhere along the way, Venture lost its way. In the customer's mind, I believe, it had ceased to stand for anything anymore. No one really seemed to know what Venture was. One year it wanted to come across as more of a sharp discounter with lots of bargain bins in the aisle, and another year it wanted to be more like an upscale fashion discounter and lifestyle store. Somewhere along the line, Venture confused its customers. I remember my dad not being sure from one year to the next whether they even had automotive items in their stores or not. According to my dad, they eventually had nothing there for him.

A Price To Be Paid For Confusion
Maybe top management really knew what they were doing. Maybe the original stores, as conceived, were never going to work over the long term in the changing landscape of retailing. Maybe upper management knew something that I didn't understand at the time. But somewhere along the line, in its effort to compete with the Walmarts and Targets of the world, Venture lost its identity. I am convinced that Venture had nothing that truly separated itself from the competition anymore. Was there anything special about it? Or was it just another discount store with nothing unique to offer its customers? At the very least, it confused itself and the public and, in the process, lost some of its customer base.

And what about the many departments that were ultimately closed or compromised after cutting payroll and service? Were they unintentionally sabotaged by the relentless effort to cut expenses? Can you compromise something so much that it has to fail? At any rate, by the late 1990s, Venture was remodeling its stores and frantically trying to return to its founding principals as an upscale discounter. It didn't work, or, at a minimum, it was too little too late.

Is There A Lesson Or Two Here?

First of all, I realize that self-service stores are just that, and I realize they cannot support higher payroll levels due to the lower profit margins in which they operate. But isn't it ironic that Venture was doing just great in the old days when they did operate with professional department managers and some level of service? Why is it that when someone (usually a senior manager who comes from the accounting side of the business) wants to reduce expenses, payroll is always the big target? I know very well that payroll is the big, big budget item . . . but is cutting expenses the only answer to profits? Must service always be eliminated in the name of making money? Is that the only way to get to a profitable position? I don't think so. As a matter of fact, I know so! There is such an outcry about the lack of service in this country. Department stores are less attractive places to shop than they were years ago, and there is a lack of service and sales help at most department stores these days. What happened? They don't operate on lower profit margins.

So my question is this: when Venture began cutting payroll and departments, were they listening and responding to their customers or were they deciding for their customers? Are today's department stores listening to their customers, or have they made some decisions for them?

One last observation to note: While almost every one of those categories were eliminated, over the years, because they were too much trouble, too difficult or too customer service-oriented, Walmart today profitably operates the large majority of those departments in their stores. Now, I'll agree that Walmart is not the paragon of customer service, but they have listened to their customers and found a way to make it all work. I would say that if you're going to eliminate service, you better have great low prices, or you better find something awfully special to replace that service. I'm not exactly sure what that is, but it better be something that sets you apart from everyone else.

By the way, the same Venture management back then also told us that little ole Walmart would never come to the big city to take on the big guys in discounting.

So What Do You And Your Stores Stand For?

What is your image to the buying public? Maybe you know what you are or what you intend to be. But what is your image, and what is your brand? Does everyone else understand what you are? Don't be afraid of making a decision, and don't try to please everyone. You'll end up pleasing no one. Venture certainly pleases no one today. It doesn't even exist. The big guys don't always have the answers either. Keep in mind the quote, "Don't be afraid to try something new. Remember, amateurs built the ark. Professionals built the Titanic!" Just listen to your customers while you build!

Things You Can Do Now To Begin The Turnaround

7

There are many areas where you can make adjustments and meaningful changes in your store. Some of them are appearance issues, some are service issues and some are merchandising issues. Hopefully by now, I've sparked a few thoughts and ideas and maybe even led you to believe your store might just need shaking up a bit. Why not begin with some basic appearance issues, and then ask yourself honestly about the rest of the list in this chapter?

We all judge things by how they look. This is extremely true in retailing. Not only should you be concerned with trends, as outlined in previous chapters, you should also remember to just update and freshen your own store from time to time.

Take A Hard, Honest Look At Your Store's Physical Appearance

Yes, I know that cleaning up a store, or adding some fresh paint will not turn around poor sales, especially during a recession. But if I had a store and sales were just treading water or, worse yet, tanking, I would want to know that I was doing **everything** in my power to attract and hold on to each and every customer. All too often over years of operating a business, we lose sight of how a customer sees us. Our goal here should be to have the same freshness we had the day we opened our store. Remember how good everything looked? Remember how clean it was? What impression do you create today? Is it one of a store that's stale or past it's prime? Or is it an exciting, vibrant and pleasant place to shop? Yes, I know you've built a base of customers and you've worked hard to get every one of them, but what about new first-time customers? You want and need those people too, don't you? What is their perception of your store?

Appearance Issues

So where do we start? Let's begin with some appearance issues. We'll start out with some cleaning issues, but there are other physical considerations as well. I'm betting that you're missing some of them. At any rate, all of these add up to a making major change in your store's appearance and your customers' perception of your image. When it comes to maintenance and cleanliness, don't tell your people they need to clean the store. Take the time via a meeting to explain to your people all of the rationale behind having a clean store. You also need to explain why a clean store is a key to better sales.

Storefront

How about cleaning the windows for starters? After the windows have been cleaned inside and out, pay attention to the windowsills and door jams. Clean and dust off the hardware attached to your doors, such as the hinges and door-closing hardware. What about the general impression as customers drive by? How noticeable is your store (in a good way)? Does the storefront make you want to stop in and check things out? When is the last time you drastically changed your storefront? How often do you change your window displays? Research shows the more often your store highlights new merchandise, the more often a browser will turn into a buyer, and the first place to do that is in your shop windows. They are extremely valuable space in your retail turf. They should be used to set the mood of any given event or promotion, and this vibe should reflect the frame of mind you want your customers in to buy the merchandise you're selling. Are you conveying excitement, summer fun, nostalgia or romance? In our fast-paced daily living, grabbing attention is important but tough, and you have only seconds to capture it.

You must excite customers! Give them a serious indisputable reason to shop and enter your store. Spark their curiosity. Be outrageous! Do something! You need to showcase or highlight new products or new themes. Do it with lighting, new fixtures, new signing . . . new ideas. Yes, you could hire a pro, but it's hard for me to believe that, between you and your employees, there's not enough creativity and imagination to pull it off on your own.

Store Interiors
How long has it been since anything substantially changed in your store? Your customer's tastes and interests change regularly, and if you have a younger crowd for a customer base, things can and will change in a heartbeat.

<u>**Inexpensive Things to Do Now**</u>: Before you get into any total store makeovers, start with one area and begin by taking a critical look at what you currently have. For instance, the sales counter or cash register area. Is it cluttered? Is it crowded and unprofessional? At the very least, stand in *front* of your counter area and take a good hard look. When you stand behind the counter day-in and day-out, you don't see what your customers see. I've seen counter areas at some stores and actually felt embarrassed for them. Consider everything that anyone can see from the customer side of the counter—on the walls, on the floor, down behind the register. Get rid of any loose papers around the check out counter and remove items that make you look cluttered and amateurish. Things like post-it notes or small pieces of paper that are scotch taped to the register need to go. Keep paperwork, invoices and packing slips away from this area. All of this gives your customers the perception that you are disorganized and second-rate.

<u>**More Expensive Investments**</u>: Have you considered whether or not your store interior needs to be redone with a theme in mind? If you can't afford a professional designer, ask around and talk to other storeowners about someone they might recommend who is innovative and can work inexpensively. Maybe you know a talented "want-to-be" decorator who has impressed you with ideas for their own home. These are all good things to keep in mind if you know you don't have the ideas or the money yourself.

Add Color

If you want a major, noticeable change, consider a fresh coat of paint in a color (or colors) that emphasizes your brand and matches your image.

Flooring

At the very least, be sure your floor is clean at all times. If it's vinyl tile, keep it well waxed and shined. If you use ceramic tile, make sure it is sealed or the grout between tiles will get dirty and discolor in no time.

Lighting

This subject is addressed under "Visual Merchandising Tips." However, let's just emphasize for now that you want to avoid the use of 100% fluorescent lighting if at all possible. This is especially important if you want to give your store some character and atmosphere. While it may be great for discount stores, stockrooms and offices, it needs to be supplemented with incandescent or halogen lights when displaying merchandise. Incandescent lighting also allows you to highlight specific merchandise as well as present it in a more natural looking light.

Keep Your Store Fresh

Do not allow customers to make a return visit only to find the same store with the same merchandise in the same displays. Keeping your store fresh and new is critical to increasing the frequency of your customers' visits. When you go back to a store, you do not want to see the exact same things you saw the last time you were there. As a merchant, I realize you can't turn the whole store over with all new merchandise every few weeks, but you can constantly rearrange, re-merchandise and redirect attention to different items on a regular basis. Just rearranging merchandise may not mean much to you when you're there on a day-in day-out schedule, but this simple tactic allows customers to notice "new" merchandise every time they come in. Try to move around at least some merchandise every two to three weeks.

"If the merchandise doesn't move, move the merchandise!"

If you bring in new product, evaluate its sales activity at least every month. Sometimes a great item can seem mediocre or poor by pricing it wrong or putting it in a location that people overlook. So if a product isn't moving, double check your retail price and re-merchandise it or move it to a new location. If you have not moved at least 50% of the product after 90 days, mark it down. Again, the sooner you can free up dollars to bring in new, fresh merchandise that will sell, the sooner you will have an opportunity to make more money.

Utilize Vertical Space
Go upwards with some small boxes or risers when merchandising on tables or countertops, and make use of wall space with higher displays on the walls, even if it's out of reach. Fixtures themselves should probably not be above five feet high, but merchandise up the walls says you have inventory and you're in stock. Remember, you are paying for every square foot in your store.

I'm not contradicting myself here. #6 just mentioned making things feel spacious, and you can't fill every square inch or you'll have clutter. You must do both. Create a feeling of space that's free of clutter while still using the room you have. In order to do this, you must take advantage of the vertical space in your store, not just the horizontal space. Go up where you can be effective, gain attention, gain space and still look organized—not cluttered. Going vertical does not mean looking like a warehouse, it means using height to your advantage to draw attention or to display more without getting stuck in the rut of going horizontal all of the time.

Signage
This is another area that's often neglected for years on end. You and your employees may know where to find everything, but you can't forget that others will not easily figure it out. In general, customers do not like to ask for help. They want to discover and find things on their own. Help them do just that. Signs need to be used to label or help identify a theme or an idea, and they make your store look

professional, as long as they don't overwhelm the store. If you have tables for in-store specials, label them that way with a sign that draws attention and makes one feel like there is something special going on there. If you have an area to highlight new merchandise, use signage that draws attention to new buys. Signage is also important to help categorize and label departments or sections of a store. But if you use signs, don't be cheap or unprofessional in the way you do it. To me, signage clearly differentiates between a professional, effective retailer and a "mom and pop" store. Most "mom and pop" type stores do not have the luxury of receiving professional signs from the corporate office, but that doesn't mean they should be forgotten or neglected. You need signs, but NOT paper signs. It's amateurish. If you're going to make signs with you own computer and printer, frame them to make them look more professional.

Empty Shelf Spaces
Does it look like your going out of business or does it just look like customers have to pick from what's left over? Make sure your shelves are fully stocked; this means finding a way to rearrange or distribute the merchandise so that all empty spaces are filled. Even if sales are slow and you've cut your inventories, an empty looking store is not very exciting for any shopper. Empty shelves sadden and disappoint. Customers also assume money problems or that possibly you look like you're going out of business. You don't want that rumor started!

Ongoing Maintenance
Designate a day once a week when everyone stays an additional 30 minutes after store closing to look for areas that have not been cleaned or have been missed during the normal course of daily activities. There are all kinds of places where dust collects. Look for cobwebs on the walls and ceilings. If you have customer pick-up areas or docks and changing rooms to try on clothes, take a hard look at those areas and see them from a customers' viewpoint.

Along the lines of maintenance is another little item that affects customers' perception of your store and has really irritated me at times. How is your ink cartridge printing out your cash register receipts? If your cash register or POS terminal is printing receipts that are hard or impossible to read because the ink is faded, your customers can get irritated or disappointed when they need that receipt with a date for a return. We're talking a very small investment on your part that can have a significant impact on how you are perceived by your customers.

De-clutter. If you don't feel you need to re-do your floor plan, create some space around what you already have. Sometimes you can't see the forest for the trees, and sometimes you can't see the merchandise for the merchandise either. Consolidate items into tighter groupings and keep in mind that aisles shouldn't be less than four feet wide.

Other Physical Issues
Floor Plan And Store Traffic
If you haven't thought about your store layout for a while because you've been so caught up in the day-to-day business of doing business, it's time to become more analytical regarding your floor plan. Since retailing evolves at breakneck speed and you want to stay interesting and fresh, it's a good idea to modify your store's floor plan from time to time. There is always room for improvement and there are always reasons to change.

Think of your layout from a profit standpoint for a second. If you have 4,000 square feet of retail space and 300 square feet is storage, and you also have another 750–850 square feet of space that is not very productive for sales, you have 26–29% of your valuable leased space producing virtually nothing for you. As a result, the other 2,850–2,950 square foot of space must be that much more effective! If you're going to maximize the use of your lease and the expense to heat and cool it, you've got to give more attention and planning to your layout. Obviously non-selling space should be kept to a minimum.

Keep in mind that the first 20 feet of real estate inside your door is generally the most valuable, so create **a positive impression or emotion with your customers in the first seconds they spend in**

your store. This can be done with displays, but it can be supplemented with smells, lighting and anything else you want them to notice immediately. From the very moment the customer walks in the door, you want them to feel, see and be wowed by what your store is all about. Sam's Club and many bakeries vent the smell of fresh baked goods to the front of the store to create an instantly pleasant feeling and help offset the warehouse experience. Best Buy puts their repair and service area in a prominent space at the front of the store to assure its customers that they are not on their own if there's a problem. For any store, it's important to give the customer that feeling of confidence and comfort.

What's the first impression immediately inside your store? There needs to be some sort of space or comfort zone—as some might call it—when customers first step inside your door. People need to be able to take it all in, adjust and "see the forest for the trees." If carried out correctly, customers should get in the store and adjust without being overwhelmed by people or merchandise crowded near the front door. But once they're far enough in, you want to wow them with an effective display that makes them feel like they've *arrived*. Creative merchandising and point-of-purchase displays were not meant for just the big stores. Spend some money, borrow some props, or rent some items from other stores to help you create more interesting displays. Remember, first impressions are important!

Think about it . . . if your customers can't find or don't notice what you have, all your efforts are shot. You've got to insure easy navigation through your store and help customers not only find what they want, but also what you want them to find. Generally, people have a tendency to move or migrate to the right when given the opportunity. Knowing this allows you to structure things that encourage people to move in the direction with which they are most comfortable. Comfortable is important. If people are more comfortable or at ease in all regards, they are more likely to stay and spend.

Position signs so that they can be easily seen from any major traffic area. Work to draw customers off the beaten path with great wall displays and attention-getting signs. I've generally observed that the stores lowest in volume are also the ones that do not use signage to effectively categorize or draw attention.

A good retail layout can entice customers to buy more than planned by drawing them through the store to see as much merchandise as possible. What you use to draw customers through the store will depend entirely on what type of retailer you are, but you need to give customers a reason to navigate to the back of your store. The obvious answer is to use popular merchandise to pull the customers to the rear of the store. Department stores will pull you through with clothing (the basics) and make you pass the highest margin items they carry—the jewelry and cosmetics counters. Jewelry stores put their best, most showy products toward the back to pull people past all the more traditional items they want them to see and pick up on the way. Supermarkets use produce, dairy and meats (basics) so that you navigate all of the higher profit processed food aisles. In a bakery, you might put the day old bread at the rear of the store to make customers walk past the wall of the enticing fresh pastries, doughnuts and specialty cakes and pies.

If possible, avoid too many straight aisles so that you don't begin looking like a convenience or discount store. Curves and angles make your layout more interesting and provide more places to highlight merchandise. If you want to lead people in a particular direction, also consider making that specific path or aisle a different material or color.

Also take a look at how you can improve dead, blocked or darker areas, as they not only hurt sales, but also can lead to theft. High profile shelving will often give you a warehouse look and prevent you from seeing what is going on across the store. But if you need additional room, building central interior walls for prime selling space may be an answer.

Consider the following questions for a moment and provide some honest answers:

- Does your store just flat-out look and feel good or exciting?

- Does your store feel open and spacious? Is there too little space in aisles?

- Can you see throughout your store relatively easy?

- Do you get customers to walk through all areas of the store you want them to see?

- Do you pull customers to the back of the store as well as you'd like?

- Does your store make customers feel comfortable and want to stick around a while, or is it an exercise in dealing with clutter and frustration?

- Does the floor plan draw attention to featured merchandise?

- Does your floor plan make it easy on your employees to take care of customers efficiently?

- Are there dead spaces within your store?

- Can more of your space be used more effectively?

- Does it make it easy to rearrange and draw attention to new items?

To improve your odds at creating a better floor plan, consider the following questions:

What works well in your store now? What do you feel good about? Where are the strongest sales consistently found, regardless of what is placed there? If your counter or register area is working efficiently, why is that? Do you have any idea what your customers like about your store? Have you ever surveyed or questioned them?

What should you keep or possibly even duplicate? Do you have one area that you don't want to mess with? Why is that? How could one productive area be duplicated with the same results? Be careful. You need to understand why it's working in the first place before you go trying to reproduce the effect.

What must change? Are there dead zones or areas within your store where any merchandise put there just dies? Why is this the case? What can be done? Is the back of your store productive? If not, why not? Also consider your sales counter. Are your people fumbling over each other when waiting on multiple customers at the register?

The general idea is to make customers walk further into the store for the things you know they are already coming to get—the items that are virtually certain to sell. If something is absolutely not selling that you know should be selling, you've probably got it in a bad spot. The answer to improving your store plan probably lies in a combination of details, from fixtures and counter area, to inventory control, lighting and merchandise placement and allocation. Ask yourself, "Has anything in my store been the same way too long?" Ask some people you respect to take a critical eye at what they might change. Ask your employees how they think you can make the most of the space you have. Remember, nothing in retail is cast in stone and your store should be constantly evolving in an effort to stay interesting and keep capturing the customers' attention. Often we (the owners) think customers are blind, but many times, it's the owner that can't see the merchandise for the merchandise.

Impulse Purchases. Create at least one area if not more, that encourages impulse purchases. The grocery stores create large end-cap displays of a single item that make you notice it (and usually give the impression that it's a special price, even if it isn't.) Impulse items should be in higher traffic areas or where customers are apt to spend some time, such as the check out lanes where all the candy and gum are at the grocery store. These items should also be higher margin items. What do you have in your store that is higher margin and may be picked up by a customer as an impulse purchase, just because it happens to be where they will notice it at a weak moment? This is where profits are made.

Merchandising. See chapter 8.

More-Important Issues to Help Sales Now

If It Isn't Selling, Move It Or Get Rid of It. Be realistic about merchandise that isn't selling well, especially once you've addressed the questions above. Use markdowns and clearance areas to move slow or problem merchandise. Do not sit on it hoping that someday a miracle will happen. Get your money out of stale merchandise so that you can invest it in new merchandise that *will* sell. Get the price down to your cost as soon as possible. Selling anything leftover at cost is not a crime, especially if the large majority of that item was sold for a good profit. If you must take a loss and sell it below cost, do so. It is not doing anything for you on the shelf. Do not fool yourself into believing that you have viable, saleable inventory of something that has little or no chance of selling in the near future.

> Many years ago, I worked with a large number of computer stores in the midwest that had thousands of dollars of software inventory in stock for their computers. The only problem was that, while they thought they were stocking a good variety, most of the inventory was—in reality—older, and meant for computers that no one was buying any longer. They couldn't bear to mark it down, so they continued to delude themselves into thinking that this large horde of software was still sellable. Meanwhile, their software sales were nowhere close to what they could have been.

Sometimes taking a tentative markdown of 10 or 20% only prolongs the misery of slow merchandise and can cost you more in the long run. You certainly don't want customers to tire of coming in and seeing the same clearance merchandise hanging around the store for repeated visits. Again, the cost of poor-selling merchandise is really lost opportunity because the much-needed space and inventory dollars are being kept from use on new merchandise that *will* sell. No matter how you look at it, it becomes very expensive to keep product on your shelves if it's not selling.

Take More Chances.
If you're afraid of ordering new products that may not pan out, you're in the wrong business. Customers expect to find the latest, newest, improved, upgraded, more stylish, state-of-the-art, unique, or eye-catching thing when they shop at a specialty store. And if they're coming to your store and not finding it, you're becoming less relevant in their eyes. Get into new products and then learn from past mistakes, but try new things constantly. Understand your cost and put some effort into how you will promote or feature new items. If it doesn't work out, mark it down and move on. This is retailing.

Sales Floor Etiquette
This will be discussed at length later in this book. For now, I'll just mention a few things. First, when a customer enters your store, I don't care what you are doing. Your customer's arrival should be acknowledged. You may know this, but can you guarantee your employees are doing it? A nice "hello" or "I'll be with you in a minute sir" goes a long way. Even a nod of the head would be preferable to what I usually see. Second, instruct your salespeople to tell waiting customers that they'll be with them momentarily. This will reduce the number of customers who leave your business without being served. I often wonder how many owners or managers have any clue of how many people leave their store without ever being served or even acknowledged.

Also, when a customer is anywhere in the vicinity of an employee on the phone, the customer should be acknowledged with "I'll be with you in just a second," or if they are on the phone with a friend or relative, they should get off the phone immediately. I'm not talking about putting the phone down on the counter and making the customer feel uncomfortable, as if they're interfering with the employee's phone call. I'm talking about hanging up. Your customers have come to your store for a reason (most likely to buy something from you). That is why you went into retail. Don't disappoint. Don't make them feel like they are interrupting something. I used to have a 10-foot banner across the soffit over my sales counter (out of customer view) facing my employees that said,

"Customers are not an interruption to your work. They are the purpose of it."

You must drill the concept of "making the extra effort" in to your employee's heads! Salespeople are there to make additional sales. If they were just there to get the customer what they wanted, they would be called order takers. It's important they avoid being too vague with questions such as "Can I help you?" or "Can I get you something else?" It would be more effective to say: "Can I find you a tie that goes with the shirt?" A truly top-rung salesperson in a service-oriented store would do even better by bringing the tie and showing it to the customer while laying it on the shirt.

Skimping On Payroll

Every retailer looks constantly to cut costs to control prices and/ or improve the bottom line. All too often, the only solution seems to be cutting payroll and employee training. And all too often, this means having store personnel who cannot answer questions about merchandise or who are too overloaded to offer real service to customers. Sometimes it's worse when the employees feel overwhelmed with work; they are then more likely to make visitors feel unwelcome, like an unwanted interruption to their job. Unfortunately, the drive to control expenses and payroll often leads to "self-help" style stores with no interaction between employee and customer until the purchase. That is, if you're lucky enough to get the purchase from the neglected customer at all.

Use Technology To Benefit Customers, Not Just You.

Spend money first on technology that will directly benefit the customer. For instance, customers will actually see the value of technology that speeds up their checkout or return process. Walmart has done this continuously over the years. As a home décor store, having technology that might allow customers to see different fabrics or colors in rooms or furniture they are trying to visualize might be appreciated. If you want customers to hang around, free Wi-Fi has been an obvious ploy. These types of benefits go directly to the customer and they become very aware of them.

Are You Offering Services That Make Things Convenient For Your Customers?

Do you offer gift-wrapping—or better yet—free gift-wrapping? How about higher end no-wrap gift boxes, free shipping or free note cards with purchase? What about local delivery? How about hot coffee in the winter? Consider anything that might make your customers' shopping experience a little easier or a bit more special at your store.

Give Attention To The Checkout Process.

If customers decide to hand over their hard earned money, PLEASE make it an easy and uneventful thing to do. Take their money. Do NOT underestimate the attention that should be given to the checkout process. If you are going to screw up the customers' in-store experience, PLEASE don't do it while taking their money! You should constantly look at how to make things quicker and more efficient for the sake of the customer. Part of the answer lies in training, part of the answer lies in the attitude and gratitude of your people, and part of the answer lies in the latest technology. Remember Apple. It has made paying for merchandise easier than ever. You also need to analyze every part of the process to streamline it and make sure your people have the supplies and tools they need at all times. And lastly, be sure your customers are sincerely thanked, with eye contact, by each of your employees. Do not allow employees to keep their eyes focused on the register when moving on to the next customer.

Know The Amount Of Your Average Sales Transaction.

You should monitor your average sales transaction on a daily or at least weekly basis. While this is not genius advice for most retailers, it is still not analyzed or monitored enough in many cases. You need to know how the things you do in your store are affecting this average. Is it going up or coming down? Is it because of a new floor plan, a new employee, a new manager, or a cleaner store? Everything going on in a store, especially your sales help, can effect your average daily sales transaction. If you want to watch and know the effect of specific employees, you'll need to upgrade to hourly tracking.

Have You Begun Offering A Gift Card Yet?

Gift cards provide customers a no-brainer solution to gift giving, not to mention a guaranteed, no return, no hassle purchase for them and for the recipient. Customers who use gift cards also tend to spend more than the amount of the card. Plus, keep in mind that retailers report that 5 to 10 percent of cards are never even redeemed.

Keep Yourself Informed.

Trade associations and organizations like GKIC (Glazer-Kennedy Insider's Circle™) are a great way to learn important information for your business. At GKIC, though not strictly aimed at retail, you'll learn straightforward marketing tips and techniques in their monthly workshops that you can implement right away to increase sales and profits. Their marketing tips and lessons are better suited for small businesses on Main Street, as opposed to some theory from a Madison Avenue boardroom. Their meetings are not lectures but interactive discussions about the latest marketing secrets that are producing really solid results for many of their members. There's no "theory"—just techniques that have gotten results. They also offer an array of educational CDs, books and even Mastermind groups for those that want much more specific help.

Aside from organizations like the GKIC, newsletters aimed at retailing can also provide valuable information, as well as ideas about what's going on in retailing that might spark your imagination.

Get Your Store Outside.

When the weather's good and if your landlord allows, set up a display of merchandise outside your store from time to time. This always creates a sense of excitement and makes your store more noticeable to customers driving or walking by. Make use of "visual movement" with flags and or balloons.

Get Yourself Involved Outside The Store.

Get involved and contribute your services to organizations and programs in your community. Serving and contributing to your community is not only the right thing to do, but it also helps you separate your store from the over-duplicated and dominating national chain stores. People do notice what businesses do and do not do to support the community.

Merchandising

8

In today's competitive environment, any retailer who hopes to have a chance at having "A Line Out The Door" cannot afford to look at merchandising as something they'll do if and when they have the time for it. With more and more competition for the customer's hard-earned money, and more and more places for consumers to spend their disposable income, your store needs to constantly strive for that extra impact and added appeal in any and every way you can get it. Don't tell me you don't have time to give this your attention. YOU ARE A RETAILER. THIS IS YOUR PURPOSE.

Even if you're operating on a limited budget, why would you want to lay all of your money on the line for a retail business and then look at merchandising as some kind of afterthought or luxury?

A Gordon Guideline

"Considering the fact that you are leasing retail space (the most expensive space in any given part of town), why wouldn't you do everything in your power to get customers in the door, keep them inside for as long as possible and get them to come back often—as in, again and again and again?"

On top of expensive rent, you've got payroll costs, merchandise costs, insurance costs, utility costs, advertising costs and more. Why would you risk and invest all of this without doing everything in your power to make it all worth it by surpassing customer expectations? Ideally, when I talk money and merchandising, I'm talking great fixtures that complement and add to your brand and store atmosphere. I'm talking about spending money on display equipment or pieces that entertain and draw attention to merchandise. I'm talking about a little remodeling or contractor work to make the store inviting and visually interesting.

Now don't get all worried. I'm not telling you to go out and spend serious money on a designer or a contractor for your store. While I do suggest putting some money into merchandising, I'll also focus on other day-to-day things that you do have the ability to improve without spending large amounts of money.

Merchandising is obviously much more than just getting merchandise on a shelf. According to businessdictionary.com the definition of merchandising is: "Activities aimed at quick retail sale of goods using bundling, display techniques, free samples, on-the-spot demonstration, pricing, shelf talkers, special offers, and other point-of-sale methods." Put another way, merchandising is looking at the customer experience—from their first approach to your front door, through their entire visual and sensory experience inside the store, until they leave your store. In order to do this successfully, you must understand who your customers are and how and why they shop. If you couple this knowledge with some real thought and strategies, you can position your product effectively to drive sales and get a bigger share of the pie.

Even the dictionary says "merchandising is the quick retail sale of goods using bundling, display techniques, etc." While you may not be able to control packaging or even publicity, you can control display. And controlling display can mean making adjustments to your product presentation until you have positively affected the sale of that merchandise. It is an educated trial-and-error strategy. The ultimate goal of great visual merchandising is to make the shopping experience better—that is, more comfortable, convenient, exciting, interesting, educational and customer-friendly—by:

1. Making it easier for the customer to find the product.

2. Making it easier for the customer to self-select or self-serve (if they so choose).
3. Making it possible and easy for the shopper to coordinate or accessorize.
4. Providing appropriate information, i.e. sizes, colors, prices, etc.
5. Highlighting and showing the latest merchandise or fashion trends.
6. Educating the consumer as to the features and benefits, of the products.
7. Entertaining the customer or visually and physically adding to the atmosphere and customer shopping experience.

The following list can affect the sale of specific merchandise and should be considered at times, *especially if the merchandise isn't selling*!

Presentation Issues & Location Issues
How does the merchandise look where it is now?

Is the merchandise clean, dust free and look like new? Is it new?

Could moving this product increase it's sales?

Is it merchandised in the right area of the store or is it hard to find?

Is the merchandise categorized?

Should it be displayed higher or lower?

Is it at eye level or down on the lowest shelf? Would moving it up or over help its sales?

Is it accessible? Can people see it or inspect it easily?

Is it behind a counter or hard to get to? Is it out of reach?

Is the presentation of a given product noticeable?

Is it lost among other merchandise or clutter?

Would it sell better next to _____?

Does it need more facings and visibility?

How many facings are needed to sell it effectively?

Should I combine this product with different types of merchandise to create a theme?

Should I display this product as a consumer would use it in their home?

Are things arranged in any kind of logical fashion? Or maybe they're too logical and too boring?

Is the most profitable merchandise in the most visible spot?

Can I use the traffic created by this item to draw attention to other merchandise I want customers to see?

Risk Issues
Is this merchandise a prime shoplifting target? Should it be placed behind the counter or secured in a cabinet?

If we put it behind the counter, will it help or kill sales on this item?

Will the placement of this merchandise contribute to a fall or accident?

Education
Does it need special attention so people understand what it is or what it does?

Does it need help overcoming poor packaging? (for example, would a portable DVD player sell better in a box on a shelf or in a display where it is set up and operating?

Does this merchandise need a sign or a description?

Demand Issues
Is it an established product that people seek out?

Do people expect to find this product in your store, or do you need to make sure people know you have it (as in, are you trying to sell socks in a hardware store)?

Is it signed? Should there be a sign for it?

Is there a price on it or will customers have to ask? If they need to ask, you've just slowed or killed your sales.

Is the merchandise in season? Also consider if it is a little early or late in the season for a particular item.

Is a sufficient quantity of the product displayed or does it look like something leftover? No one likes to buy the last one or an old item. (A whole end cap of soup in a grocery store will always sell soup better than 6–12 cans on a shelf somewhere.) So, will having more of the item help its sales?

Assortment Issues
Would more variety help?

Would more variety hurt?

Shake things up a bit. Retail merchandising is trial and error. All these thoughts should be constantly going through a retail merchant's mind!

Note:
Merchandising, or merchandise presentation as we just described it, refers to the more basic and traditional methods of presenting products in an orderly, understandable, profitable and findable way possible. Today's successful and more cutting edge merchants are taking merchandising to a whole new level. The term merchandising has been somewhat re-defined as "visual merchandising," thanks to more imaginative approaches in retailing.

"Visual Merchandising" (The Total Approach)
I get a kick out of the term "visual merchandising." Isn't all merchandising pretty visual? To an older merchant like me, the term still means the same thing. Does it look good? Does it grab your attention? Does it draw attention to what you want attention drawn? And finally, how do we make it look better?

The words "visual merchandising" has likely evolved because it is no longer just about putting merchandise on a shelf. It's about combining product, environment and space in some sort of *stimulating* and *engaging* display to increase the odds of the sale. Over the years, visual merchandising has become a more and more important element of retailing. For large retailers, it may even start with the building design itself to more accurately showcase the store's products and put them in a special atmosphere that not only creates comfort, but stirs emotions and engages the customer.

The only real rule in visual merchandising (VM) is to increase sales and profits. While some might say it's a science, I would call it an art. It should involve most or all of the senses to create an effect: to entertain, excite, educate or cause an emotional response, all in an effort to increase sales and relieve the customer of his/her hard earned money and give the customer something he or she either wants and/or needs

In order to get these kinds of results, many different elements can be used to build interesting displays. Effective displays make use of color, lighting, space, product information, sensory inputs such as smell, touch, and sound as well as technologies like digital displays and interactive installations. In effect, a store is making good use of almost anything at its disposal to highlight the merchandise and create emotions in order to stimulate the consumer's decision to buy. Not only should VM use all of these effects well, it should also make your store a more attractive place for customers while still reflecting the image you want for your store.

Yes, visual merchandising can be expensive. But it is also key in using all of these areas to help reflect your own store's style and brand. It's still about displaying 'goods for sale' in the most attractive manner with the end purpose of making a sale and if the merchandise really begins to sell, then your extra expense and effort in visual merchandising becomes insignificant.

A close sister to visual merchandising is "retail experience" or "customer experience." Customer experience looks at the same issues from product presentation, but it considers the customer's perspective rather than the retailer's needs. In the best retail stores, such as the Apple's retail stores, the visual merchandising, customer experience, and store design are all in synch to create an environment that makes customers comfortable enough to buy, and it has helped create unbelievable sales for the retailer.

Visual merchandising can step up all
merchandising efforts a notch or two.
Visual Merchandising:

1. Can present products with more three-dimensional props and displays that can create a more memorable or impressive experience. It visually displays the product in a more appealing and exciting manner, often making use of large displays (such as a boat or table setting.)

2. Educates or tells a story to the customers about the product/service in a more creative and even entertaining way. This might include, video, photos or a brief story for customers to read.

3. Clearly separates your business and store from the competition via the shopping experience including sound, theatrics, fun or active and interactive displays.

4. Focuses on the product or product line and visually ties it to current marketing and fashion efforts, i.e. a manikin wearing currently promoted merchandise or a large cardboard Santa at a holiday soft drink display.

5. Can grab the attention of the customer by providing an "experience" thus motivating them into an easier or faster buying decision.

Basic Visual Merchandising Tips

When customers enter your store, they are affected within seconds by impressions including sight, sound and scent. These impressions can have an immediate positive or negative effect on the customer's frame of mind. For example, color is a key element in these first impressions as it not only grabs customers' attention but can affect their mood as well. I cannot stress this enough. Selling products through visual merchandising is about creating an emotion and telling a story. If you go into a Ralph Lauren Store, you can feel the frame of mind and persona he is trying to create. You might find a saddle, rope and other props in his stores. While he's obviously not in the saddle business, he is using these things to create a feeling and tell a story. And stories create connections and emotions for people (customers). What persona or emotion does your store create? Although I'm guessing that many of us believe our store's current visual impact is fine or sufficient, the truth is a person who is less connected to your business may have different ideas about whether you've accomplished your mission or not.

Change Displays as Often as Possible.

Customers want to see new and different things every time they enter your store. Changing displays and drawing attention to new items are a part of the entertainment element that retailing is all about, but merchants often forget to make these changes regularly. Once a customer makes a couple of visits to your store to find nothing noticeably changed, they lose interest in returning anytime in the near future. If your customers have seen the same three tables or same end caps for the last two months, your store looks stale and is no longer an interesting place to shop—that is, until things do change. If your competitor down the street constantly looks fresh and interesting while you do not, which one would *you* want to visit again?

Color

Color commands attention. A new coat of vibrant paint can make a world of difference. Any merchandising plan should make use of bright or contrasting colors to grab attention or focus a buyer. Color can also evoke or stir up certain emotions or moods and thus influence buying decisions. If you have a well-designed logo, consider tying the colors of your store in with your logo and theme. Choose colors depending on what you sell, since a darker color usually makes the merchandise displayed against it appear to "pop". A rich deep color can add some class or offer a more sophisticated feel. Combine good colors with intriguing aromas and you've got a killer combination. Consider applying some special splashes of paint in your store to create more colorful focal points and draw shoppers to where you want them to go.

Accent Lighting

People are drawn to light like moths. Lighting brings colors to life and generally puts merchandise in a more flattering "light." Focusing light on a large wall of product will enhance any display and draw the customer's attention as well. Illuminating a particular product automatically says, "this is special" or "your attention should be here". Lighting can also be used to create shadows and depth. Something fluorescent lights can't do. You don't want to be totally dependent on the typical evenly lit "schoolroom" effect of fluorescent lights found in most stores when addressing your own lighting situation. Besides, all fluorescent lighting only makes you look more like a discount store.

Whenever possible, you need to add some incandescent lights or halogen lights for highlighting the merchandise. First of all, it more closely resembles natural lighting, which is important to customers when judging appearance and color. But the use of spotlights can accomplish that focus and that highlight you are looking for. Also try to be consistent with the color of incandescent bulbs you use. They do put out different types of white light and a mix can look very unprofessional. Planned lighting is just one more element to include when creating visual interest for customers, and it can positively impact a customer's impression of almost anything—not to mention the positive affect it can have on your profits.

Add-Ons & Themed Merchandising
When building a display of a particular product or products, look for products that are natural add-ons or complementary products to the main merchandise featured. For example, if I built a display of sun tan oil, my display—while certainly full of suntan oils—would also feature sunglasses, some brightly colored beach towels and maybe a large bright red or yellow umbrella over the entire display. If I owned a candy store, I'd build a colorful bulk display of different flavored taffy, highlighted with piles of fresh citrus fruits—lemons, oranges, limes, pineapple—to make the mouth water. And then maybe I'd add a tall tree display of large brightly colored 6" or 8" diameter suckers. I might even cap it all off with the same large red or yellow umbrella. This is visual merchandising, and it needs to be practiced day-in and day-out as much as possible throughout your store.

Themed merchandising pulls it all together to help create a picture in the customer's mind. Grouping products together is another way of saying, "all of this could go together in *your* home" or "maybe you should add this item too". For example, in a home décor store, an obvious grouping would be a dining table complete with table settings and a centerpiece. Napkins and interesting bowls or plates combined with coordinated fabrics or scarves thrown over the chairs could all be added. For Valentine's day, there are any number of combinations, depending on what you were trying to sell—from candles with jewelry and romantic movies, to lingerie, chocolates, jewelry, romantic CDs, picture frames, special novels or stuffed animals. Even a display that combines a muffin mold with a classy potholder, a cookbook on muffins or gourmet cupcakes, a pair of wine glasses, and a rose or two create a warm fuzzy homey feeling for all the Valentines out there. While it requires some imagination and planning, theme merchandising is a great way to communicate seasonal ideas, activities or projects. It helps your customers connect with other ideas, projects, and once again, "emotions". As a result, these connections translate into a better bottom line.

Add Motion
Moving merchandise always catches the eye. If you have anything that moves—from toys and wind chimes to fans and music boxes—put it on display to capture attention. Do not keep everything in a box. Let customers see things working. If your merchandise doesn't move, use something that does in your displays.

Create a Main Focal Point.
Give your customers something on which to focus their attention. We're going for a "knock their socks off display" wherever possible. Leave them with a lasting impression that makes them want to spread the word. Create at least one eye catching area in the store that tells a story or makes a bold statement as to what your store is all about.

Create Displays That Pop.
Merchandise that is central to your store's offerings should always be displayed in the best manner possible. Work toward making your presentation impressive, bold, informative, eye-catching, inviting, exciting, mouthwatering . . . Do any of these words describe the merchandising of your important items? Use signage, quantity and mass, or make the display interesting by placing products at different heights with special props or display pieces. Use color from the merchandise itself, where appropriate.

Using Props
The list of props you can use is only limited by your imagination. However, often I wonder how much of an attempt some storeowners really make. The following is only a very limited list to help spark your imagination and keep the expenses down:

Paper is a basic tool, as it can be used to help fill out shopping bags for the display or serve as a background. Wrapping paper is also good for a variety of uses. If you make a trip to a display supply house, you will find heavy-duty papers on large rolls ready to use for all kinds of displays.

Fabric is one of my favorites. It's relatively inexpensive and when it's stretched over some frames like a canvas, it can be used for everything, from serving as a back drop, to covering an ugly wall, to creating a new atmosphere by hanging a series of stretched fabric panels from the ceiling. It can be draped over things and used under things. It can cover boxes or concrete blocks to build staggered height displays. Just remember to brush or clean it regularly so it doesn't become a major dust collector over time.

Tree limbs and branches can support hanging items as well as serving as decor. Use some spray paint on them and you can create some pretty effective and wild looking displays. Don't forget about combining them once in a while with the miniature lights, too.

Foam board is another basic for people who want to use their imagination. You can find this thin covered Styrofoam in an array of colors. All you need next is a utility knife to cut out the shapes you want.

Miniature lights and rope lights like those used at Christmas, have a myriad of possibilities; use them around windows or inside of items to light them from within. These little lights will help any display seem a lot more special, and best of all, they're cheap, too.

Photographs can create a mood or add some whimsy to a display. These days, depending on where you go, you can get huge 20 by 30 inch enlargements for less than $15.00. Stick a large photo to foam board and you've got a focal point for a window theme.

Video Screens are becoming cheaper by the month. A large video screen introduces color, movement, education and it draws attention. You will need to find the videos to keep it going day and night.

Again, the list of props available is limited only by your imagination. Visit a fixture warehouse that offers used retail fixtures, or find a store that might let you borrow something for a while. Below are a few more quick ideas:

→Ask your employees to loan the store something that might be laying around at their home.

→ Borrow or buy movie paraphernalia from a movie rental store.

→ Spray paint some old large frames to highlight or "frame" a product for visual effect.

→ Spray paint old wooden chairs, luggage, bedposts etc.

→ Visit garage sales and look for old items that could be given a new life.

→ Buy artificial clearance flowers to create a spring display.

→ Take a walk through a large craft or hobby store, especially when they're running a clearance sale.

→ Sporting goods stores and flea markets also often have items that make for interesting displays from small boats to coolers and outdoor equipment.

A little humor perfectly illustrates merchandising, taken to the ultimate degree:

"A new supermarket opened in Henrietta, Texas. It has automatic water misters to keep the produce fresh. Just before it goes on, you hear the sound of distant thunder and the smell of fresh rain.

When you pass the milk cases, you hear cows mooing and you experience the scent of fresh mown hay.

In the meat department there is the aroma of charcoal grilled steaks with onions.

When you approach the egg case, you hear hens cluck and cackle, and the air is filled with the pleasing aroma of bacon and eggs frying.

The bread department features the tantalizing smell of fresh baked bread and cookies.

It's all great. . . but I don't buy the toilet paper there anymore.

Author Unknown

In Conclusion:
Remember, your working to create a mood or atmosphere that translates into the perfect emotion (the type of emotion you want to for *your* customers.) Have you ever walked into a store for the first time and felt like the mother ship has landed? You are home! You may have never been there before, but the store effected you, and that feeling most likely came from the mood or atmosphere created by the décor and the displays. This is your goal for YOUR target customers if you want to become more than a mediocre merchant. Every store creates some sort of feeling. (Hopefully it's by design) You might want anything from a fun, lighthearted candy store to a dignified and classical feel of a high-end men's fashion store. Your job is to decide what that mood or feeling should be and then create it throughout your store and in each and every display. Approach it all with a creative and open mind. Don't be intimidated or inhibited.

If something doesn't work this time, CHANGE IT AGAIN! Try something else. Get some input or help.

Are there a lot of retailers who aren't too good at displays? . . . YES. Are some people better at it than others? . . . YES. But your store needs to become good at it. Retailing, more than anything else, is effective merchandising. Find someone on your staff that has an eye and a knack for this kind of merchandising. Put that person in charge and give him or her the ball to run with it (within some parameters, of course). You already have a great deal invested in the merchandise. So make the most of it. Try it, **change it**, adapt to customer patterns and behavior. And become a student of other retailers and their methods. No matter how effective or wonderful a display is, they still must be changed to stay fresh. More importantly, you must make your store look good through the eyes of *your* target customers. Your displays must reflect your store's image and brand. Do NOT use average lighting or cheap display items if you are trying to maintain a high-end image. Last, but not least, remember that no matter what you do, your store will not appeal to everyone who walks through the door . . . no store does. Nevertheless, your job is to make sure your store works for *your* target customer.

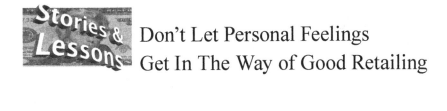

Don't Let Personal Feelings Get In The Way of Good Retailing

When I started my experimental full-line pet department for Venture Stores, I had about 1000–1200 square feet turned over to me to create a "live" pet department. I created the merchandise mix, merchandised it, and even decided what types of live pets we would carry. It was a unique responsibility for someone only 21 years old. In addition to the stress of being new to the company, I had the eyes of upper management on me to watch the progress and the success or failure of this department.

In developing the merchandise mix for this department, I eliminated all of the products typically carried by dime stores and discount stores at the time. The large majority of them were Hartz Mountain products. My goal was to create a department that rivaled many independent pet shops, with top quality merchandise and a depth in selection not found in any discount store. I was proud of the merchandise mix we carried, and I had a lot of confidence in the products I had selected.

One day after the department had been open for a couple of months, I had a visitor from the corporate office. He was vice president and general merchandise manager for the company, and I had a lot of respect for him. Maybe it was because he was the one who initially called and selected me as the man to create and manage this first department? (No . . . couldn't be that!) He began walking through the store, inspecting my merchandising efforts, general cleanliness, and he questioned my reasons for most of my decisions, including the mark-up percentage on the merchandise.

We got to the dog products area, and he noticed my various facings of flea collars, which were very big back in the 70s. He really seemed to be zeroing-in and concerned about something in this area. He asked me if the flea collars I was offering were selling well, and I quickly responded that they were selling fine. And then there was a long pause, with a slight look of concern on his face, and he said, "Tell me what the two best selling flea collars in the market are. What brands are they?" I answered with some bit of hesitancy, "Hartz Mountain and Seargants Brand Flea Collars were number one and two." Then he followed up, "And tell me why wouldn't we be selling the two most popular flea collars on the market?" I answered that I didn't believe those brands were any better than the ones I was carrying, and my brands were the same as what all the really good pet stores carried. He shook his head somewhat frustrated and said, "Hartz Mountain and Seargants spent millions of dollars in advertising virtually everywhere, telling people to buy their brands, and that is one of the main reasons they are the most popular." He then explained that, due to their advertisements, all kinds of customers were coming into my store looking for those two brands. So, WHY WOULD I WANT TO DISSAPPOINT OUR CUSTOMERS BY SAYING NO, WE DON'T CARRY THOSE?

I sheepishly nodded in agreement and said that I understood. And with that, I learned a valuable lesson. In my zeal for getting rid of all things that I considered inferior, I violated the cardinal rule of not listening and catering to my customers. I let my feelings and opinions dictate what the customer would buy instead of letting the customer choose. I also neglected to consider the power of the millions of dollars in valuable advertising by the two (2) manufacturers who were driving traffic into my store. Why would I turn my back on that?

 Tips For Pricing Your Inventory

9

Retail pricing is about finding the best price at which to sell something—the price where you get the maximum margin while still maintaining the best rate of sale you can achieve. (I keep telling you, I'm a genius.) While you can obviously sell at a much faster rate if you practically give something away, that probably doesn't get you the best profit margin. I also consider this part of retailing an art, since you will find many different opinions on how to achieve all of this. The key in my experience is to understand and address many of the following points and apply them to your business, location, market, etc. Many of them should be in the back of your mind for virtually every pricing decision you make.

Key Issues That Come into Play for Retail Pricing
1. Price Sensitivity To Customers

You need to know your customers' preferences for different products and if price is an important issue. You need to have a good idea of what people will pay for the product. What is the high and low price point for merchandise in order for a customer to buy? Other times, if the product is a higher ticket item that is comparison shopped or bought on a very regular basis as a consumable, your price may become much more important.

2. Prices Must Fit Who You Are.

Does your planned image have anything to do with being priced right on this item? Is it about the best service? Is it about having the best variety? Is it about finding something unique and hard to find? If you are about high quality products supplemented with good and knowledgeable customer service, you should be able to sell the product at top dollar (assuming you have chosen a location that will demographically support higher-end products).

If you sell popcorn, are you the neighborhood snack bar where people stop by and pick up a hot dog, a soda, some candy, etc.? Or do you sell gourmet popcorn at a premium price? Are you cultivating an image of selling upscale, gift oriented premiere products and want to avoid the neighborhood snack bar image by selling to neighborhood kids coming in for sodas, snow-cones and candy bars? I assure you that if you are trying to be the place where people will spend top dollar for a gourmet product, you will fail if you look and act like the neighborhood snack bar. And vice versa. If you want to be the neighborhood stop for a quick lemonade or a bag of popcorn, you will fail if your store is perceived as too upscale and posh with prices to match. You must decide who you are, what image you will project, and to whom! Other questions you need to answers are as follows:

Will special customer service (such as delivery, gift-wrapping, alterations, or free installation) affect profitability on this item?

Will you offer unusually generous return policies or warranties with these items?

Will special sales events, with a combination of sale prices and advertising expenses, be consistent with the store image you are creating?

3. Shop Your Competition, Especially If You're Offering The Going Price.

That means internet retailers as much as it means the business down the street. You can't know if you're priced right if you don't know what the going price is. By the way, this isn't exactly a strategic reason for pricing anything, but if you're going to use this as your only pricing strategy, you need to be giving customers other reasons to shop your store.

You don't need to be the cheapest; you just need to be in the ballpark.

4. Are You Going For "Prestige" Pricing?

Selling at a price higher than everyone else is a great place to be if you are really unique. When you provide a top-notch store or entertainment experience, over-the-top customer service and/or when you are in a pretty exclusive or unique location such as a tourist spot or high end shopping area, cache pricing can work. Another way to achieve prestige pricing is to almost exclusively offer top quality merchandise.

5. Regular Sales Promotions

Will you have regular sales events where special savings or discounts are combined with advertised promotions? Does this approach fit with the image you are trying to build? (Also remember that many large department stores have gotten themselves into trouble by running regular sales promotions too often, which resulted in training their customers to not buy until there was a sale!)

6. Pricing Below Competition Or Discounting

This is a tough world to exist in these days because now you have to contend with all of the normal street competition plus internet retailers. If you're going to exist in the world of discounting, you better be able to keep costs down, operate as efficiently as possible and buy at rock bottom prices.

7. Treat Pricing As The Art That It Is.

Avoid key-stoning (where merchandise is marked up to double the wholesale price) or using a single strategy for pricing every item.

Remember that you have to consider freight costs, the pricing of comparable merchandise in your store, competitors' pricing, the customers perceived value of the item, income demographics of your area and more. Take into account your store image, identity and demographic location as well as competition and the going price range for the item. Well-known branded goods should probably be priced at the manufacturer's suggested retail. Retailers will rarely get brownie points for being slightly under the market on this merchandise, and, over a period of time, it can add up and negatively impact your profit margin. You have more pricing flexibility on merchandise that is lesser known since it's difficult for the customer to comparison shop. Be honest with yourself. What would you honestly consider paying for the merchandise? If a unique necklace or unusual home decor item can sell for more, price it for more.

I loved to experiment and use some imagination and psychology when pricing merchandise. When I worked in a discount store, I made sure that, on well-shopped merchandise, I was always lower than my competition. But on merchandise that was unique, a one-time buy or more of an impulse purchase, I marked up as high as I possibly could. Walmart and mass merchandisers have been using this tactic for years. While in general they are the place to buy at the lowest price and they have created that reputation, they will also use a higher mark-up where they feel they can get by with it. Unfortunately, many small retail owners don't take advantage of this tactic.

A Gordon Guideline

Make an intentional decision about whether to be below, at, or above the market place on any given item. <u>Do Not</u> mark up all products or categories with the same mark-up percent. You can be losing sales if you're automatically too high, and hurting profits if you are needlessly too low!

8. Consider Current Popularity

Is this item at its popularity peak? Or is it more of a normal, everyday item at this point?

9. Employees are Good Sounding Boards---They Shop Too!

Ask your employees what they feel a particular product is worth. Don't tell them what you paid for it. If your employees are similar to your customers in demographics, you may get some interesting input.

10. For the Best Margins, Find a Niche.

Everyone wants to sell high volume and easy to move merchandise, but this isn't necessarily the merchandise that will help separate you from everyone else; certainly not from Walmart. Look for appealing but unique merchandise that everyone and their brother isn't selling. Selling the same "me too" items as found in most stores is tough to do, especially if you want to make a healthy profit margin on it. Private-brand merchandise may also help in some product categories.

Other Pricing Strategies To Consider

Other considerations when you are structuring your margin on certain products are special discounts you might offer, special buys, loss leaders, stores that offer trade-ins, coupons, and flexible pricing due to negotiated prices.

In Conclusion:
While no one considers all of the above issues when pricing a product, the point here is to avoid just arbitrarily picking a price or doubling up from your cost or even blindly going by your business' planned mark-up percentage. There is a lot to consider before pricing any merchandise, so it is almost impossible to tell you where your store should be and what component of all of these considerations are most important to your business at this point in time. I believe that if you

really use pricing creatively—going low where you need to be low and selling high when it makes no difference—you can increase sales and profitability both. However, you need to learn which products are price-sensitive and at what point a slight increase in price, will lead to a drop-off in demand. And, remember that the right price is whatever most of your customers are willing to pay while still giving you the best profit possible. Not always an easy task!

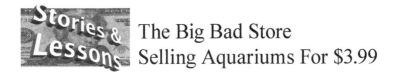

The Big Bad Store
Selling Aquariums For $3.99

I was 21 years old when I started the original department for Venture Stores, which was located at 95th and Metcalf in Overland Park, Kansas. My first goal was to show shoppers that they could find the same quality merchandise in my department as in any first-rate pet store. My next goal was to show that they could buy these supplies, tropical fish and other pets at real savings over the typical pet shop. We stocked an array of aquariums, which ranged from the typical 5 and 10-gallon glass aquariums to much larger 80-gallon hexagon ones, and even L-shaped aquariums. We were serious about the pet business, especially about tropical fish, as they were a very popular hobby in the 1960's and 70's.

From time to time, I ran huge tropical fish sales where one could buy three (3) or four (4) small Angelfish for as little as a dollar. Neon tetras could be purchased in groups of 10 for only a dollar. These huge sales garnered us a lot of attention and brought in many new customers. Originally, my thinking was that even if someone was afraid of buying their tropical fish and supplies at a discount store, the tropical fish sales were too good to pass up. Thus, anyone who was into the hobby would have to check us out. At the same time, my goal was to attract as many new people to the hobby as possible by showing them that they could get started very inexpensively. Initially, I ran 10-gallon aquariums on sale for $3.99 each. This was close to half of our regular price and meant even more savings when compared to other pet stores.

At that time we were really shaking up the pet business in Overland Park with our low prices on the same merchandise sold in area pet stores. It seemed that my competition only knew one way to fight back. They told customers our fish were sick and unhealthy. How else could we sell them for those ridiculously low prices? The fact was that we purchased our tropical fish from the same distributors and fish farms out of Florida and California as any other store. And our fish and aquariums were just as healthy and clean, if not more so, than those at any other pet shop. They hated us. The problem was we were taking business away from them.

One day after the first year or so, I was invited to a local seminar held by one of the national pet supply manufacturers. I was sitting in the same room with my competition, all of the other pet shop owners and managers, only they did not know who I was or that I had even been invited. Somewhere along the line, we were asked to stand up and introduce ourselves and name our business. When I stood up and announced I was with Venture Stores, there was total silence. You would have thought I was the devil incarnate. At the end of the meeting, the host (who had noticed the tension) asked the other dealers why they seemed to have a problem with my presence. The responses amazed me, mostly because these people displayed a total ignorance of what I was all about. The major problem with Venture was that we were supposedly and "unfairly" selling tropical fish and aquariums at lower prices than they deemed appropriate. They felt that because of my tremendous buying power, I could buy aquariums below their cost and sell them below what they could afford to do.

Here's the painful truth of it all. I was buying for one test store at the time. Some of these owners had two (2), three (3), or even four (4) stores. The fact of the matter was that I was paying $3.92 for my 10-gallon aquariums at the time, which was the same price that they were paying in any kind of reasonable quantity. I put those aquariums on sale for $3.99. I was making a whole seven (7) cents on each aquarium. I believe I sold somewhere over 100 of those aquariums, bringing all kinds of new customers to my relatively new department. As a result, those same customers bought thousands of dollars in tropical fish and supplies from my department. I did the customers some good by offering good prices and I did the tropical fish business some good by bringing in all kinds of new people into the hobby. That was great for all of us!

Tropical fish were priced for owners and managers like me who wanted to buy a large number at a time. Generally, one would purchase 100–500 of each type of fish. Any of these stores could have done the same, but they never did. Actually one of them did later on hold some pretty good sales of their own. The trouble is that many small businesses want to find a villain to blame for their problems, when what they really ought to do is use their imaginations to create some excitement and hype about their own store.

The host ended up giving me a chance to explain myself and my position, and I think it did do me some good; however, there were still many at this seminar who were convinced I was a liar and that the big bad Venture Store bought aquariums for a dollar each or some such nonsense. The fact of the matter is that I made sure to undersell my competition. I actually shopped other stores to guide my own pricing. Many of my full-price competitors, on the other hand, just marked up their merchandise in an across-the-board fashion. That isn't much of a strategy, if you ask me! I always made sure that any big ticket items (that shoppers might have compared) were priced competitively. And the same thing went for any regularly purchased products, such as consumables, which were very aggressively priced. I took advantage of impulse-purchase items that shoppers would not bother to compare and marked up the prices. It's not some sort of genius strategy on my part. It's basic common sense for many of the smarter merchants in this country.

Sam Walton didn't make Walmart the 800 pound gorilla it is today by giving away merchandise without a profit. Yes, he might price something at cost now and then, but he always had a profit motive behind it. He built Walmart by being smart, efficient and constantly trying to find a way to keep prices down. He built Walmart by making a good mark-up wherever he could get away with it. And he constantly worked to make innovative improvements at his stores and his distribution centers to reduce costs and maximize benefits to the customer. Shouldn't these be the objectives of any retailer? Walmart has the most efficient distribution system in the world which translates into very competitive pricing. That is not unfair. That is smart!

Being More Creative

10

"We should learn to detect and watch the gleam of light which flashes across our own minds."

—Emerson

I can't tell you how you become the next Mrs. Fields Cookies or Build-A-Bear Workshop. I don't know what the next great concept will be that will make someone millions. If I did know, I'd be doing it myself! I can, however, help you understand how to be more creative with your own business. And that is a key asset in becoming great.

I'm sure that persistence and determination are a big part of any entrepreneur's success. The ability to open your mind to new ideas and ways of doing things can go a long way in leading to your success or failure as well. Giving serious consideration to some of the thoughts and concepts in this book might be a good start! Fortunately for all of us, our own creativity and imagination is something that *can* be developed, or at least improved. So yes, open up your mind if you want to be more creative . . . I believe that all of us want to keep fresh with new ideas and show customers a commitment to innovation and a better experience and better service.

No owner or manager has all of the best ideas. But you can bet that if there is a better idea out there, your competition is trying to find it. You need to be looking for it also.

"All mediocrity will be challenged and beat eventually."

Even if you have some great ideas, you can bet they will be copied eventually, so exercising your creativity really has to be an ongoing thing. Considering its ongoing importance, wouldn't you rather have others (your employees) helping to think about your business creatively? I truly believe that the key to success is working to build an atmosphere within your business based on creativity, innovation and a constant search for a better way. If you can create a culture like this in your company, you can instill a sense of importance and purpose in your employees. I'd call it pride in the ownership of ideas.

Do You Want Your People to Be Creative for You?

There may have been some times while around your employees when you've thought the words, "Am I the only person that thinks around here?" Wouldn't it be nice if your employees would think about your business the way you do? Well, that's not going to happen! No one will ever think about your business the way you do. But, if you haven't thought about it before, you do want your employees to be at least somewhat mentally invested in your business and its products or services.

Try to find ways to get all of your employees to think about how to do things better and to challenge how things have always been done. Yes, you will need to sort out the useful ideas from those that are uninformed or totally off-the-wall. But that's why you're the boss. Just don't be too quick to dismiss the seemingly crazy concepts or the ideas that aren't on the same wavelength as your thought process. Some really great ideas can come from some pretty unexpected people. If you do get an idea that seems a bit bizarre, challenge it and question it further, rather than dismissing it. This strategy is another one of the many reasons why Walmart left the competition in the dust.

15 Ideas for Increasing Creativity in Your Business

1. Cultivate Your Employees' Creativity

Convey clearly to everyone and create an atmosphere that lets your people know at every opportunity that you value their ideas and you want to find new and better ways of doing things. Many employees are often hesitant to suggest new ideas, especially if they feel there is the possibility of being laughed at or rejected out of hand. So be tactful in the way you deal with employee ideas, as you don't want to discourage any enthusiasm for ideas with a negative remark or facial expression. And when you do get some good ideas, you need to reward those ideas.

2. Encourage Employees To Challenge Ideas, Policies And Procedures
    Arrange meetings where different ideas can be expressed by any employee. One way to bring ideas out, is to intentionally appoint a good "devil's advocate" to take the other side of any given suggestion. While you could appoint yourself as the devil's advocate, it's probably better for everyone if you appoint a different person each time. The only condition you need to give to this person is that the criticism on any given idea or subject must be constructive in nature. Shooting down an idea just by being negative gets you nowhere.

3. Take A Hard Look At the Common Practice Within Your Market.
    Look at common approaches and ways of doing business of any competitor in your market. What are the things that are never done in this competitive arena, especially at your price levels? Why not? What would a customer be pleasantly surprised or shocked to see in a store? What would make a customer come in and say, "Wow, I didn't know you did that," or "Hey, I've never seen that done before!"

4. Bring In Some Retail Outsiders With Your People.
   Bring your employees together with some outsider people who don't usually deal with your store's daily problems and issues. These outsiders will see things from a whole other perspective and open up new possibilities of thinking. They may even ask some seemingly dumb questions, but that's ok, because they won't be limited by a familiarity with your usual practices.

5. Ask Why?
   One of the secrets to creativity is curiosity. Ever had a new employee ask, "Why do you do this?" or Why don't you _____?" Sometimes we get irritated by these questions. Something to the effect of, "Just do it this way!" Don't rock the boat. Maybe everyone in the organization needs to ask, "why" more often. Remember without "why" there is no reason to improve or change anything.

6. Flip The Problem, Or Turn It Inside-Out.
   A common practice to creatively approach problems and ideas involves reversing the problem or issue. For example, instead of asking "How can I improve service to customers?" you ask, "How can I make the service so bad that it scares customers away for life?" Or, "What could we do with our front windows that no one would ever want to do?" It may sound crazy, but it really does help with ideas and solutions. Remember, "success is failure turned inside-out".

7. Be A Great Observer Of Everything Around You.
   Constantly watch and take note of how people and businesses address specific objectives or problems. What makes it better? Or, what makes it worse? What makes other businesses more noticeable or impressive than you? Has any business, marketing effort or display effort knocked your socks off recently? If so, what did they do, and how might a business like yours do something

similar? How can anything you've seen that's moved you be adapted for your business? See the chapter "Observing Other Retailers" for more on this topic.

8. Have A "What If" Brainstorming Session On A Regular Basis.

Make it an event. Bring in lunch or desserts . . . whatever. Ask each participant to voice their most creative and interesting vision of "What IF the company did _____ five/ten years down the road?" It might have to do with a new product category, a new location, a new approach, a new policy etc. Another approach is to have everyone generate as many ideas as possible to solve a problem. It doesn't really matter how crazy these might sound initially. Set a time limit or shoot for a specific number of ideas before you stop. Make sure someone is assigned to write all of the ideas down. Even where the ideas may sound outlandish, don't judge them as they pop up, as one idea can lead to another that really will work after some massaging.

9. Get Inside Your Employees' Heads.

Conduct a little soul-searching exercise where each employee is asked to write about how they see themselves within the company. Let the employees know that no one but you will see what they write and that you want some sincere thoughts behind this. How do they see their value in the scheme of things? How do they make a difference? What is the one thing the company should know about them that might make a difference? How do they see their role in five (5) years? How do they feel the boss could make them and the company better at what they do? You will be amazed at the information and revelations that can be gleaned from this exercise. Worst case, you will know your employees better and they will appreciate your interest!

10. Make Use Of Mind Mapping.

Mind mapping starts with a central idea that you want to brainstorm or develop further. Write the main idea down in the center, and then jot down whatever immediately comes to mind around the central idea like the spokes of a wheel. Try to develop at least 6-12 new ideas. Now, take each one of the new ideas or words and do the same with them. The goal here is to record whatever comes to mind, without judgment. The resulting diagrams can give you a new way of looking at or linking ideas together to spark creativity. It really works!

11. Do Something Different.

Do something you wouldn't normally do or take a class that is totally different for you. Spend some time in the company of individuals with whom you generally do not come in contact: persons of a different age, race, sex, sexual orientation, national origin, educational background, religious background, etc. Talk to people you wouldn't ordinarily talk to and go somewhere you would not normally be found. You don't need to feel like an artist or be an artist to let out your own creativity. Just try something different. If you can make a habit of doing these things on a regular basis, you are more likely to have an open mind.

12. Drill Down With Questions To Get Answers.

Ask every question you can think of related to the task, opportunity or problem at hand. Question every answer or explanation that is given. For example: Why don't we gift wrap purchases for customers? Answer: Because it is too expensive and time consuming. Question: Why is it too expensive? What would it cost? How could we make it cheaper? What makes it too time consuming? How might we shorten the time? This "drilling-down" will regularly produce high value possibilities and answers—and also crystallize your idea, problem or opportunity so you can produce better quality and more concise responses.

13. Know Your Current & Potential Customers.
You hear this a lot in this book. A lot of your own creativity can be mustered by getting to know your customers in a way you've never known them before. The best way to know your customers—really know them—is to research via questions. Find a third party or perceived third party to sit down and question your customers with carefully prepared surveys to get inside their heads. You need specific information, not generalities. Questions might include:

What do you like to do in your spare time?

What do you dislike most about doing business with us?

What made you consider us in the first place?

Why did you ultimately buy from us?

Where might you have shopped instead of here? Why?

What do you like best about our competition? Why?

What kinds of web sites do you visit? Why?

If we went out of business tomorrow, where would you go? Why?

Would you shop here again? Why?

What could we do to make you come back here more often? Why?

What is the one thing you would change about this store immediately?

What is the worst thing about your day? Why?

What kind of music do you listen to?

Knowing the answers to these questions and countless others like them can give you great insight into what direction to take your business if you will only look at the information and use it. What are you missing? Why haven't certain prospective customers bought from you? There has to be a reason. Whatever the reason, don't dismiss it too easily. There are a lot of potential customers who haven't bought from you. WHY?

14. Reward Innovative And Creative Ideas.
Recognize good ideas that lead to improvements with personal gifts, gift cards or cash. Make sure everyone in your organization knows how much you value such assistance. Reward the best suggestions received. You don't care about quantity. You want quality. You also don't want to turn this into WORK by imposing some quota where employees must turn in some specific number of creative ideas to receive a reward. Remember you're looking for help.

15. Visit The Competition Whenever Possible.
Have a field trip and ask each person to try and find something that the competition is doing better or differently that could be considered or researched more. If you're worried about manning the store, send your employees out individually.

"Creativity can solve almost any problem. The creative act, the defeat of habit by originality, overcomes everything."

George Lois

"Creativity comes from trust. Trust your instincts. And never hope more than you work."

Rita Mae Brown
(American Writer)

 Change Focus:
& Turn Things Around!

In 1948, a company owned by a man named Earl Tupper made products out of something they called Poly-T. We call it polyethylene today. It was molded by this company into all kinds of unbreakable containers, without the drawbacks of cracking or splitting like other plastics. The big customers at the time bought his "nesting" cups for thermos bottles and snack bowls, which were sold or given away with Canada Dry soft drinks. The owner of the company managed to make other non-packaging related products such as ice cube trays, poker chips and bowls with close-fitting caps. By the way, those bowls with the close-fitting caps were really appreciated by a Massachusetts insane asylum, as they were much quieter than aluminum containers. I'll let your imagination kick in for that picture. One of the improvements Earl's products provided the unique seal he had developed that made the containers waterproof and airtight.

Unpaid Product Demonstrators?
Earl became obsessed with selling his products to the housewares departments of retailers around the country. He believed his products would be great for preserving foods. Unfortunately, consumers of the time were very comfortable with using glass and tin lids to preserve their food and leftovers. As a result, a lot of the inventory he sold to retailers of the time was just sitting on the shelves. Retailers put it in their stores, but no one seemed to understand exactly how the product was supposed to work, and retailers felt they weren't in the business of demonstrating bowls and lids and containers. The feeling was that they were not Earl's "unpaid product demonstrators". As a result, a lot of inventory was returned to Earl and his besieged business.

A New Approach!

Eventually, in about 1951, a lady by the name of Brownie Humphrey Wise came along. She had been using Earl's products to supplement her current sales of Stanley Home Products. She had been successfully selling her Stanley products in a "home party" format. The friendly in-home and rather relaxed atmosphere was a low-pressure situation, and there was generally an average of at least two (2) hours to demonstrate and show products. This atmosphere and the extra time with customers to fully explain products or demo them to housewives seemed to lower buying resistance and motivate homemakers to buy. In that same year, Tupperware Home Parties, Inc. was formed. Tupperware decided to clear all of its products out of the retail stores and focus on home parties as their only sales vehicle. It just so happened that as women came back from working in the plants during World War II, many of them weren't quite ready to "go back to the kitchen," and Tupperware became one way to give women a toehold in the post-war business world. By 1954 the company was doing $25 million in annual sales. By the time Earl Tupper died in 1983, there were an average of 75,000 Tupperware parties being conducted every day around the world!

That Was Then, This Is Now?

Isn't it interesting how things change and yet they stay the same. Retailers back then resorted to what they had always done, which was to put products on the shelf and wait for them to sell. When they didn't sell, the products were considered no good and returned to the manufacturer. Then along came someone else who recognized that some products need to be sold and demonstrated. A friendly, laid-back atmosphere was created via the "home party" and the sale became a bit of an event. The sale of something as insignificant as a "mellon baller" became more of an event, and the purchase and the party made the customer experience fun. Meanwhile, the occasion, the atmosphere and the entertaining nature of it all simultaneously lowered buyer resistance and served to educate the buyer. What a concept! Isn't this what Williams Sonoma, Trader Joe's and Build-A-Bear tries to achieve in their stores?

They educate the buyer.

They make the atmosphere fun.

The customer spends additional time with the products.

They demonstrate the products.

They create a no-pressure atmosphere where the customer feels comfortable.

They lower buyer resistance through the friendly atmosphere.

The combination of all of these factors has transformed the way these products are sold. Now Apple is taking it one step further by de-emphasizing the purchase!

Some of my large popping equipment

Rich at the original Store

A FEW PHOTOS FROM MY OWN BUSINESS

My daughter Lindsey at the original store

Counters & menu on wall at right

Some of the candies & chocolates we offered

Space was always at a premium at Christmas, as our packed
shelves were always full of merchandise.

"Football Cardinal Hall of Famer" Roger Wehrle autographs tins
for customers at one of my grand openings

A cover page from a Christmas brochure

A brochure from the tin design business I started

Interior of Store #2

Exterior of store #2

Rich & his very pregnant wife Ellen

Why Separate Your Store From The Pack With Service?

11

Retailing in my mind, is a form of show business. I know what you're thinking. You think I'm stretching the meaning of show business a bit, right? Maybe I am. But it is a business of promoting and inviting guests into your theatre (your store). It's about keeping your guests happy, interested and entertained while they are there, entertained with interesting merchandise and attractive and interesting displays. We hopefully do it with the right performers (our employees) and an atmosphere that is uniquely ours (with lighting, colors and sometimes even smells and motion). Our goal is to do all of this so that our guests will buy more and return again and again.

We may spend a lot of money trying to do everything in a first-class way. We may even buy the best quality merchandise available and put it in a location and store that we pay top dollar to have. And yet, after all this, it can be totally wasted by the appearance, remarks, inattention, indifference, poor mood or poor choice of words from one employee. Regardless of what you think, you are very dependent on the words, actions and even attitudes of your employees. If they're not trained well, treated well, chosen well, or supervised well, ALL IS LOST!

Too Many Retailers Don't Get It.
Today's educated and more savvy shoppers know what they want from their shopping experience. And most of the time, believe it or not, too many of them don't really seem to be getting it. According to 2010 article from CSM, an eMagazine for customer service professionals, 68% of customer defections take place because customers feel poorly treated. What constitutes poorly treated? Who knows? But it doesn't make any difference. It's the customer's perception that counts. In the same article CSM eMagazine claims that 68% leave because

of an attitude of indifference towards the customer by the staff. Furthermore their source (Lee Resource Inc.™) points out that for every customer who bothers to complain, 26 other customers remain silent. But here's the problem . . . a recent study conducted by Empathica, Inc., a provider of Customer Experience Management (CEM) solutions, found 55% of U.S. consumers feel customer service in the U. S. is getting worse; I personally feel that it's a higher figure than that.

It doesn't take a genius to know that shoppers have always wanted a friendly environment with a knowledgeable staff. So why would retailers react over recent years **by continuing to do a poor job of meeting customer priorities and expectations**? If 68% of shoppers say the most important thing is the treatment they receive from store staff, then why is it that customer service seems to be getting worse? Believe it or not, less than 10% of all shoppers name price as the most important reason they shop at a given store, so it seems to me that it really comes down to service and the customer experience. Studies and statistics from the U. S. Small Business Administration and the U. S. Chamber of Commerce in 2007, indicate the reasons why customers leave your business are as follows:

1%	Die
3%	Move Away
5%	Friends' Recommendations
9%	Price
14%	Dissatisfied with Product or Service
68%	Upset with the treatment they've received or indifference of sales clerks

♦ They also estimate that customer loyalty and the lifetime value of a customer can be worth up to 10 times as much as the price of a single purchase.

And I love this statistic, also from them:

- A dissatisfied customer will tell up to 10 people about his/her experience. Thirteen percent of those unhappy customers will tell up to 20 more people!

Other Reasons Given for Not Wanting to Return to a Store Are as Follows:

- Store personnel or owner were on the phone when I needed assistance

- No one at check-out when I was ready to purchase

- Store didn't have what I wanted

- Long lines

- Advertised merchandise not in stock

- Sales clerks lacking in knowledge

- Sales clerk too pushy

It seems to me that getting the first visit may not be the real problem. Based on the above information, it seems the real solution would be to take good care of the customer while they're in the store the first time. If you think that a purchase or two at your store means you've just added a new customer . . . think again! I say that each time the customer comes in, your goal should be to take great care of them and make them want to come back . . . again and again and again!

Here is a list of today's most common issues for retailers as I see them.

Customers Want: Pleasant experience.

They Get: Long waits at the sales counter or check-out line.

Customers Want: Quality merchandise made in USA.
They Get: More & more products made overseas.

Customers Want: New and unique merchandise for their lifestyle & tastes.
They Get: Same old brands aimed with ads focused on the same merchandise from week to week.

Customers Want: Knowledgeable, well trained and friendly staff.
They Get: Indifferent employees who make you feel like you're interrupting them. Salespeople who are poorly trained and don't know products. Understaffed stores.

Customers Want: Professionalism.
They Get: Employees with body piercings, often dressed like they're working at a garage sale.

Customers Want: Fun, unique or somewhat entertaining experience and atmosphere.
They Get: Rows of shelves and fixtures lined under the same fluorescent lights & elevator music, while they find their merchandise and take it to the register.

Customers Want: Better and more unique store ideas.
They Get: Malls full of the same stores.

Customers Want: Rewards for loyalty and appreciation.
They Get: Same old ads aimed at everyone, built around price.

Customers Want: Information and answers on products
They Get: Employees read off the product package as if the customer couldn't have done that. Customers turn to the internet more and more for information.

Do you see anything here you can improve in your store?
Did you notice that half of the issues above involve customer service or the actual experience? When asked, most retail shop operators will also tell you that they have a good, well-trained, service-oriented staff. But I'm not buying this answer at all! In fact, even having service-oriented, trained employees isn't really enough any more.

NOTE: You will find me approaching this subject from different angles, and you may even feel that I'm repeating myself. Well, I am repeating myself to a certain extent, but I am trying to make a light bulb go off in your head that, too rarely, doesn't seem to go off with people concerning this subject! I don't care how well you think you take care of customers, I assure you that you will get some important perspectives and ideas from these chapters. The following chapters are the most important in this book. I wouldn't have said that 20 years ago, but I've learned too. READ THEM ALL.

Some Thoughts on Getting Customers Back Again & Again
Getting customers to come into your store is not generally the big problem. The market is becoming increasingly competitive and the bar for grabbing and keeping that customer has been raised as well. The retailers who win the war for customers are the ones who know their customers best and capitalize on their "wants and needs" to get them back in the store. They use this knowledge to make shoppers happy by creating customer relationships and loyal fans or advocates of the business.

Believe it or not, we all generally buy with our hearts and our emotions rather than with our heads. All things being equal, the stores that do the best job of dealing with human emotions will usually have the best success. People buy because they are happy, excited, inspired, eager, anxious, envious, jealous, selfish, comfortable, in love, turned-on, desperate, depressed, lonely, hungry and even mad. These are all emotions that effect customer actions, and overall, the store that does a better job of creating the necessary emotions to sell its merchandise will be the most successful. In other words, if you are doing a good job of making customers feel the way you want them to feel, you will have a much better chance of success. On the other hand, if you are just counting on customers to buy from your store for totally logical reasons, you may be in trouble.

Customers today don't always buy products or services because they need them. They buy things because they want them. They may buy things that they happen to need too, but <u>they must also want them</u>. There are many things we all know that people should buy because they need them, but they won't buy in any case unless they want them too. "Wants" are stronger in all cases where human emotions are concerned than "needs". That is not necessarily logical. How to get people to "want" things is at the heart of marketing and even <u>retailing</u>.

One thing for sure is that if a customer doesn't get a good feeling when they come in your store, or your employees don't make them feel welcomed or happy or impressed, your customers won't purchase much from your store over the long haul. **<u>People don't buy from places and people they don't like</u>**. How we get customers to not only like your store, but love your store is at the heart of what this book is all about.

"Do what you do so well that they will want to see it again and bring their friends."

Walt Disney

DO YOU REALLY HAVE GOOD CUSTOMER SERVICE?
. . . I'm Not So Sure

12

Marketing is usually thought of as advertising, packaging or even creating a brand. But there is one major area that seems to be neglected by most businesses, including the big guys. It comes down to holding on to your current customers by concentrating on **outrageously** great customer service. There is a cost to this to which you must commit. However, it's cheaper and smarter than constantly going after new customers. Great customer service can be much less expensive than always trying to dig up new customers, especially if you look at your return on investment. Are you still thinking . . . "I already have good customer service"? Maybe you do. But odds are that you don't. I assure you that the large majority of business owners out there believe they have good customer service, but they are often clueless or sadly misguided. If everyone who thinks he has good customer service really had it, we wouldn't all be complaining about how service has gone down the dumper in this country over recent decades.

Everything still comes back to service. It doesn't make a difference whether you are trying to win customers over the first time or if you're trying to keep customers after years of service. People will always remember the times they received poor service or they had a bad interaction with your business, even if the product was great. And in many cases, it doesn't matter how long you have taken care of them, they are more likely to remember the last time when your service disappointed or irritated them. The whole point of the next few chapters here is to get across the attitude, the benefits and the steps necessary to do a better job than just "good customer service."

AN IMPORTANT QUESTION:

Do you ever go for days, weeks or months on end without a complaint? . . . Is your service really that wonderful? Here's a couple of facts that should concern you. *[1]

1. Only 50% of customers with serious problems ever really bother to complain at all.
2. More than 90% of customers with more minor issues never take the time to say anything about them.

The fact is that if any of these people had been to your store, you wouldn't know about it would you? . . . Yes, most of them will continue to shop at your store as long as you didn't really tick them off. But what about those who just don't feel like your store is providing them what they want or giving them the kind of treatment they expected or hoped for? What happens over time is that more and more of them will just gradually and quietly slip away, never to be noticed or missed. Somewhere along the line, some other store comes along that they like better. The customers begin spreading YOUR money around at a variety of other retailers. And you never have a clue what happened to them. You chalk some of this loss up to the big bad box stores. Some of it you chalk up to the economy . . . and some of it you just figure is gone because people's circumstances change. None of it, you figure, had anything whatsoever to do with your wonderful store's appeal.

Unfortunately, most customers would rather just switch than confront someone over most issues, no matter how minor the reason for the switch. Many, like my wife, just don't like any kind of confrontation. They don't want to be one of those pesky complainers. If and when I ask for a manager to complain, I even get that look of disapproval from my wife. But I tell her that if I was in their shoes and I cared, I would want to know. But she, like many customers, wants to avoid any confrontation whatsoever. Some customers don't really believe

---

1   Statistics from TARP Worldwide, Arlington Virginia (a customer service research firm)

any complaint or conversation will result in any real change, so why bother. **<u>And in most cases, they are absolutely right!</u>**

The fact is that the people who complain are **<u>fantastic opportunities</u>** for your business. You need and want to know what is wrong and how you may be disappointing your customers because in many instances, it's the only way you'll learn how to get better.

Having a Long-term Relationship

Inviting customers into your retail environment is about creating a relationship, just like having friends over to your home. You may look at it as strictly financial, but it isn't. RETAILING IS ABOUT PEOPLE. If you want to maintain a long-term relationship with your customers, you will have days when you disappoint them. Why? **<u>Because stuff happens!</u>** Out-of-stocks happen. Defective items happen. Misprints in ads happen. Deliveries are late. Some employee forgets to follow up on something. An employee has lost a lot of sleep and becomes a little abrupt with someone. Computers go down. STUFF HAPPENS!

In order to maintain good, long-term relationships, there has to be communication between your store, your employees and the customer. You want and need to know what goes on in your store from both employees and customers, even when you're not there. (Seriously consider installing a video system that you can access via your laptop computer to monitor what goes on when you're not there—you want to know, believe me).

<u>Think about working harder to find out what is wrong because there are things that need to be addressed whether you believe it or not</u>!

Don't be afraid of finding out how disappointed a customer is over some situation, even if you don't think you can rectify things for the customer at the time. The problem is that, too often, your employees respond to customer comments or complaints with some answer such as, "Yes, that happens once in a while" or, "Yes, you're right, but there's nothing we/I can do about it". How many of your employees are answering customers, "I'm sorry. That's our policy." This kind of employee reaction or word choice scares me to death, as I know those comments stick in the mind of the customers and fester, until one day that customer is gone. Hopefully, you're beginning to get the picture.

Keeping Customers Happy

1. Train Everyone To Be Courteous.

Have you ever walked into a small store, especially where teens or young adults were working, and felt like an accountant in a blue suit walking into a biker bar? Many people, especially teens, don't even realize when they're being rude or making someone feel uncomfortable. Don't take anything for granted with your people. We all have a different idea of what being courteous really looks like. Things like, "hello", "please", "thank you", "we're sorry about the inconvenience", "you're welcome", and so on, may seem like they go without saying, but again, you should take nothing for granted. Some younger people especially don't even understand what it means to be friendly. Employees must understand that customers on the sales floor come first, over ANYONE on the phone. Do not make a person in your store wait for a phone call. If necessary, have your employee take the caller's phone number and promise to call them back promptly. Then keep the promise! However, all employees must understand that every interaction with a customer—whether by phone, e-mail, letter or in person—leaves some kind of impression, and those impressions are representations of you and your company.

Treat customers with respect and dignity at all times. Take note, there is no excuse for being rude or discourteous to a customer . . . even one who is rude or upset. You DO NOT show frustration, disgust, disbelief or sarcasm. Listen closely to customers when they believe they have a problem. Did you notice I said "believe" because that is all that's really important. It's not about whether they do or they

148

don't have a legitimate complaint. It's about what *they* believe. Belief is their perception and perception is reality to them. So you must understand their point of view and respond by speaking to them in a calm tone and reacting with concern, as you would want to be treated.

I also realize that working with the public is tough, and your people on the front lines can be nailed regularly by impolite, moody or angry customers. By the end of a long day or tough week, the employee is likely to have the patience of a TV football fan on a Sunday afternoon with a remote control in their hand. Their frustrations can bubble up in any number of unpleasant ways. Aside from stressing the importance of being courteous at all times, the next best thing you can do is to carefully interview and choose the right people at the beginning. Then you've got to teach them exactly how you want them to treat your customers, especially customers with complaints.

2. Provide Prompt Attention

No employee should be allowed to be so focused on a particular little job they've been assigned that they ignore customers who stand and wait for attention. Nothing irritates me more than for some employee who is self-absorbed in some minor project behind the counter with their back to me (or worse yet, facing me) as if to say "I'm too busy for you, you'll just have to wait." No one should be reading a book or doing anything that even appears like they are not ready to give the customer their undivided attention, EVEN IF THEY ARE ON BREAK. All employee breaks, personal phone calls and personal business should be conducted out of the view of customers; and cell phones and lunches should not exist on any sales floor if you are a retailer or have a showroom. Customers don't understand why they're being ignored and shouldn't have to understand. In addition, no employee should arrive in the morning right at opening while a customer waits at the front door. **<u>Customers should always feel like they come first.</u>**

3. Have A Dress Code.

People who deal with customers should NOT look like they were at a beach party or they just stepped out from cleaning out their garage. I don't care how Walmart employees look, your store doesn't offer the lowest prices on the planet. People don't come to you as a last resort because of your low prices. Having your people look nice is part of what helps make them noticeable and makes your store more professional and polished. A dress code may be as simple as no shorts, no jeans, no cutoffs, no T-shirts, no shirts with any messages or artwork on them, no halter-tops, no piercings, and no visible tattoos. Remember this is YOUR business and, whatever type of business it is, it should reflect the image you want for **your** store.

4. Be Ready For Business.

No one should be fumbling around looking for receipt tape, shopping bags, staplers, order forms, etc. And no one should arrive looking like they are still dressing or they just got out of bed.

5. Your Employees Must Know Your Products.

Your employees must demonstrate and talk with confidence about the products, your business, as well as any policies or special knowledge needed in your trade. Being well versed in the company's services and return policies is another area that gives the customer confidence in whom they are dealing with. You and your employees should talk at your meetings about possible types of questions that might be asked so that everyone is ready with the best answers.

6. Listen

It's an undeniable fact that the majority of salespeople (retail or otherwise) do not routinely listen closely enough to their customers. Typically, they respond with an answer or a suggestion that does not match the problem because they were not paying attention or they thought they knew what the customer was going to say.

For example:

> Salesperson: This is a really hot selling item right now!
>
> The customer: I'm not so sure I like the way this dress looks on me.
>
> Salesperson: It fits you fine.
>
> The customer: I'm just not sure it looks right.
>
> Salesperson: I'm telling you it fits you great and it's been real popular.
>
> **The reality:** The customer told the salesperson earlier that she doesn't believe the color pink ever looks good on her.

7. Make It Easy or Easier to Do Business.

Your product or service must be easy to buy and your customer choices or promotions should enable a clear or relatively simple buying decision. The harder you make it to select or decide on, or do business, the less likely you may get the sale. The buying experience in your store, your web site, or even the ordering process in a catalog should also be as easy as possible. Help customers find what they need, understand what they're buying, and do whatever else you can to smooth out the purchase process.

8. Streamline The Actual Purchase Process.

Make it easy and simple to get customers' purchases taken care of. Take the time to offer employees a procedure and process for taking care of each sale so that it is smooth, quick and professional. One of the biggest single complaints from customers is WAISTING TIME. The salesperson should not need to run back to you or anywhere else to find out how to handle something or to get a price, confirm a discount or whatever. Your salespeople should not be making one customer wait while they train another employee or straighten out their problem. Everyone should know how to hastily handle inputs of register information and credit card or debit card processing and what to do if something doesn't work properly. No employees should be seen shrugging their shoulders as to not knowing what to do next. Have you ever seen a customer help an employee calculate a sale price of 15% off because they couldn't seem to get it right? The bottom line is not to test customer's patience in line while your employee attempts to figure what to do. Customers don't care who's at fault, and they shouldn't have to wait while an employee calls someone else for help. THEY'RE TRYING TO GIVE YOU THEIR MONEY! Customers should not be waiting while your employees learn to make change or get a math education. Customers really don't care for employees to be trained on their time. Get the process down to a science. And if there is a problem, your employee needs to address the customer's concerns promptly and then figure out what went wrong later.

9 . Keep Your Promises (implied or otherwise).

Deliver on your promises or commitments. Whether it's the quality of the product or service you're touting, you need to deliver on your pledges, assurances, guarantees, promises etc. . . . whether these are in writing or are just implied. If you promise a customer that something will be ready by Monday morning, then it should be there by Monday morning. (Am I a genius or what?) If or when the time comes you cannot make this happen, you don't make excuses, and you don't feed them a line of B.S. The only words you need to remember are "We're very sorry", backed up by an extra special over-the-top effort to really make the customer happy. This might be in the form of a discount, or free delivery or a small gift sent to their home afterwords with a sincere note of apology and appreciation for their business.

Always provide what you promise. Again . . . Always provide WHAT you promise. When you fail to do this, you lose both credibility and customers. If your business guarantees a quote within 24 hours, get the quote out in less than 24 hours. The bottom line is to only, ONLY, make promises that you know that you and your business can keep. This goes for marketing also. In marketing, we make subtle and bold promises everyday when we advertise what we are about, or what we'll do. **Do NOT write checks for marketing efforts your store or your service can't back up**.

10. Don't Rely On Automated Voice Systems.

If you do rely on voice mail or something similar, it should be only to buy you a minute or two before answering. If you haven't heard people make jokes about being shuffled around via automatic voice response systems and not being able to get to a real human being, you haven't been living on this planet. Companies who actually answer a phone with a real human being on the other end are real standouts in this world today. Here is your first chance to be different in a positive way. Automated systems should be your last line or back-up for customer service, not your primary tool. Many employees actually ignore the phone as a way of allowing them to goof off or avoid dealing with customers (especially when your not there). Too expensive, you say! I say it's too costly to keep doing it the "poor self-service" way. Find a way to afford it.

11. Accessibility To You, The Boss

If you refuse to give responsibility to take care of customer issues to your employees, or if you have a website where there is little face-to-face contact with your business, you need to be more accessible to your customers. If there is no customer service department or it is difficult to contact customer service or speak to a manager, you may be losing buyers in a very subtle, slow fashion while you remain clueless! You must create a way for customers to have their concerns or problems addressed easily.

12. Cross-train Employees

Try to avoid situations where one employee has to plead ignorance and pass the customer on to someone else. Every employee who comes in contact with the customer, should know your products and be able to help the customer for the most part. Another benefit to cross-training your employees is that you will then have ability to react and be flexible on days when one area is busier than another, as well as better able to handle unplanned employee absences.

13. Do NOT Allow The Buck To Be Passed.

When someone walks up to a sales clerk or calls for customer service over the phone, they should expect a qualified person to handle or service their problem. On the phone, a customer service representative should be the first or second person to whom they speak. In a non-retail environment, a customer service representative should be at least the second person to whom they speak after talking to a receptionist. You wouldn't like being passed around from person to person or department to department, and customers don't like it either. Passing the buck or the customer around is the first step to passing your customer on to your competition.

14. What Is Your True Attitude About Returns?

The reality is that—sooner or later—every customer will be unhappy about something. During my years with the mid-western mass merchandiser Venture, I learned something very important that has served me well for decades. When I asked my first boss why we would allow customers to return merchandise and take advantage of us, when we knew they (the customer) had broken or damaged the merchandise after they bought it, I got an interesting answer. And I received a similar interesting answer when I asked why we would allow someone to bring back live plants that had been perfectly healthy when they were purchased in the morning and yet totally burnt to a crisp from sitting in a car in 107 degree heat the same day.

It was explained something like this . . . "When a customer returns something to us for cash or an exchange, we believe that 90% of them have a legitimate reason. We also believe that another 7–8%

of them believe that they have a legitimate reason even when they may be totally wrong. And then there are another 2–3% of them who are just out to take advantage of us or rip us off. However, if we can keep all 100% of them happy, then no one can complain about us or badmouth us. Why make a scene with a customer and get someone really steamed over a few dollars?" That answer has stuck with me for many years.

"It takes 20 years to build a reputation and five minutes to ruin it. If you think about that, you'll do things differently."

Warren Buffett

15. Build Adequate Marketing & Service Into The Budget— ALWAYS!

Experience has proven time and time again that companies that spent more to increase sales during a recession have a higher success rate holding on to market share. Cutting payroll and service is not always the best place to cut. Consumers DO notice changes in service (good or bad,) and they do remember poor experiences over the long haul. Yes, when things get slow, everyone must watch and cut expenses. Just take careful note of where you cut and what will be remembered when things get better!

16. Don't Hide Behind Your Internet Website.

Hopefully you aren't using your website to weed out unhappy customers who just aren't persistent enough or aggravated enough to fill out your online form. While the Internet has become a great communication tool, it has also become a tremendous way to help management to hide or become invisible. How many businesses today are hiding behind websites with "frequently asked questions" and cold standardized and programmed responses? The frequently asked questions portion of a website may be helpful to some customers, but it has also become a frustrating substitute for personalized, human interaction for many companies to hide behind. There should always be a very *simple way* for a customer to contact someone who can address their concerns to their satisfaction, both in the store and out of the store.

17. Consider Using A Suggestion Box.

Yes, you probably won't see many suggestions. But if you get one (1) or two (2) good ideas, it could all be worth it many, many times over. Just catching the right criticism or suggestion could dramatically improve a part of your business. Make the box very noticeable.

18. Accept All Major Credit Cards

You should be accepting ALL of the credit cards, including Discover and American Express. I have actually avoided a store in the past because they didn't accept American Express and I didn't want to start a balance on another card. If a particular card is charging you a higher percentage than you like, so what. You don't put percentage in the bank. You put dollars from a sale in the bank (and you keep a few more customers happy). You may be hurting yourself more than them. Make shopping convenient for ALL of your customers.

19: Other Ideas In Brief:

♦ Offer gift wrapping.

♦ Offer delivery service.

♦ Consider seating areas. Chairs send a strong message that you care, that you welcome visitors to stay a while. If you don't have chairs, people will often improvise by sitting on the nearest shelf or merchandise.

♦ Consider after-hours shopping for special customers.

- Upgrade your restrooms—this could set you apart from the riff-raff.

- Offer layaway.

- Offer a personal shopper (phone orders) service.

- Offer personal "thank you" or "we miss you" notes.

- Consider if your business hours are convenient for your customers.

- Offer longer store hours during the holidays.

In Conclusion:

Be consistent over time. You will build your reputation through a daily commitment to quality, service, good prices, etc. . . not by telling everyone you're wonderful. You shouldn't be telling customers you're great. You should be setting their expectations by steadily and consistently delivering on your promises or warranties (implied or otherwise). It doesn't matter how big or how small your organization is, customer service has to be emphasized on every detail you can think of, from answering the phone to handling a return.

If you are truly worried about being taken advantage of and you can't afford the monetary loss, then you can tell the customer you disagree and why you disagree in a pleasant and professional way. However, for the most part, "The customer is always right, even if they're wrong." Yes, it may not be fair to you, but who said business was always fair?

WHY GOOD CUSTOMER SERVICE ISN'T ENOUGH

Now that we're finished talking about good customer service and whether you have it or not, let's talk about "great" customer service or even "outrageously" good customer service. We are talking about making the customer experience so memorable and positive that the customer becomes your best form of advertising. Wouldn't you like to have dozens, even hundreds of advocates and spokesmen out there, touting your business and the exceptional experience they have in your store? This is when you have successfully separated your store from the pack. Your marketing will be done for you, without cost! There is actually a huge majority of the population out there that really wants to spend money on quality and service, or an upscale first-class and unique experience.

The Little Shop Of Horrors

Picture this: You've just entered a health food store. The sign above the store is painted and obviously faded from years in the sun. The front door is dirty and full of finger prints that are noticeable, as a result of a number of small pamphlets taped to the inside of the door.

You begin walking down the aisle of the store and notice that many of the boxes and bottles of supplements on the shelves are in disarray and that quite a few are dusty. There is a bag of sunflower seeds on another shelf that has a large hole in it and there are sunflower seeds spilled out all over the shelves. You notice over in the corner a large box of strawberries with a discarded soda cup laying on top of the strawberries. You've been trying to get the attention of a young female clerk who seems to be rapped up in a conversation about a movie with two young male admirers from her junior college.

You proceed to the front checkout counter after finally finding the glucosamine supplement you were looking for, but there is no sign or prices visible anywhere. You decide to approach the front check-out area, but the female employee at the front counter is talking on the phone (apparently to her son) and signals you with her hand to give her one minute while she finishes up her conversation. She finally hangs up and begins looking through a book of prices for what seems like an eternity to find you a price. "I think the price is $24.99 + tax," she says. You hand her two twenty dollar bills, but she seems to be out of quarters and has only one dollar bill left. She hollers to the young girl who was talking to her male friends to get her a roll of quarters and some singles from the back room. You stand there waiting for the change and just about the time the quarters and singles arrive, the phone rings at the checkout and a customer calls, evidently asking if the store has any organic blueberries in stock. The customer obviously continues to ask a few more questions of the cashier, who finally decides to try and give you your change after the 3rd or 4th question has been answered. You pick up your bottle of glucosamine, which now has some sticky residue on the bottom of it from the counter. The cashier, while still on the phone, tells you that she thinks she can find you a bag for your bottle. You answer back, "don't bother". At this point you beginning to feel like the store is really testing your patience, so you ask the cashier—who has finally gotten off the phone—if the manager is around. The cashier points to the back corner of the store where an open door is visible. "The manager should be in there," she says, totally oblivious to your rather disgusted look.

As you walk back to the open door, you wonder whether you'll ever come back to this store again. You stick your head inside the doorway and you see the manager at a desk with three (3) or four (4) cups and an array of debris scattered across the desk. A small area has been cleared for an egg salad sandwich, an apple and a candy bar. The manager has just taken a bite of his sandwich and his mouth is full of eggs and mayonnaise when you ask, "_____."

What do you ask?!! Do you think there really is any point in saying or asking anything? Do you really think anything will result from your conversation? At this point, do you think the owner or the manager has a clue or understands whatever point you might try to make? No, you turn around and leave the store, and no one is the wiser! And no one at that store seems to understand why sales have been gradually deteriorating. It must be Walgreens' or Walmart's fault!

"For every sale you miss because you're too enthusiastic, you will miss a hundred because you're not enthusiastic enough."

Zig Ziglar

Start With Being A Good Host!

13

Being a good host is about building loyalty with your current customers by treating them like important guests, and then setting in place policies and procedures that your guests (customers) will love and value. But if you're going to be a good host, you've got to be ready for guests well in advance of their arrival. **It's not unlike giving your friends a good time in your home because you want them to come back**. Think about it.

You invite them over via your marketing efforts. Now that the guests have arrived, you want them to be comfortable and to enjoy themselves. The following gives you an idea of exactly what I'm talking about:

♦ Make sure your home (your store) is clean and ready before guests arrive.

♦ Make your home (or store) inviting and welcoming on the outside. At home, your grass is cut. Your walkway is clear. Your house is well-maintained. At your business, the front window invites customers in through interesting displays. Your front door is clean. Your store sign is visible and well-lit. And is there a banner or sign in the window that peeks the customer's interest? Or is it the same sign that's been there for three (3) years?

♦ You decorate your home to make it uniquely yours. Your home is not a copy of any other home anywhere. It reflects YOUR personality and your tastes. Your store must uniquely reflect your brand and your identity in the same way. As your guests arrive, they need to feel like they've arrived in YOUR home.

♦ Is it obvious who the visitors or guests are and who the host or employees are?

♦ Make your atmosphere reflect your home or store's personality and make it an interesting place to visit.

♦ Once your guests (customers) are in your home (store), you want them to be entertained and comfortable. To entertain them in this case, you must have new, fresh and interesting merchandise; attractive and attention-getting displays. Just as you want your guests to feel free to move about in your home, you want your customers to be enticed to move around the store. You also want them to be coaxed by interesting or informative displays and signs that help them find their way to what interests them. Your salespeople become the good hosts by showing off their home (your store.)

When you do talk to your guest, avoid the typical, "Can I help you?" (translation—what can I sell you today?). Try welcoming your guests by saying "Nice to see you again", or, "Thanks for coming in." You can ask them their name (or preferably know their name) and talk to them about what brought them out today. As a good host, you make the conversation about the guest (your customer), not about yourself or your store. As you or your people are listening to the answers given by your guests or customers, you can then focus on their needs.

What Might Happen Inside An Average Store
Think about a customer coming into a pet store and asking where the dog toys are. One store, which we'll call "Mediocre Mac's Pet Store", might be like most stores, where the salesperson tells her the chew toys are on the back wall, to the left, and points in the general direction of the toys. Our customer finds her way to the back of the store and sees the chew toys with a much healthier price on them

than she was used to seeing in Walmart, and her buying decision will probably be based on those prices. She is then asking herself, "Why should I pay more for a chew toy here? What's the point? No one has given me the slightest reason to hand over more money for what appears to be the same basic item." And she might be right to think this way.

What Might Happen Inside A Better Service Oriented Store
In a store across town, which we'll call "The Splendid Turtle" pet store, the same customer asks the same question as she enters. But Joe Sales Star goes a step further by greeting the customer with a live Macaw Parrot sitting on his shoulder. He gets the bird to say "Hello," then he walks the customer to the rear of the store and says, "we've got the most fun toys right now." As Joe hands the customer a highly textured and hollowed out rubber ball, he points out that by putting a great snack inside, the dog will play with the ball forever trying to get the snack out. He asks the customer what her dog's name is and what kind of dog she has. He is told that "Fluffy" is a mix-breed Schnauzer/Poodle or Schnoodle! He further points out that this store's toys are "guaranteed fun", meaning if the dog doesn't play with it and the toy doesn't live up to the owner's complete satisfaction, she can return the toy for a full refund. Now a good salesclerk might let the customer go there, but Joe Sales Star isn't satisfied. Joe then ask the customer if she has any good fresh treats for her dog at home and, after hearing "I'm not sure" Joe says, "You really should try these. Dogs really love them and they're good for their fur coats, and besides, they fit inside the ball really well."

By now, Joe Sales Star has just separated himself from every other pet shop clerk and most any retail sales clerks at any store, because of his outstanding customer service.

As he walks the customer to the register, Joe mentions that in two (2) weeks they will be having a special event to insert a security chip under dogs' skin and the pet shop will be doing it at cost, with a vet performing the task. He tells the customer if she will give him her email address, he will send her a reminder via email.

As the customer pays for her merchandise, it's evident there was virtually no real buying decision made by the customer—it was almost automatic. Walmart has been totally forgotten. Joe places her purchase in a bag and drops a couple of small treats inside the bag, telling her to give the treats to "Fluffy" when she gets home. He then walks around the sales counter and personally hands the customer the shopping bag as he thanks her for coming in.

At this point, Joe Sales Star has just separated himself and his store from every other pet store that the customer has been to in years, not to mention Walmart! Do you think she'll be back?

I'm sure that, in your home, you also tell or show your friends something they didn't already know during the course of your friendly conversation. And, being a good host, you would expect these guests to return again. Why wouldn't they? And why on earth wouldn't a customer return after that experience at "The Splendid Turtle"?

In Conclusion:
There are a myriad of strategies and approaches toward making your store ready for your guests and getting them to come back. It is not just one thing. It's new displays, it's cleanliness, comfortable lighting, and even aromas. It's pleasant, fun and knowledgeable sales people who are there to help. It's fresh and new merchandise to see. It may even be entertainment in some form or another. It's all of these collectively that make the real difference.

"You have to perform at a consistently higher level than others. That's the mark of a true professional. Professionalism has nothing to do with getting paid for your services."

Joe Paterno

"The way to a customer's heart and wallet lies in how well we initially serve our customers and recover from poor service."

Author Unknown

"Right or wrong, the customer is always right."

Marshall Field
(Founder of Marshall Field & Company)

Raising The Bar Above Basic Customer Service

14

(OR Delivering "Over-the-Top" Customer Service)

If you want to grab your share of customers in today's business world, you must impress them to get their attention, and then you've got to deliver the goods. Again, you must continually work to give customers compelling reasons why they should patronize your store. Because if you don't, I'm betting there is another business out there that will be more than happy to oblige! Your stores overall long term objective should always be to use the software, have the people, implement the processes, and invest in the equipment that will help you consistently deliver the best customer experience possible.

If you're looking for sales increases that come from great or over-the-top customer service, then start by taking a look at all of the following tips:

1. Go Back To Your Mission Statement.

Hopefully your mission statement is reminding you and your employees of just what the experience should be for customers shopping in your store. **<u>Work with your employees in developing an over-the-top customer service vision with some specific objectives</u>**. Your employees can be invaluable in providing you input about what customers see and want. Think about it . . . your people know from firsthand experience where your business doesn't measure up. Your customer service goals should include the following:

a. A clear, understandable statement as to what your objectives are.

b. What you need to provide over-the-top experiences, i.e. how will you generally impress and keep your customers returning because of the great service or people at your business.

c. Tie in "what you need" with your business plan, your training, your policies and any mission statement as you translate it into specific action points with your employees.

d. Decide what will set you apart from your competitors to make you special or distinctive in the eyes of your customers. Apple Stores are known for good service, the "Genius Bar" customer assistance, and innovation. Build-A-Bear is known for offering a fun family experience. Nordstrom is known for its person shoppers and their fantastic return policy. Yes, I know you're probably a small business, but it doesn't make any difference. You must offer something that will cause people to talk and spread the word about your store.

e. More than just offering something distinctive, you need to look at what your store can offer that your competition can't. Is it really unique merchandise? Is it a staff with special talents or knowledge? Do you have a unique location or ability to perform a specialized service? Do you have access to something your competition does not? Think about it for a while! Don't treat this question lightly.

f. Talk to customers. Survey them about what they like and what they experience elsewhere that impresses them, as well as disappoints them.

Once you've done your soul searching, brainstorming and customer research, you will know where and how you plan to excel. Whatever it is, it must grab the customer's attention and separate you from the pack with some clear difference in words and actions. And when it comes to action, you will need to come through "as promised". If you don't, you may be in worse shape than if you'd made no promises at all. Customers aren't blind . . . or at least, not for very long. You certainly don't want to under-perform on any expectations you set by reputation or even marketing.

Think about what you want customers saying about your store?

While your vision and objectives may come out of your own imagination, they still need to be grounded in some realities, including your own ability and financial capacity to actually do what you set out to do. If you see your employees rolling their eyes or shaking their heads with comments like "that'll be the day", or "no way that's going to happen with our payroll and schedule", you're not really accomplishing anything because your employees are not buying into the goal. They must buy into your goals as you're going to need them to believe it—to live it and breath it on a daily basis. It should be the main topic of conversation and focus for you and your employees.

Over time, if you've successfully conveyed the dream, the goals and the pride of being the best, you should actually be able to see and feel the improvement in your employees and their attitudes. Those who care and are worth keeping will begin to feel your stores unique position and their special place in the whole effort.

2. Focus On Helping Customers—Not Making Sales.

Remember that keeping a customer's business is generally more important than closing the sale. Don't be looking at immediate gratification by focusing only on getting the sale. Remember, it's about providing solutions and getting customers to come back the next time. Customers learn very quickly when you are taking care of their needs (rather than just interested in making a sale). These are the people who can become your stores advocates.

3. Anticipate Your Customers' Needs.

If you will take the time to truly and thoroughly understand your customers' unique needs, it will pay off. There is no way you can serve your customers adequately if you don't even have a clear picture of what your customers expect and want from your business. Find out what they need, what they wish for and what they feel like they missed. Use questionnaires or polls and dig deeper into details. Talk to customers about their experience with your store or your company and really listen to their complaints, opinions and observations.

4. Special Attention And Recognition For Regular Shoppers.

Regular shoppers should be recognized and acknowledged like an old friend or acquaintance. A simple "nice to see you again" can be important with regulars. People love feeling like they are special. Learn their names and use their names when talking to them. Train employees to identify regulars. Patrons in a restaurant love to feel like they are getting special attention because they are regulars or because the owner knows who they are. People want to feel like someone cares about them and values their business. Have you ever had one of your people call and follow up with your customer to be sure they were happy after a purchase? Can you imagine how unique this would make your business compared to your competition? Customers who feel valued will come back.

5. Evaluate And Rate Your Service Performance.

Be honest about every aspect of the customer experience. Again, it's not about your impression. It's about your customer's perception. When you have a chance, ask your customers what they like best about your competition's store or services compared to yours, or how they would rate you on a scale of from 1–10. *You can't fix it if you don't know what's broken.* Even once you have great service, you can't become complacent and assume you know how things are going. From time to time, you must send out or e-mail a customer survey to make sure your services, products, efforts and understanding of your customers are all on track. You need to know why they are doing business with you and why they are, or are not, buying from your competition.

6. Ask Some Key Questions And Change What Doesn't Cut It.

Get your best people together and analyze what can be done to improve. You will certainly want to include your sales help for specific service issues. Your people hear things and see things you don't, and they can often provide some very enlightening information and answers. Consider the following questions:

Are you and your people really listening to customers or just going through the motions?

Are *you* listening to your employees?

Have you ever acted as a customer and called your own business? What did you learn?

Does a process or a policy need to change?

Do you need better equipment or better training?

Do you know what the competition is doing to serve customers better?

Do you know what you're doing that surpasses the competition?

Can the job, the service, the repair, the response be done faster?

Can it be done better? (Can the experience be better?)

Do you have independent contractors or vendors that are performing in a substandard manner? Do you even know for sure?

Is your store meeting the customer's expectations or surpassing them?

If you can easily address all of these questions during one meeting, you're not looking at the questions seriously and hard enough (or you've had one very long meeting)! Once you think you have it fixed, go back and check again.

7. Your People Are Your Personal Representative.

Have you ever been at a business and had someone take care of you with such care and interest that you just assumed they were the owner? This is the kind of person you really want taking care of your customers. You also want someone who actually cares for your customers and who will take ownership of a problem and make it their goal to take care of that customer as your personal representative. It's all about having people who want to deliver a memorable experience, as opposed to having people who are indifferent to customers and just want to put their time in.

By the way, a great deal of what I'm talking about here can be avoided by doing a better job when hiring your people (we'll talk about hiring later). However, if you hear things from your people such as "that's not my problem" or "that's not what I was hired to do", you may have the wrong employees and will probably never get where I'm talking about taking your business. You'll need to deal with it now. Do NOT put it off, because an attitude like that will most likely not correct itself.

8. Reward Exceptional Service.

Implement a customer service awards program that recognizes employees for exceptional customer service. No plaques or awards.

Consider offering a gift certificate for special recognition from a customer, or possibly a partial day off. Be creative.

9. AGAIN. . . . Handle Inquiries, Problems And Complaints NOW!

The customer comes first. And then after that, the customer comes first. Do NOT leave customers in the waiting or "limbo" mode. Orders should be filled promptly and delivered promptly, even if it is a hassle or an extra expense for you to do so. Inquiries, repairs, e-mails, complaints and callbacks need to be handled with a sense of urgency. Customers want their products to be fixed or their service problem to be resolved. They should not have to wait or wonder if their problem will be addressed.

While in the new home construction trade, I watched many homebuilders really miss the boat time and time again. They would go through the whole process of building a home for the customer and do a pretty good job, and then, after closing day, when little things came up such as bad paint jobs, doors that don't close right, noisy dishwashers, or squeaky floors, the builders would take forever to either respond or correct the problem (if they did anything at all). To the builder, it's a minor annoyance. To the buyer, it becomes a growing aggravation over time and sometimes an embarrassment when they're trying to show off their new home. Customers in all areas want immediate resolution, and if you can't give it to them, it will be this lack or delay in service that leaves the bad taste in their mouths—and that's what they'll remember!

> Research has shown that the likelihood of repeat business goes up tremendously when complaints are resolved on the spot. Your loss or cost should not usually be a factor. There is no way you can tell me exactly what devastating effects will come from poor word of mouth, especially when coupled with the continued loss of your original customers.

The following figures are cited by CSM, and eMagazine for Customer Service Professionals © 2010:

The average "wronged customer" will tell 8-16 people about it. Over 20% will tell more than 20. Source: Lee Resource, Inc.

A typical business hears from only about 4% of its dissatisfied customers. 96% just go away and 91% will never come back. Source: "Understanding Customers" by Ruby Newell-Legner.

91% of unhappy customers will not willingly do business with you again. Source: Lee Resource, Inc.

70% of complaining customers will do business with you again if you resolve the complaint in their favor. Source: Lee Resource, Inc.

- 95% of complaining customers will do business with you again if you resolve the complaint instantly. Source: Lee Resource, Inc.

Admit your stores mistakes, then ask your customer how you can make amends and please them. Apologies should come immediately for any problem, followed by a quick solution. Depending on the issue or mistake, a small gift or token of appreciation helps set you apart. Think about the value to a business over a period of years, if when a mistake or problem took place, your store went out of its way to correct the problem AND gave the customer a small token of appreciation as well. You would turn something negative into a really memorable positive—one that your customer is likely to talk about.

A Gordon Guideline

Problems or complaints are your very best opportunities to show "over-the-top" customer care and service, and these are the absolute best times to set yourself apart and generate loyalty and tremendous "word of mouth" advertising.

10. Empower Your Employees.

If you allow or teach your people in any way to say "Sorry, that's company policy. . ." or, "If I do that for you, I'll have do to it for everyone", you've just given the go ahead to the mediocrity train and it's leaving the station soon with a number of your customers. You need policies and training in place that make it very easy for employees to address any given situation or problem for a customer. Employees should not be running to you to find out how you want a particular customer handled in a customer satisfaction situation. The goal is to have such a clearly spelled out customer satisfaction policy that you avoid putting your people in the position of coming to you to and asking you what you want to do. You also don't want your people to be fearful of doing the right thing for a customer. (See the chapter on "Empowering Your People".)

In Conclusion:
Consider a commitment that says:

"We want our customers and our competition to be in awe of us, in every way possible."

One Little Warning!
Do Not Boast about Your Customer Service!

If you think about it, everyone says they have good customer service. So how are you separating yourself in the world of marketing by claiming to have great customer service? Do you really believe that, if you list great customer service as a selling point, new customers will get in line to take their business to your store because it must be true?

If McDonalds hamburgers touted great personal service or a fine dining experience, would you buy into that? However, if McDonalds says they'll have your order in 60 seconds or it's free like they did in the late 60's, that might have a real impact on your decision. That is a claim that has merit and is backed by more than just boastful marketing propaganda!

Let me ask you to consider these typical marketing claims for a moment:

"We're Number One"

"Top Quality"

"Best Service"

"Best Tasting"

"Superior Customer Service"

My question would be, according to whom? Do any of these slogans really help anyone make a buying decision?

What about the words "Top Quality"? Again my question is, as opposed to what? Is the advertiser saying that those who don't make this claim have **Less Than** "Top Quality"? If a company doesn't say "Best Service", are they saying that they give **Less Than** the "Best Service"?

The consumer is becoming more savvy and cynical everyday. Do you really believe that people are really impressed by your claims. If you're going to claim in your marketing efforts that you have the best customer service, my response is, "Yeah, I've heard it before!" The only good way to promote customer service is by *providing it!*

A Gordon Guideline

Claiming great customer service lumps you right into a group of hundreds or thousands of other companies in your market area that are all making the same meaningless claim! Wouldn't it make much more sense to take the customers who are already coming to your store and then wow them with great customer service? This is where you separate your store from the pack.

Which do you think impresses a customer more? Telling customers you have great customer service and then having them find out that it was true, or having them do business with you without any real expectations and then being surprised or "wowed" by the experience?

If you promote your store as having great customer service, the best you can hope for is either meeting their expectations or worse, disappointing the customer's expectations. Since everyone has a different idea of what great customer service really is, how can you possibly deliver on your promise to everyone?

Entice And Keep Customers By Truly Knowing Them

15

If you want to entice and keep customers returning, you'll need to provide what they need, but (more importantly) **what they want**, and maybe even what they don't even know they want yet. You can't do this without having a clear idea who your customers are, what they like, what's important to them and what they've wanted before.

Now, do you really honestly know your customers, or do you **just think you know**?

The big retailers I've watched over the years have spent mind-boggling sums of money on advertising to drive customer traffic to their stores, and yet they don't even know who these people are. Generally, retailers of all sizes do not know who purchased any given item. Most of the time, all they know is what zip codes they send their ads into. They can't tell how old their customers are, much less their names and addresses, and they probably don't have phone numbers or e-mail addresses either. Years ago, that was fine, but not with today's competition and technology. Your cash register is no longer there to just ring and total up sales when the cash drawer opens.

Is This Your Business on a Smaller Scale?

Wouldn't it be smarter (and certainly cheaper) in these days of technology to drive customers in the first time with advertising and then try to hold on to them and get them back again and again with some specific offers tailored to customers because you know them? Wouldn't it be even better to personally invite back the customers you want, or try to benefit from collecting information so that you know exactly with whom you are dealing?

Identifying Your Best Customers

Wouldn't it be great to know the overall characteristics of your best customers? Let's put it another way . . . at the very least, wouldn't it be good to know your customers better than your competition does? Couldn't this be a key part of winning the wars with your competitors? Think about it from a marketing perspective . . . once you know what these characteristics are, it becomes a heck of a lot easier to go out to target and attract more customers just like the ones you already have.

The Easiest And Cheapest Way Is To Ask Them.

I have benefited greatly in the past by using well thought out surveys (either sent in the mail or conducted on site). They can be really eye opening in terms of how you're doing in addressing customer needs and wants. They can be very instructive in pointing out weaknesses in service, product assortment and convenience. In some cases, you can also learn a lot by just calling some of your better customers for their feedback. In addition, calling can show the customer you care about them and value their business as well as their thoughts. However you get feedback, take what they say seriously and try to implement processes to integrate their feedback into your service. While I am certainly not a survey and research expert, some of the great questions (most of them open-ended) that have served me well via some customer surveys are as follows:

If you could change one thing about this business, it would be _____?

The thing I like best about coming here is _____?

I have been disappointed when _____.

Why can't your store have or do _____?

Your competition does a better job of _____.

I could have shopped at _____.

I don't like _____ about them.

I would like to see more of _____. Why?

This is the reason I would recommend this store to my friends...

This is the reason I could not recommend this store to my friends...

My age bracket...

My zip code ...

A Company That's Been Practicing What I'm Preaching.
As mentioned earlier in Chapter Two, "Hot Topic" is a teen fashion chain whose efforts are regularly based on daily feedback from their customers. They even encourage their own employees to report on trends. Almost everything it does to improve sales is based on consumer input. The company places a report card or comment card into every shoppers bag and then the company actually reacts to the responses it gets. The company CEO even reads many of these customer report cards. Company employees monitor concert halls to be aware of the hot bands and fashions at the time so that they can react to customer trends. In addition, Hot Topic's website offers a "community" link that allows for feedback on all kinds of issues as well as discussion forums. All of this results in close customer-employee-management communication and better understanding. This is what helps lead to better odds of making a connection with the very people you value the most—your customers (we'll talk about social media later).

Begin Seriously Using Your Sales Transactions To Collect Data.

I'm sure you know that the easiest way to gather information is at the "point of sale," through the use of your store's retail computer software and point of sales system. The first and most obvious goal has always been to determine what's selling. Any decent retail computer software should provide an effective sales analysis that would, first and foremost, be based on the following:

1. Total sales volume

2. Total number of transactions, per hour, per day, per week

3. Number of units per transaction

4. Average sales per transaction

5. Sales and transactions by merchandise category

If you use the information collected by your system, you should be able to put this information on a spreadsheet on a month-by-month basis. With the right software or spreadsheet, patterns and seasonal trends show up, and if you do this religiously, you should be able to see weaknesses as well as real opportunities for change. As an example: if your sales trend was up, could it be because you had more transactions and individual sales, OR were your average sales just higher? If your average sales are higher, is it because of a change in sales people, better training, re-merchandising of a product category or have you drawn more attention to items with higher price-points? I could go on with more questions like these. Obviously, in your store, you would know the answers to these questions.

Next—Who's Buying The Items That Are Selling?
We all want profitable merchandise, and you probably know what that merchandise is in your store, but how about knowing more? Wouldn't it be even better to know who's buying what, or what kinds of customers are buying it? Wouldn't it be great to know who the more profitable customers are? Once again, the best way to do this is to collect and capture this customer information at the point of

sale (your cash register). The ideal goal should be to link certain customer information with the specific transaction information (i.e., the item, price, date, etc.). Today's cutting edge retailers are using this information to better understand their customers' buying preferences and offer useful advice as a result. Then, they use customers' e-mail addresses to say thank you and to present personalized shopping lists, offers and promotions. Customers get used to this kind of service, and they increasingly demand more from their retail experience. Hopefully you have a P.O.S. system that can have some additional information keyed into it. What information might you collect from each sale besides the usual bar code information?

You could collect zip code, gender and possibly age by simply typing in another digit. Your people wouldn't even need to ask the customer about their age. They could just casually guess and enter an age code. While this wouldn't be entirely accurate, it will still serve your purposes over the long haul. You might even enter another digit code to indicate whether the item was a personal purchase or a gift purchase. Gathering this minimal information is not time consuming and it can become much faster once it becomes more routine for your staff.

Just Think How You Could Use This Information!
With information on a customer's age, sex, neighborhood and type of purchase all coming together on one page, and then coupled with the actual SKUs of what they bought, you can see and interpret all kinds of statistics. Your best customer's preferences would really begin to stand out. You could find out the age range of customers and exactly what that age group is buying. And could learn whether they're buying full-priced merchandise or if they're bargain hunters who are picking up the cheap and low-margin finds. Once you know which customers are buying full-priced merchandise and what category of merchandise appeals to whom, you can begin to target advertising for the customers you really want to cater to, especially via e-mail. You could also focus your advertising on those items that are the most popular with your best customers. Other information could determine if people are buying for gifts more often than for themselves. Then

you can begin to analyze why that would be. Another question might be, "does your percentage of gift purchases hold up or increase during the holidays?" I worked at a store where people were buying men's shirts and ties for themselves during the year, but the gift purchases actually went down during the Christmas season because customers didn't want their gift recipients to be able to find out that it came from a discount store. In other words, they liked the quality of clothes for themselves, but they were hung up on the lack of a brand name when buying a Christmas gift.

Knowing what customers you want, who they're buying for and who's buying the most profitable merchandise, allows you to react and cater to them much more effectively via the store atmosphere you create, the music you play, the brands you carry, the type of sales you have, and possibly even how these people are approached.

Furthermore, with information that is tracked by zip code, you begin to learn which zip codes are your stronger areas. Or maybe you already know your best zip codes, but for some reason that's not where you're traffic comes from. If you did a little research on the internet or at the library, you might begin to get a more clear demographic picture of who these people are. You may find some zip codes give you a good response percentage but those zip codes could be full of bargain hunters or more elderly buyers. Or maybe a lower response zip code may still net you more upscale buyers or maybe even more teen buyers. If you then wanted to appeal less or more to a certain group, you could make adjustments accordingly.

*Can you think of any information
that could be more important for your business?*

Create "The Experience" (Surpassing Expectations with a Wow Factor)

16

Look back on the best, warmest memories you can recall, and you will find that they all involve people—not things. Think about the commercials on television that affect you most, and you'll find they touched something emotionally inside you. If we can take a lesson from these "warm fuzzy" feelings and situations, it doesn't take long to realize the fact that material possessions are not what become priceless and memorable as we look back at what we truly value in the end. The memories and experiences we've had interacting with real people, especially loved ones, are the most important. Sounds like the word "emotion" is back in the picture once again. If you recall, that's the word I said that was so important in causing someone to buy. Remember: needs vs. wants. Wants, and the emotions connected with them, are what usually win.

We've been dancing all around the word, *"emotion"*. So wouldn't it be great if you could create a positive *emotional* experience in your store. If we look at some other companies who've built great reputations, we know that they earned their customers by surpassing expectations and impressing buyers on an emotional basis. They also work very hard to keep those customers by maintaining consistently high standards and working to create more emotional connections that set them apart for their competition.

If you think about it, we're all always anxious to tell someone about an unexpected surprise or experience. What I'm saying here again is that if we could create an emotional experience or surpass customer expectations (which is an experience in itself), the word about the positive experience generally spreads. Let's also remember that positive word of mouth doesn't cost you a thing! It's the cheapest form of advertising there is!

Here are four solid examples of companies who consistently surpass expectations and provide pleasant and memorable experiences":

- Apple computer provides hassle-free and smooth running computers and software. Then they wow customers with superior customer service and "genius" bars in their stores to support their customers after the sale.

- Cheesecake Factory markets great desserts, then surpasses customer expectations with great entrees and oversized portions!

- Panera Bread promises great freshly baked breads and good sandwiches. They surpass expectations with sparkling clean stores, friendly staff, a comfortable atmosphere and free WiFi!

- Nordstrom provides a comfortable clean and spacious environment to find trendy fashions, but then goes a step farther by providing superior customer service. For example, a good customer returned to their store with a pair of shoes that were damaged and only one year old. The shoes were repaired free of charge by Nordstrom, even though the store manager knew that they never ever had sold that particular shoe brand.

Providing the Experience & Surpassing Expectations
As I said before in my chapter on observing other retailers, some of the retailers who are doing the best job, are creating "experiences" for their shoppers. They are de-emphasizing the actual "purchase" part of the transaction and focusing more on the customer's personal needs or wants.

This is where some crazy and fun brainstorming, along with some research, might come into play. First of all you need some creativity and imagination. As a secondary goal, you might want to work on how you can de-emphasize, speed up or simplify the transactional side of your store. The bottom line is to make it less eventful. But this can all be greatly assisted and enhanced with the answers to some questions that you need to ask.

1. How can you help your customer forget about what is going on in the world outside of your store?
2. Can you make them laugh or say "Wow!" or "Unbelievable!"?
3. What kind of unique experience can you create that your target customers will remember for years to come?
4. What would competitors never do because it is too outrageous or too expensive?
5. Is it possible to heighten interest and emphasize the more exciting and fun aspect of owning a product from your store?
6. What might make your customers feel better about themselves or improve their self esteem?
7. What will make the experience in your store totally over-the-top in terms of expectations and value?
8. What can you do to tie any positive store experiences to the customer's memory?

A Gordon Guideline

You can create memorable or remarkable moments in your store by working to ensure that your customers experience something special, emotional or outstanding that makes a lasting impression on them. The goal is to tie the customer's memory regarding visits to your store to small daily positive memorable experiences or big "wow" moments when possible. Over a period of time, real emotional ties develop and become much more powerful than any advertising campaign.

Memorable experiences are usually tied to some emotion or feeling, whether it's surprise, warmth, extreme gratefulness, happiness, pain, trauma. . . do you get the picture? Feelings are what stick in our memories, much more so than words. Sounds, scent and music can bring back those feelings. I'm sure you've heard a song from your past that instantly takes you back to a feeling or a time from years ago. A scene or place can bring back feelings. They can be very powerful, which is why sales are best made via creating emotion rather than just rattling off features. Do you ever remember your mother telling you to keep your hands away from the hot stove or you'll get burned? You probably forgot about what she said—as it went in one ear and out the other. But I'll bet you remembered not to touch the hot stove after the first time you burnt your fingers. That stayed with you. Pain is very emotional. (I keep telling you, I'm a genius.) Events or experiences at your store do not need to be life-changing events. They need only be memorable in a positive way. Regardless, memorable experiences are extremely rare when visiting almost any store.

Giving customers a memorable moment or experience can also be accomplished by offering an escape from the usual. Again, think about doing something that isn't expected in your market arena. As a beginner, think about doing some little extras that are never done at a store in your market. For a motel, it might be something as simple as cleaning the ice and snow off the guest's vehicle on a cold winter morning. For an oil change store, it might be cleaning the inside and outside of the customers windshield or car before you're done. These experiences don't all need to be on the Disney World level, and they certainly don't always need to be expensive. But collectively, they add up.

Consumers evaluate experiences in four (4) ways:

1. Comparing the experience to what they *hoped* it would be;

2. Comparing the experience to what they *expected* it would be;

3. Comparing the experience to other *related experiences* they've had in the past;

4. Comparing it to *experiences others have had*.

(Source: '*The Paradox of Choice*' by Barry Schwartz).

For example, you hope your purchase will be uneventful and reasonably brief. You expect the cashier to be pleasant and accurate. You compare the experience to your last purchase at a store, but when the experience is compared with experiences at the competition, you realize you were treated unusually well. Your cashier went the extra mile. She smiled and remembered your name. She carried on a sincere pleasant conversation with you and asked about your children. She then offered to gift-wrap your package at no charge, opened the door for you as you left and helped you carry your packages to the car as well.

These things ad up and go a long way in being memorable. A cashier at a drive thru window could also have a smile. They might make a positive comment about a child or pet in the car. They may keep treats available for kids or for Fido. They may even hand a regular customer a special coupon for a free drink or sandwich the next time around.

One of Nordstrom's nice touches comes when they finish ringing up the sale. They don't hand the package over the counter to the customer or let them pick it up off the counter, they walk around the counter and present it to the customer . . . Nice Touch!

Make the effort to surpass their expectations. Every customer expects good customer service. Unfortunately, they still don't get it enough. Your job, if you want to set yourself apart from the competition, is to not only meet customer expectations, but to go above and beyond and deliver an exceptional experience.

A Gordon Guideline

"Work to find and emphasize the little things you can do for your customers that let them know they're very much appreciated! Replace the usual and common experience with the pleasingly unexpected."

Now I have two (2) questions for you:

1. What kind of experience are your customers having?
2. Do you even know for sure what kind of experience your customers are having?

If you think I'm getting carried away on the "customer experience" bandwagon, read everything you can on the internet regarding Zappos.com's customer service, and then do some soul searching as to how you might provide memorable moments.

A Memorable Moment for Me
A memorable moment for me came when visiting the Coca-Cola Store at the Coca-Cola Museum in Atlanta, Georgia. Having been a Coca-Cola memorabilia collector for years, when I arrived, I felt as though the mother ship had landed once again. I was home. The variety, the class, the color just blew me away. Unfortunately, this is something that a large corporation can do that we little guys can't.

But It Doesn't Always Require a Big Budget
Another memorable moment came from a store I visited in Fort Walton Beach, Florida. It was a Coca-Cola memorabilia store. It wasn't pretty. It wasn't merchandised all that well. It wasn't even open and spacious feeling, as I often preach. But they made up for all of that with two (2) things, the product selection and the variety. It knocked my socks off! I couldn't believe the new and old collectable merchandise they had there. The other thing that made my visit special was the friendliness, patience and stories from the

shop owner. He was extremely patient and gracious with his time and information. He had story after story of things that had been bought and sold there, as well as a great story about his live parrot there at the counter that had been in an old Coca-Cola commercial. Who knows if it was all true, but it didn't matter. He had what I wanted and he had things that I hadn't seen anywhere else before. I drove home with my car packed with great Coca-Cola buys!

One of the best opportunities to surprise and exceed a customer's expectations comes when a customer has a problem or complaint connected with a purchase from your business. They come to you wondering what you're going to do about it. This is the opportunity . . . the magic moment, so to speak. . . when you have the opportunity to get and keep a customer's respect, love and loyalty. The easier you make it for them to get their problem solved and the more gracious and enthusiastic you are in accommodating them, the better it is for all.

Creating Memorable Moments

1.   Memorable moments are hard to create without some kind of human contact and caring attention to a customer. This isn't very likely to happen for businesses that don't treat their own people well and are too interested in just getting the sale. No one seems to get emotionally attached to a vending machine, no matter what it's selling.

2.   They are almost always a result of a store employee or owner. Yes, the Coca-Cola store was impressive, but it never would have stood out if I hadn't been comfortable spending time there and if I didn't feel welcomed as well as entertained by the owner.

3.   They usually come from someone who likes and cares about people. I've never heard of, or can't imagine, a special moment for a customer being created by someone who is indifferent to customers or wants to get customers out the door so they

can get back to what they were reading or doing. It almost always happens because someone who cares took some extra time and effort.

4.   Employees who have paid close attention to their customers and listened well, have very good chances of creating a memorable moment. It's usually a result of listening intently to a customer and then seizing upon some opportunity. However this is not so likely if the employee has not been given some freedom or been empowered to go out of their way to take care of customers. It's also not very likely where customer service is not highly emphasized.

5.   Some memorable or "wow" moments may be created by an overwhelming variety of merchandise to choose from, that the customer highly values and seeks. This happened for me at my Coca-Cola store. Once again however, if I'd had a poor experience with an employee, this would have tainted and obscured my experience.

6.   Memorable moments can be created by attention to design and store interior. A really "over the top" moment can be created by some imagination and design of an over-the-top store atmosphere or store interior. This of course, requires the larger dollar investment. However, the human interaction with store employees must still be positive. You may be wowed upon arriving at the Hershey®Chocolate Factory Store, but if the employees were to treat you like chopped liver, most of the experience would be dulled.

Another great retailer that I've mentioned before is Build-A-Bear. Maxine Clark is a prime example of a CEO who understands the importance of entertaining the customer. Her entire chain of stores is built around this premise. In her book, she quotes a former chairman of the May Department Stores, Stanley Goodman, from a speech she heard him make years ago. He says, "When a customer has fun, they spend more money." Her stores are entirely about creating fun, putting smiles on her customer's faces and creating the experience. She says that reading that statement was a defining moment for her. Keep the "entertainment" idea in the forefront of your mind when mapping out the original concept of your store and while maintaining the ongoing daily operations, and you will be miles ahead of the average retailer anywhere!

Think of retailing as entertainment. The first act is when customers walk through your door. The shopping, the discovery, the lights, the colors and the interaction between store staff and customer are the storyline. The finale becomes the purchase and the sincere appreciation shown for the customer's business.

Memorable moments can be created by any store on any kind of budget. You may need to give some thought as to "How can I wow my customer?" But the real challenge comes when you ask, "How can I make it a *regular* part of my customers' experiences with my store?"

"Lifelong customers and loyal company advocates such as the loyal customers of Apple Computer, are created as a result of ongoing experiences of either small pleasant surprises or "over the top" memorable "wow" moments in your store.

Music is One Inexpensive Idea to Help Enhance the Odds for a Memorable Experience

Many people are affected by music in their lives. I certainly am. Music can make you remember a special girlfriend from the past. It will remind you of a vacation or event. It will bring back the actual feeling and vision of a movie. In fact, movies would be much less impressive and emotional without the music. While I understand that not everyone is affected by music like I am, I would venture to say that most people have felt an emotion or a mood based on music they've heard, whether they are aware of it or not.

One of the things that just kills a store, in my opinion, is an environment that is too quiet (like a library). Those who do play music (like every chain store and office building in America) all seem to be playing the same thing so it ends up becoming almost like beige paint on the walls of a store. Who remembers any of it? And isn't a beige wall in one store just like that of another? It all becomes the same no matter where you go. After all, does the music in a Walmart sound any different from Kohls, or the mall, or Target or the airport? So why wouldn't you want to use music so that it's more than just beige paint, to help define your business and set it apart? Make it part of the experience.

Pottery Barn has typically encouraged their customers to "feel" the experience through music from vocalists such as Mel Torme, Frank Sinatra, Dinah Washington, Nat King Cole and Sara Vaughn. These recordings help create an atmosphere that represents the Pottery Barn lifestyle. In fact, you can find "Pottery Barn" CD's on Amazon.com. Do you think that a company like Disney has given great attention to the music played in its amusement parks? You bet they have! Starbucks has been so successful with their ties to music that they have sold the music they play on CDs at the register. Chipotle has also made music an important element of their identity and atmosphere. They offer Chipotle radio on their website to hear the music played in their stores.

Music can help create a feeling about your retail experience at a store, because it creates emotion and that emotion latches on to the customers who visit your store over time. But it has to be appropriate for your store's special retail experience and the emotions you want attached to that experience. The music that you personally enjoy may not be what is best for your target customers.

For starters, look at the age of your ideal customer and then choose music that is appropriate and pleasing to that audience. It doesn't need to be so loud that it rattles merchandise off the walls, but it does need to be loud enough to be a significant part of the environment. Remember that you're also in the entertainment business. But more importantly you want to maximize sales.

Studies have found that classical music caused shoppers to spend more money including the purchase of more expensive wines. Another study found that music (specifically low-tempo music in a grocery store) increased sales by 39.2%. A 1991 study commissioned by Muzak, reported that sales to shoppers under age 25 increased 51%, age 26-50 increased 11%, and over age 50 increased by 26% when music was present. All of this entirely depends on the market you are in, as well as the mood that is needed. There is no doubt that the right sound can increase retail sales. On the flip side, studies have shown that the wrong music can hurt your image as well as your sales. For instance, as an extreme example, I really doubt that classical music would be an asset in a teen clothing store or that rock n' roll would be too wise in a funeral home's casket selection area.

Music can elicit feelings that make customers feel upbeat, classy, hip, romantic, adventurous—and cause them to linger in your store longer. All of the things I have been talking about are what separates the great stores from the mediocre stores. It all comes together to become very powerful with customers. When you connect emotions, experiences, and good people together to create a great personal and visual experience in a store, it's like adding the strength of 3 + 3 together and getting 8.

Consider Offering a BOLD Guarantee
Let your customers know right up front (via your warranty or promise) that you will do something to back purchases at your store. A really great guarantee serves one very important purpose to prospective customers. It eliminates or reduces the risk that would keep them from making a purchase from your store and, believe it or not, it's generally not an expensive proposition.

Why do I say this? Because the percentage of buyers will be insignificant who will need or ask you to honor the warranty. And again, as I said, if you have confidence in what you're selling, then what's the problem? Think about what your competition offers in your marketplace and how you can step up your offering to customers in order to make them more comfortable in buying from your store.

Fill in the blank. The competition's policy regarding purchases or dissatisfaction is _____.

My store will offer_____.

(Statistics indicate that the large majority of those who ask for refunds will do so within 30 days. But meanwhile, how many more sales could you have because customers were more confident in buying from your store?)

For example:

The competition offers a warranty of 90 days parts and labor.
Your store offers: A one-year warranty on parts and labor!

The competition offers a return if not satisfied.
Your store offers a 30 day trial and a discount on their next purchase.

The competition offers delivery sometime between 8:00am and 5:00pm.
My store will deliver as scheduled for a specific time that will be on time (within 1 hour) or delivery is free, plus you'll buy them dinner. Will you have to step up your game? Yes, but shouldn't you be doing that anyway?

Are you creating some expectations with these guarantees? Have you set the bar for your service or product a bit higher? YOU BET YOU HAVE! And now you are a standout compared to the rest of your competition. You've raised the bar another notch and separated yourself from the pack again in a world of mediocre competitors. Now just try to be organized enough and perform well enough to avoid needing to honor your guarantee too often. The reality is that these policies can also help force you into being a better business.

Customers really don't want to come back to you and use your guarantee. They really just want to know that your mouth (sales pitch and marketing) matches or comes close to the quality of your product or service!

So again, what is the best way to earn new customers?

<u>**Exceed Expectations!**</u>
<u>**And what is the best way to keep customers and build a reputation?**</u>

1. *Tell customers what your store offers or what it can do for them.*
2. *Back it up with a bold guarantee.*
3. *And then deliver better than they expected and better than your competitors.*

In Conclusion:

DO NOT allow your salespeople or your store's marketing efforts to make promises on which you can't deliver. Your people may consistently provide decent customer service, but decent service isn't so remarkable if it falls short of the initial promise. In fact, it's worse than not promising at all.

Any experienced business person worth his salt will tell you that it takes a lot more effort to get a new customer then to hold onto a new one. So treasure them, spoil them and treat them all as you, yourself, would want to be treated. Start out by doing an unexpectedly great job with the little things. It might be as simple as having a real human being answer customer calls within three (3) rings instead of making them work through the maze of an automated response phone system or voicemail, but it's a start.

Truly loyal customers are your crops or your farmland, and you must learn how to plant new seeds of business by listening to them and delivering what they want. Listen, plant the seeds of service, and reap the harvest by continuing to give them TLC as you would any crops growing in your field.

 Raising The Bar With
Your Sales Staff

17

Separate your store from the pack right from the moment the customer walks in your store! How about being the one store that doesn't ask them, "Can I help you"? You know what the customer is generally going to say anyway. . ."Just looking". So, why not start with a better approach than most other retailers? Maybe one of the following tips will get your store on a new approach.

1. Let Your Customers Know That You Recognize Them.

What are a retailer's most important two words when dealing with a customer? No, it's not "thank you", "thanks again" or even "please". It's your customer's first and last name. The sooner you can learn names, the sooner you've taken the service element up a notch in the customer's eyes.

> **Have you ever walked into a store or restaurant where the owner or a clerk greeted you enthusiastically by name and let you know how glad they were to see you back again? You almost feel obligated to buy something when you feel you're among friends!**

Any sales class ever taught has always emphasized the importance of using the customers name often. Everyone likes to be recognized and everyone likes to hear his/her name. It makes people feel more secure . . . like they're among friends. Wouldn't you rather buy from friends?

So what if you don't remember the customer's name? You can at least let them know that you recognize them and are glad to see them again. How about, "Hi, nice to see you again." Again customers like to go to where they are recognized. So show that you recognize them and help ensure they keep coming back.

2. Acknowledge, Acknowledge. . . . and Oh Yes, Acknowledge

Restaurant waiters are often guilty of this sin. Of course acknowledging the customer is better than not saying a thing. The customer knows your employees have seen them or heard them, but the employees act like they haven't noticed their presence anyway. In the case of a restaurant, you aren't sure if your waiter has seen you or not. This is a big no-no in retailing also! Estimates are that 68% leave because of an attitude of indifference towards the customer by the staff according to CSM (an eMagazine). I don't know if these percentages are really correct, but what if they were even 20–30%? Isn't that still too many customers to needlessly lose?

3. Haven't You Been Here Before?

Another really good greeting alternative: "Hi, you've been here before, haven't you?" Or, "I've taken care of you before haven't I?" It all comes back to being recognized and acknowledged again. You could add, "I'm trying to remember what was it you bought here last time. How did you like it?" These words show that you do care that they're happy. Or, it gives you the opportunity to deal with any concerns if they weren't.

4. Compliment Them

IF you can do it sincerely and come across that way, then don't be afraid to pay someone a compliment. Specific comments about something are always better than a more general "you really look nice today" comments. How about, "Wow what a great purse or jacket" or whatever?

5. Have a Sense of Humor and Smile.

Smiles work, and if you have someone that can skillfully use their sense of humor to lighten things and get someone engaged in conversation, empower them to have some fun.

Three Poor Customer Approaches
That May Handicap Sales in Your Store
Stop these immediately:

1. he Lowlife Stare when employees look at the customer like "What are you doing here?" or, "Why can't you people (the customers) just leave me alone?" Don't you think your customers can feel or sense something here . . . and it isn't positive? (And this isn't going to happen while you're there in the store with the employee.)

2. Saying, "NEXT!" Talk about treating someone like a piece of meat or like you're doing them a favor . . . Or maybe it sounds more like you are selling meat in the deli! . . . Remember the soup Nazi? . . . NEXT! Very cold.

3. The Canned Greeting or Speech that might as well be recorded—do not say anything that sounds like you just came from a training class, such as, "Thank you for shopping our store today, we're having a great special on _____, How may I help you?" Next customer arrives: "Thank you for shopping our store today, we're having a great special on _____, How may I help you?" If you want this type of greeting, you can get a parrot.

Selling Skills in Retail Stores Have Hit Bottom!

Is This Your Store Too?
As a customer, have you ever led a salesperson to a product to ask a few questions, and then you find that his only helpful attempt is to read the same thing off the box or display that you already read? Is this sales help? Real selling skills in any retail stores is a rarity today. This is even more true in the large mass merchandisers. Although,

I don't even think the large, full-scale department stores are doing a much better job than their discounter cousins. However, this provides the opportunity for you to gain one more advantage over the large store competitors. Of course, having some selling skills does require at least some minimal and informal training. Following are a few common issues and some basic ideas for fixing them:

Three (3) Basic Goals For Your Salespeople
1. Your people must have the personality and credibility for the job.
2. Your salespeople need to know the products and services you're selling.
3. Your salespeople need to learn how to ask questions to determine what's important to the customer. They've got to tune in and listen to customers.

Three (3) Important Factors to Having a Good Sales Team
1. Finding the Right People

Yes, it is hard to find good help. (It's hard to find good bosses, too!) What most managers/owners don't understand is that a lot of the problem is created when they hire their employees. First of all, do you really understand the type of person you want? Is this person clearly defined in your mind and in your help wanted ads? If you don't know exactly who you want, how will you find them or how will you even know when you've found them?

For more on this subject, see my chapter on interviewing. In brief, you must sit down and list out some job specifications, as this exercise forces you to think through exactly what the job requires and provides at least an outline for judging the necessary capabilities of prospective employees. Obviously, if a job requires the sale of big-ticket items, you would look for people who have big-ticket sales experience and closing skills as well. In all cases, you want someone who **enjoys** serving people!

2. Training the Right People.

You need regular sales/training meetings. We're not talking some fancy formal training program, but we are talking about regular and frequent (one (1) per week, at a minimum). It's too easy and tempting to put them off or cancel them. All this does is to set the example to your people that maybe this isn't so important after all.

Use your meetings to discuss new products, changes in store policies, new merchandising strategies or other matters relating to the store's merchandise and services. Get input from employees to solve problems or issues in handling customers. The more involved your people feel in creating new policies or procedures, the more likely they are to enthusiastically participate, and the more likely they are to emphasize these same policies and procedures to new employees. There is nothing like a company culture that has employees saying, *"Here, customer service is everything!"* or *" Here, we do it this way!"*

This is also a great time to show what over-the-top service is all about and why it's important, or possibly how to handle an unhappy customer. It may sound corny, but act out the customer-salesperson relationship between you and your people. Role-playing can help your people see and experience various situations from the customer's point of view and more importantly, it can also help employees to quickly "size up" customers (learn about their needs) or recognize when a customer's body language or words signal a problem in the making. Use your better salespeople to help with suggestions or tactics they've used before. Often, a good sales personality loves to boast about his little success stories. The bottom line is that there is no shortage of subjects to talk about, but you've got to do it regularly. If you do, you will be pleasantly surprised at how much your salespeople improve.

If you won't train . . . (you're making a big mistake).

If you can't or don't want to train, try encouraging your salespeople to take a formal course in salesmanship or to attend informal sales seminars. You may even be able to get a manufacturer or distributor to hold an informal class at your store. Consider some training CDs or check some out from your local library. Just find a way to ensure that your people listen to them, perhaps by offering a reward.

If nothing else, consider sitting down with your salespeople over a break to discuss ways your products might be better presented or maybe cover some bad habits you've observed with customers. Just remember that, over time, even small but regular efforts can pay off.

Get New People on the Right Track.

When you can begin working with a fresh face, try to encourage and stimulate their enthusiasm before bad habits or day-to-day problems wear them down. If you want new hires to develop the right attitude, take it upon yourself to convey the enthusiasm and purpose you originally brought to your business in the beginning. I've never understood an owner who takes off and leaves the store as a new hire begins the first very impressionable hours. Be involved!

3. Compensation.

Your type of retail business and other factors will largely determine the type of compensation that will work for you. Again, depending on what you sell, any compensation plan can and should be based on the employee's and the store's performance. Consider also:

How you will define the employee's performance?

Performance should also be linked to customer service and other issues that affect the overall image of the store.

Try to reward the performance of other jobs or tasks under your roof, such as stocking, merchandising or cleaning. There's more to having a great store than sales.

Good salespeople are hard to find, and if you have one or more you want to hold on to, you've got to find a way to reward them. Find a way to reward your good people and let them know you appreciate them, regardless of what they do. See chapter 27 on "Motivating Your People."

Empowering Your People For Over-the-Top Customer Service

18

Have you ever thought about the times in the past when you made a simple request of someone in a hotel, a store, a convention hall or an auto dealer? Maybe you asked for an exception to the typical standard policy. Maybe you bought something and the instruction book was missing, but the store clerk just shrugged his shoulders and seemed too indifferent about things as he told you to call the manufacturer. Maybe there was a time when you thought a restaurant shorted you on your main entrée or glass of wine. Wouldn't you have walked away with a much better feeling about the establishment if someone had made a decision to bend the rules a little and please you?

Hopefully you're not part of the problem in your store. You need to remember you're always watched by your employees. Your own actions with customers automatically set the stage for how you want customers to be treated. However, when your out of the store, wouldn't it be much better to have a customer who feels that the owner (who's out of the store) wants his customers taken care of in the best way possible? The fact is that retailers who do provide the best service have learned they must allow a significant degree of decision-making authority if they really want to take care of customers well. This is not about giving up control, it's more about removing barriers and employee fear to allow rapid, on-the-spot ("we all want you to be happy here") customer service!

Is there something standing in your way? I can't tell you how many small business owners I've heard about or even observed, who seem to be afraid of turning over any control to their employees. Giving up control just scares the daylights out of them. My question is, why?

Maybe the real issue is that you are hiring people you didn't trust or didn't train to handle customers appropriately. Regardless, your business will never grow beyond where it is if you don't have people who can take the ball and run with it besides you! (By the way, do not go turning this page because you want to ignore this part of the book!)

Yes, I understand you may want to maintain some degree of control. You can always establish some parameters or limitations for your people and then train them while reviewing their decisions on each situation, so that you and they can learn.

Empowering your people is critical for any retailer that wants to offer over-the-top service and a memorable positive experience. Empowerment is not about the day-to-day work in your store. It is also not about neglecting your return policy or giving away the farm. It is about letting your employees have the ability and authority to take care of any customer whom you may be about to really aggravate, dissatisfy or lose.

There is no doubt that the longer it takes your store to take care of a simmering and potentially explosive situation, the more damage you've done to the customer's attitude about your business, even if you later address the situation to the customer's satisfaction.

A Few Empowerment Tips

1. If you want your people to be involved in improving customer service, they've got to feel they are part of a greater purpose or mission, instead of just sales clerks. (This is what chapter 5 was all about.) You want people who will go the extra mile for customers because they care and feel part of accomplishing something special..

2. Treat employee errors in judgment as a training opportunity. If you have people that really care, you may want to ask yourself if your employees are getting more grief or more praise for their efforts and

the decisions they make? If they're getting more criticism or grief from you, more training may be in order.

3. Establish some parameters. For example, you establish that your average sales clerks can make a decision up to a certain dollar amount, say $200, and any decision that would exceed that amount needs to go to a manager (if you have one). Then your store manager has authority to make a decision up to $1,000. Also give your people examples of what might be done in certain situations, as well as what others have done to provide over-the-top or memorable service to customers.

4. Try to recognize and reward employees who've taken the initiative and done something special in front of others, even if it doesn't seem all that important to you at the moment. The goal here is to encourage your people for even the small steps they take towards better customer service.

In Conclusion:
There are other benefits in empowering your employees to take action for the customer. It's a great way to show your own employees that you respect and trust them (assuming you hired the right people to begin with). Having people who can make these decisions when you're not in the store also helps give you more time to work "on the business" as opposed to physically being there at all times. Lastly, this is also one more way to gradually prepare employees for more responsibility later.

"Washrooms will always tell if your company cares about its customers."

Author Unknown

"If the shopper feels like it was poor service, then it was poor service. We are in the customer perception business."

Mark Perrault, Rally Stores

"If you don't care, your customer never will."

Marlene Blaszczyk Editor & Publisher,
Motivating Moments (MotivateUs.com)

16 Obstacles That May Hold Your Store Back

19

Sometimes, owners and managers need a reminder about how seemingly trivial things can become a big deal to our customers, especially when we're accustomed to the same policies and routine day in and day out. Over time we all begin to accept or get used to certain poor habits or unattractive things about our stores. Keep in mind, it's hard enough to get customers in the store without disappointing or aggravating them. The fact is that most of these issues cost little or nothing to correct, and we certainly don't need to give customers ANY excuses to leave. Even if they're costly, how costly is it to look like a second, or third-rate store? Are you in this as a hobby, or are you running a business? So let's consider this chapter a wake-up call. If you're not guilty of any of the following turn-offs, congratulations! (I'll bet you're profitable too!) Regardless, take an honest look around your retail store and determine if you're guilty of any of the following:

1. Dirty Bathrooms

Dirty bathrooms are high on anyone's list of turn-offs. Restrooms in a retail establishment should always be extremely clean, *even if they are not open to the public.* Things happen and sometimes a customer needs to be allowed to use your restroom, even if it not normally made available. Let's face it, a dirty bathroom is a reflection of your standards. It says that all the clean, shiny things out front are a bit of a façade. Keep the restroom clean and stocked with paper products and soap. Do I really need to say more?

2. Crowded or Cluttered Aisles

I always felt the one thing that makes Target such a clean and attractive store (even for a discounter) is the clean, wide and uncluttered aisles they have throughout their stores. Shoppers want to be comfortable and they do NOT like navigating through narrow aisles, stepping over or around things and bumping into other people. Cluttered aisles and areas around fixtures just make merchandise harder to even notice. Make sure your store is laid out to allow plenty of space in the aisles, and work to keep aisles free of merchandise or any kind of clutter.

3. Apathetic Or Uncaring Sales Help

You could have the greatest store around, but if your people treat your customers as though they were an interruption instead of the purpose of their work, you'll lose customers. *Generally, most employees aren't stupid enough to be indifferent or uncaring to customers when you're present, but how are customers treated when the boss is nowhere to be found? Apathetic employees, in my mind, are signs of an apathetic owner!*

4. Not Being Able to Find a Price

Yes, I realize you're not a large store or self-service store, and you have sales people who can help; however, people today are busy. They want quick answers, and they like to be able to shop without having to ask a question every time they pick something up. If you want to sell your merchandise, people need to know how much it costs, and they tire of asking. They often start making assumptions or just decide it's not worth the effort.

5. Handwritten or Amateurish Signs

Handwritten, poorly worded or misspelled signs just say "amateur," or "mom and pop"! Why would you want to appear that way? And yet, I see it everyday! It is too easy in this day and age to print a sign from your computer or have signs made by someone else. Just keep in mind, if you're going to print a sign from your computer, it should be on card stock, framed, and have correct spelling as well.

6. Loud, Inappropriate Music

Just as having the right music is important for creating the best environment for customers, the wrong music is just as influential. Music that is inappropriate for your customers, too loud or even poorly transmitted through bad speakers can make customers spend less time in your store or even totally disappear. Do NOT allow employees to play whatever they wish, *especially in your absence.*

7. Cluttered or Dirty Dressing Rooms

Many owners of clothing shops rarely, if ever, go into their dressing rooms. But they should be inspected daily by a responsible employee. Look for dirty mirrors, pins on the floor and items that don't belong, including chewing gum stuck almost anywhere. Tags, hangers and packaging do not make a customer feel like they are buying from a first-rate shop. Merchandise left lying around in these rooms also encourages theft. It's just too easy and tempting to cop something for free, even if it's not the right size. You might even consider decorating them a bit.

8. Disorganized Checkout Counters

Ever noticed how clean and clutter-free a bank counter and bankers desk is? Yes, I realize they're not in retailing. But retailing does not give you an excuse to have a counter area that's a disaster. Merchandise returns, boxes, papers, excess hangers and many other items including employee drinks and food make an area that doesn't look or feel very appropriate for a financial transaction. Again, it also makes you look unprofessional, unorganized and even lends itself to theft. And let's face it—if you want be a first class store, look like one!

9. Stained Ceilings or Flooring

Regular vacuuming and mopping is a must. A professional service should be considered at least on a seasonal basis. Stained ceiling tiles can be replaced or even painted. And while I'm at it, does anyone ever clean your HVAC vents in the ceiling? I've sat in restaurants right under absolutely filthy air vents. Does this say clean and healthy? You don't want your store to look like it's one or two steps up from a garage sale. Anything that is dirty is a problem, but floors and ceilings are the most visible and noticeable!

10. Confusing Promotions Or Misleading Signs

Nothing takes the zest and enthusiasm out of a customer about to buy like finding out all of a sudden that the price is significantly higher than they thought it was, even if the price is still reasonable. Once the expectation and price has been put in someone's head, anything higher is a turnoff. All of a sudden the word or feeling of "rip-off" becomes the customer's unconscious perception. Misplaced, misleading or confusing signs are often sales and attitude killers.

11. Burned-Out Or Poor Lighting

Professional retailer stores should be well lit or appropriately lit for their image and atmosphere. Inadequate lighting is really hard on seniors or those with problem eyesight, and poor lighting just looks dingy and dirty. Missing light bulbs are just one more display of low standards, and low standards reflect on your business in ways that you can't even predict. It may not bother you, but you're not the judge . . . the customer is!

12. Stores That Aren't Open When Expected to Be Open

Have you ever arrived at a store first thing in the morning ready to shop and find the store isn't opened yet, according to their posted hours? The disheveled store clerk arrives 10 minutes late and asks you to wait while he turns on the lights and opens the register. It's irritating and unprofessional. Even worse is arriving at a store during what would be considered normal shopping hours to find the store closed. The owner has taken the day off or doesn't open on Mondays or Tuesdays or Saturday afternoons or at lunchtime (whatever it is). You have taken the time to drive, park and seek out their store, and the owner doesn't have enough respect to be there for you. If you're not open when they do visit, they might not come back to try again.

13. Regularly Understaffed Stores

Most customers understand unexpected or busy situations in a store. Although customers are not required to understand anything, the real problem comes when a customer regularly has trouble getting questions answered, getting a price or just getting checked out. Even if the customer has not yet made a conscious decision to stop shopping at your store, there is often the feeling in the back of the mind that it's a little too much trouble or a little too time consuming to go to your store.

14. Out of Stock Position

The customer comes into your store with credit card or cash in hand to give you their business, but you can't sell them what they want. I guarantee they are blaming your store, not the manufacturer or the trucking company. It happens to even the biggest and best retailers at times. But coming into a store for a basic blue dress shirt or a repeat attempt at something that you never seem to have when they want it gets old very quickly. Eventually, the attitude becomes "why bother?"

15. Offensive Or Unexpected Smells

Customers expect certain smells from certain stores. You pretty much know what you're going to get at a pet store, a bakery or a lawn and garden store. But customers do NOT want to smell body odor from an employee or unpleasant whiffs from a trash can as they enter a store. Even popcorn coming from a microwave can bother some shoppers. Do what you must to eliminate or neutralize any unpleasant or unexpected smells.

16. Store Temperature Is Too Warm

A store that is too cold is rarely a problem, especially when someone is wearing a winter coat to begin with. The problem comes when the air conditioning hasn't been turned on yet for the season or an owner is trying to save some money on their air conditioning bill. Stores that are hot or uncomfortable do NOT encourage customers to browse or stick around. Shopping in a stuffy, warm building just isn't worth the "close" clammy feeling!

Are You Ready
To Promote Your Business?
20

"Doing business without advertising is like winking at a girl in the dark. You know what you are doing, but nobody else does."

Steuart Henderson Britt

Marketing Must Begin with What Your Store Is All About.
I think the large majority of small business people I meet consider themselves marketers, in some sense of the word; and maybe by some definitions they are. When most people think of marketing, they are thinking about advertising, promotion, signs, flyers, publicity and, yes, direct mail. But marketing is more than even these things. In the future, I suggest thinking of marketing as just about anything that helps or—possibly even hurts—your sales or reputation. When you think this way, we're talking everything from your business's physical location to your logo and name, as well as your policies, people, service, prices and overall image. So, if we start thinking in these terms, then getting your store involved in a charitable fundraising event would "be an element of marketing" because it effects the way you are perceived by the public. So if this is the case, the word "marketing" expands to include how your front windows and restrooms look as well. If you're going to launch any kind of successful marketing program for your store, then you need to answer to three (3) key questions first:

1. What Are Physical Assets That Help Bring in Sales?

2. What Emotional Assets or Weapons Do You Have (if any)?

What is bringing in customers right now? Do you have a couple of really great employees? Is it your location and the surrounding area? Is it your advertising? And, if so, what about your store is working? You need to know. Make a list of everything that is a real plus.

3. What Obstacles Stand in the Way of Bringing in Customers Right Now?

Is it location? Competition? If so, what is it about the competition? Is it the way your store looks from the outside? Is it expertise? Is it your assortment and display of merchandise? Think of everything you can think of and make a list.

You need to know these things because, until you know what's wrong and what's right with your business, you can't say 100% for sure what attributes to highlight and what to cut out!

What is the point of drawing customers in to your store with a great ad only to have customers disappointed by your store atmosphere, a filthy bathroom or indifferent employees?

So take your list and highlight the negative things you can do something about easily or in a relatively short time. Work on eliminating the negatives from your store now! Remember, when we bring customers into our store, we invite them in to see the negatives as well as the positives. Why compromise or reduce the effectiveness of your advertising dollars? The cheapest, quickest and easiest negatives to correct should be the things that you correct immediately. Again, that means NOW!

Take a look at your positives and determine which are your strongest and which you can most easily emphasize, highlight or expand (depending on what we're talking about). Any advertising you plan to do should take advantage and work from some of these strong points. These strong points even become more important if you can emphasize the ones that truly separate you from everyone else (especially your competition).

Differentiating Your Store from the Competition.
We talk about this a lot in this book because it is key to surviving and standing out in this overcrowded and super competitive world of retailing.

> My question again is this: Why would anyone want to open up a store that is not much different or substantially better than one down the street? Why put up with all of the aggravation and negatives of retail just to have another mediocre me-too store out there?

> *You can't be totally satisfied with being just another store, if you're taking the time to read this book!*

There needs to be differences, whether they are subtle or major. And they need to be significant enough in number or in quality that you easily set your store apart from the competition. The fact is that customers are looking for differences, and they will notice them over time. The question for you is, are the differences positive or negative?

Aside from merchandise assortment, which is easily adjusted, what else do you have that really connects with the customer? I think you've heard this word "connects" before. You must find ways to connect with your customer. Look at what everyone else does in your business and what you already do, and find some areas where you can do something positive that is never done or never expected. How can you do it better or differently in a way that will be valued by your customer? Develop a list of these areas and talk with your people about what would really impress your guests and exactly how will you go about delivering these differences. Write it all out.

You Believe Your Own Store Is Wonderful
(Unfortunately, No One Cares!)

Often, the problem is that our advertising focuses on what we have, how much it is, how much variety we have and to hurry in and buy it! Our marketing becomes too much about us and how special we are. Customers care about themselves and their own situations. They want to know what you can do for THEM if they walk through your doors!

Think about the old quote, "People don't care how much you know until they know how much you care." If there is one message you need to understand about your brand, your store and your marketing, it needs to be this: Personal branding and marketing has nothing to do with what WE think we offer in our stores. It has **everything** to do with what **customers** feel about us and whether we can make them care about us . . . If you really want to leave a positive marketing effect on potential customers, then find ways to make them feel good about your store and your name. You must find and connect with something that your customers care about. It's always easier to get a sale from a customer if you've connected with them first. (This is good advice for any type of sales activity.)

Consider these basic marketing rules before you begin your marketing efforts:

What: Let customers know who you are and what you're truly about.

Feature: What is special or important about your store that is also important for THEM (what might attract them)?

Benefit: What can your store or service do for them? What "want" or "need" (at least want) can you satisfy or address?

Connection: How will you make them feel or what can you do for them on an emotional or personal level? (Why will they care?) (How can you show you care?) Is there a way you want them to feel different when they leave your store compared to the competition.

LET'S GET REAL!
Wouldn't you like to believe that, after your customers decide what they're looking for, they would research the market and product information and add up the pros and the cons to see where the best place would be for them to shop based on affordability? . . . DOESN'T HAPPEN! . . . at least not with most customers. I'm sure you would still like to believe in the tooth fairy, too! If that's not how it works, then how do customers decide all of a sudden where and when to buy something?

Think about these questions:

How many books have you bought that you've never read?

How many clothes have you bought that you never, or almost never, wore?

How many CDs (remember those?) have you bought where you only liked 2 or 3 of the songs on the album?

How many wives just had to get the large, marble soaking tub installed in their newly constructed home, but never actually use it?

How many times have you selected a product, which you didn't know anything about, from a group of similar products because the packaged looked sharper?

Is this logic? Are your shopping decisions logical?
The fact is that no one really knows how customers make the decisions they do. We do know that most are emotional and some lesser amount are logical. You need to constantly assess and ask, why did this person buy this product? Asking them directly certainly helps, and following up after the sale can help also. Think about this. You really

don't need big expensive studies and marketing advice if you will talk and listen to your customers. Just think about some of the following questions and ask yourself:

How valuable would it be to learn the information below from 20-30 customers? What if you could ask it of 100 customers? Do you think you would have some very valuable information if you could act on it? Do you think this would help your marketing efforts? So why not go out and get it? I can't really think of too many things more important than getting answers to these questions for your business:

How did you first discover this store?

When was the last time you shopped here?

What brought you back to this store?

Where else would you have gone if you didn't come here? Why?

Why didn't you go there?

What do you like best about us? Why?

What is the one thing you would change about us if you could? Why?

The negative thing that surprises me most about this store is _____.

The positive thing that surprises me most about this store is _____.

What would make you come here more often?

I wish you would do_____.

I wish you would sell more_____.

The employees here_____.

My favorite store to visit in the whole world is _____. Why?

What could we do to here to make your visit more enjoyable? How could we make you smile?

Why did you ultimately buy from us?

What could we do here that would really surprise you, if you were the customer?

If you doubt the value of this exercise, **what if your competition knew the answers to these questions and you didn't?**

Take a hard look at these questions as well as the others listed in this book and decide which of them would benefit you most.

 Watering Down Ideas & Concepts

During the eighties, I worked with Apple computer dealers and other consumer electronic dealers across a 4 ½ state territory. In those days, we were all trying to figure out where the personal computer was headed. We knew big things were in store, so many entrepreneurs were headed into the computer business and wanted a piece of the action. Accountants, lawyers, techies and anyone else with deep pocket books were jumping into the business and throwing a lot of money our way to meet Apple's minimum inventory requirements. There was one big problem though. Very few of these guys really understood what having a retail store meant. One thing for sure was that many of them were floundering.

My job was to work with the dealer base in my territory and help the dealers think and act like merchants. I would talk to them about how to merchandise and lay out their stores. I talked to them about promotions and co-op funds from Apple computer. I also explained why they should stock many of the products they didn't seem interested in stocking.

Now I realize that no entrepreneur gets into business to listen to someone else tell him or her how to run a business. I realize that I didn't have all of the answers and that they all had their own ideas. But somewhere along the line, everyone needs to realize that there are people out there who have some expertise and experience that could help them. Supposedly, that's why you bought this book. (Maybe when something comes from a book, it automatically carries more credibility. I don't think that should be necessarily true, because I've read a lot of bull in books!)

When someone comes to you with expertise and makes some solid recommendations about how to deal with aspects of your business, I hope that you would listen very carefully and maybe even take some notes. And yes, it is your prerogative as to what you listen to and what you don't. If you make a decision not to listen to someone, that is just fine. It may be a mistake, but that is YOUR mistake and YOUR choice. But I will make one strong recommendation. If you decide to listen to someone—to implement an idea or a concept that they can explain and back up with years of experience—IMPLEMENT THE IDEA FULLY, WITH NO COMPROMISES, AND GIVE IT YOUR BEST, WHOLE-HEARTED EFFORT. There, I've said it.

The ONLY way you will ever find out if the idea has merit and will help you is to actually give it a try. Don't water it down and compromise the effort. Because if you do, then you still haven't tried the recommendation or idea. Sometimes compromising one part of the idea or concept ruins the whole thing. If I told you that cutting the price by a dime and filling a whole end cap with cans of Pork n' Beans would increase its sales drastically, that doesn't mean you fill the end cap with 6 cans or 20 cans or even 100 cans. It means you FILL the end cap from top to bottom. If I told you that you needed to reduce the price on the beans by a dime, that doesn't mean that you lower it a nickel or that you don't lower it at all, because then you have still not really tried what I recommended, and you can't come to me and tell me it didn't work!

During my visits to the computer stores, I continually talked about carrying all of the accessories that people needed for their computers. That meant stocking cables, printing ribbons, daisy wheels (remember those?), diskettes and computer paper. Customers needed to know that their stores were the place to go for those things. So what did I see as a result? I saw stores buy ONE box of computer paper and set it in the corner somewhere (maybe even behind the cash register). Did I see a display stacked up with paper? NO! Did I see an end cap of paper? NO! Did I see a sign or price on the paper to encourage people to buy? NO! They had it marked up as high as any other merchandise in the store (consumables carry a lower markup, generally). But what

I did hear from many of them was, "This computer paper just doesn't sell!"

Now, what do you think? Do you think computer paper sold? Somebody must have sold it. It was that special paper with the holes down each side so the printer could pull the paper through while it printed. This was the only kind of paper anyone could use back then. So either it did sell (just somewhere else), or no one printed anything in the eighties and printers just collected dust.

I told them they were losing sales to other retailers who stocked paper, accessories and a better variety of software, but they didn't care. They just wanted to sell computers even though they constantly complained about the eroding profit margins. I also told the store's owners that if they didn't stock these kinds of products for their computers, somebody else would. And I believe I was right! These places are now called Office Max, Office Depot, Sam's Club, Walmart. . .

Considerations Before You Advertise (a Crash Course)

21

If you were planning to advertise for your business, a typical thing to do (especially in the past) would be to buy as big of an ad as you could afford in the newspaper of your choice. And it's possible that may still be the way to go for you. But what if your local direct mail expert called you and proposed also spending money on a direct mail campaign for your business? Then what do you do? Depending on the quality of your ad in the paper and the quality of the direct mail piece, the answer could vary. If you factor in other variables like the quality and the customer demographics of that mailing list, it becomes even more complicated. The fact is that you don't know what you should do in this situation and neither do I . . . yet.

I'm sure there are some others out there who would say don't waste your money on either. But before you can make any decisions about how to spend your money, you have to consider many different issues if you're not going to waste your money!

Before you start any campaign, I would ask you to consider a couple of more questions:

   • Has the advertising money for this campaign been planned as a part of your overall budget?

   • Who are you trying to reach? (Telling me "customers" isn't specific enough.)

   • What will be the most cost-effective way to reach YOUR customers?

A Gordon Guideline

Too often in advertising, a retailer goes to someone out there who puts a sign over their door and calls themselves an advertising agency, and that supposed agency will just do whatever is asked of them while taking their money. An artist or a graphic designer may also do just what you tell them. But is that what you need? This will likely result in you having spent good money for few or no results. You could do better with a true marketing professional who can actually advise you and keep you from wasting money (and can give you some good references on their results rather than their skills as a graphic designer) to boot.

Consider All of These Issues For Any Advertising Campaign

What Is the Purpose of the Ad?
Do not make the mistake of many small business owners by advertising just to get your name out there. You need a much more specific goal, as there is no evidence that just "getting your name out there" will ever payoff for your business (especially not right away). Are you educating customers, building the name of your business, or trying to get an immediate bump in your sales figures? As I told you in another chapter of this book, you should not spend ad money just for brand building. This is for the big guys like Coca-Cola, McDonald's, Macy's, etc. You don't have that kind of budget. I'm guessing you want to increase sales now. And if you're focusing on getting sales and you want an immediate response, you need to create a sense of urgency.

Advertise for the Right Reason.
So, what is the right reason? When you should seriously consider parting with the dollars is another question. The reason shouldn't be because the Yellow Pages or newspaper rep walked in through your door with some space to sell! Outlined below are some typical

(and legitimate reasons) to advertise. Do any of these apply to your business?

♦ **Announce new products or services IF they're important to your business.**

Advertise when you are introducing an important new product or service. Communicate the benefits of your product or service (fight competitor claims or let potential customers know you are filling a particular need). If you've been around for a while, your customers pretty much know what your store is about. But if you are trying to change your image or to get into a new line or service, then get the word out through advertising

♦ **Advertise at the right time when the market is truly your market.**

An ice cream store is pretty much wasting their money if they advertise in the dead of winter. Nobody is looking to make an impulse purchase of a sundae in 20-degree weather.

♦ **Advertise when you can't reach your customers any other way.**

If you're in a low-visibility location and you need people to know who you are and where you are, you probably need to advertise. Your advertising might be in any number of forms and media, but you do need to find something effective to make your company visible—even if your storefront isn't.

♦ **Match your media to YOUR customers.**

Advertise when your targeted customers primarily use a specific media type. If you're advertising to a group of customers or a geographic area of customers who basically only read the paper or a particular magazine or listen to a dominant radio station, then use that media as much as possible. If your business is seasonal then use that media only at your time of year. Do not advertise on any media that does not really match your target customers. If you are a small, local nursery with one location, do you really need to be in a large metro area paper or on television stations that broadcast to the entire region?

Advertise if you're trying to win new customers or increase market share.

Inform customers where to obtain certain products or services.

Drive business for a particular event, such as a sale or show.

♦ **Market directly to customers in order to get a direct response back.**

♦ **Marketing through direct mail, catalogue advertising or direct TV offers are easiest to measure.**

♦ **Announce a new business.**

Advertise when you need to get the word out to announce your new business, new location or a major product that is critical to your success. Advertising for your retail store should generally come before any product though. Emphasize the name to increase awareness of your store, or service, alongside of any specific product if you're offering a new service or entering a new market. Also, don't make customers look for your name in the ad!

Can You Afford It?
Advertising, if it's used wisely, is first and foremost an investment. But you still need to be able to afford that investment. Make sure you know what your goal is with your advertising and make sure that you use the right advertising vehicle at the right time. If you can't afford it, then find some other ways to build your retail business. Unfortunately, affordability often becomes the only criteria when choosing a particular mode of advertising. In addition, advertising is often done in some halfhearted way because deep down inside you really don't expect your ad to produce business all that well. You

just know you need to advertise and thus it becomes "just another necessary expense." The ad(s) don't produce. "Affordable" or "low cost" are not reasons to choose a particular advertising vehicle when there are so many other critical issues that should effect your decision.

NOTE:

Keep in mind, that with many of the less expensive publications, you get what you pay far. Some of them are actually free to their readers, thus they have no audited circulation numbers. While I'm not saying these types of publications are bad, you just need to be certain that they are what your customers actually read.

Create a Plan.
When your advertising dollars are limited, it becomes even more important that you budget a percentage of sales for advertising and marketing and that you create a marketing plan. Be specific about your goals and detail what you need to do to reach them. For instance, if your objective is to increase sales by 15% during the next 12 months, you need a specific schedule and plan for meeting your objectives. If you sold 100 widgets as a result of the last ad you ran, will you sell 115 if you increase your budget by 15%? . . I wish it was that easy. The fact is, that there is very little correlation between the amount of money you spend and the results you get from advertising, so you've got to be much smarter than that.

**Advertising Should Pay (and You Should
Be Able to Measure the Results).**
If you are going to spend good advertising dollars to build sales, you'll need to measure and determine if this advertising produces enough to make it cost effective. If you can't tell, then you're out of control and most likely throwing money down the drain. If an ad costs you $800 and you have a 50% markup on the merchandise you are selling, you've obviously got to do an additional $1600 in sales above your norm, just to break even. How sure are you that it will be

cost effective? Now, if you're not losing money and it is helping you bring in new customers and increasing awareness of your store, then maybe you can say that it's worthwhile. But don't forget the cost of creating the ad as well.

If you want to be sure that your advertising produces, your objectives need to be stated in a measurable goal. This should be agreed upon up front with your advertising person. In other words, what would define success for your ad?

Measuring doesn't always tell the story of ad effectiveness.

For example, your advertising may do a great job at generating traffic for your store; however, other sales factors or customer issues may mess you up, such as your sales prices, your merchandising, your staff, your warranties or even the product features. It's important to measure your results, but don't rule out the possibility that your advertising could be working and boosting your potential even when you are not getting the sales for reasons that have nothing to do with the advertising.

What Appeals to Buyers?
No, I can't tell you exactly what your customers want, or I would be a lot more successful than the guy writing this book. However, there are some important wishes or "wants" that run true to what all customers are trying to satisfy. The absolute most important are as follows:

- **Convenience**: If you can save a customer time or effort, everyone wants that.

- **Self-Preservation**: If you can appeal to a customer's health and safety for them or their family, you've hit on an important theme for many people, (i.e., "will give you more energy," "will make you look 10 years younger," "will lose 20 lbs," "will prevent arthritis").

- **Security**: Financial gain, freedom from financial stress.

- **Self-Improvement**: Spiritual development, a need for knowledge, or educational benefits.

- **Avoidance of Worry**: If it will make someone feel better or worry less, (i.e., "will protect or prevent something," "we'll warranty this item for 3 years, parts, and service").

- **Recognition from Others**: Appeal to image, vanity, respectability, idol. (i.e., "you are a preferred customer/ member," "the same dress worn as _____" or "endorsed by _____," "special benefit")

If you can promote or connect with customers in one or more of the above areas, you have a much better chance for sales success. If you haven't noticed, the one thing that all of the above have in common is that they are all sold based on appealing to a customer's emotions. (There's that word again: emotion.) Self-preservation may involve some health "need," but the fact is that all of these may connect with people via their emotions, comfort, or "wants," not their actual needs.

Are You Creating Emotion?
An absolutely ungodly amount of money is wasted in advertising every day because the ad does not connect with the intended customer, due to any number of reasons, including the offer itself or it's lack of emotional appeal. I wish I had just 20% of the money I feel like I wasted over the years on ineffective advertising.

Are you selling something people need or is it something people want? If it's a want, you are talking about an ad that definitely needs a more emotional appeal. People generally buy things they want because an emotional button has been pushed. And even "needs" items will do much better if you can turn them into wants. Everyone needs a car, but what car do they WANT? Do you create a reason to buy or a need that's emotionally felt? If you're selling computer printers and your ad says you have a couple of computer printers for sale or even on sale, is that enough? Aren't these printers on sale in other places from time to time? So why do I need to buy one from you, NOW? What's wrong with the printer I have at home now? . . . You must give them a reason to want the printer, and want it now, more than the money they have in their pocket. You need to make them want this printer over the printer they already have! Will it save them time? Will it save them money? And why should they buy it from you?

Are You Taking a Knife to a Sword Fight?
Who are you selling against or competing with in the media you are using? If you've got house paint on sale and Walmart does too, whose ad do you think will get more attention? You need to be aware of how the competition's merchandise or services are sold by the competition. If you're selling against another paint store down the street and he typically runs a little ad in the corner of the paper, you may do well. But again, if it's Walmart and you're selling something that is perceived by the public to be basically the same item, you're going to lose, and you're going to waste your money.

Are Your Advertising Objectives Attainable?
Your ads could be great, but if your product or service is priced too high or does not do the job that the prospective customer is looking for, no amount of advertising will achieve your goal. Make sure your objectives are closely in tune with your marketing goals and research. Years ago, I watched Smith Corona (a well-respected name in typewriters for decades) fail at introducing a new line of computer printers because the market research didn't measure up to the goals they had established. No one in the computer world really valued their name, and there was nothing else special about the product, so their efforts failed. They never had a chance with the way they went about their product launch.

What Is Your Message And Who Is It For?
Is it targeted at your customer? I don't mean appealing to your broadest idea of a customer. I mean, who is your best prospect who

will most likely buy now? Often in an effort to go after everyone, you end up appealing to no one. You need to grab the attention of a much more narrow range of prospective customers and gear your message toward the given people who have a reason to buy now. That doesn't mean listing an item and sticking a price next to it. Everyone out there is not just waiting for your ad to hit the street. Your specific, target customers need to understand why they should buy the product from you today!

Sell Substance Over Style? (Better Yet, Have Both.)

Consumers are more and more sophisticated, and even jaded, when it comes to advertising. Do not believe the old saying, "Sell the sizzle, not the steak." Today's consumers know the sizzle from the steak and prefer the steak every time. Your substance (product quality, benefits, service, etc.), and your ability to grab attention and satisfy wants will serve you much better in the long run over a pretty ad.

Bigger Is NOT Necessarily Better.

If you have a limited budget and think that making a big splash with an ad would still be the best idea, think again. Unless you've got money to burn, you are almost always better off with smaller ads run on a regular, more frequent basis. The fact is that most people do not respond right away after the first time they see an ad. They seem to have to warm up to it and get used to it first. Don't ever be in a newspaper or magazine once and then wonder why everyone didn't beat a path to your door!

Repetition

If you're going to advertise, you need to be in the marketplace on a consistent basis. While this doesn't mean you need to be there in the same amount each week or month, you do need to be out there on a fairly regular basis. You can't just be in the marketplace whenever the mood suits you, when you have the time to put forth the effort, or whenever some media person comes to you with a special promotional scheme. If your going to be remembered when the consumer is ready to buy, you must be out there regularly, *whenever* that consumer is ready. (Note: I am not telling you what media you must use for this).

You need to stay in the public eye until they are ready to buy! Repetition greatly increases the success rate of advertising response. You must repeat the message over and over. Repetition breeds familiarity and helps ensure you are there when the potential customer is ready to buy. Repetition and consistency are key to visibility. A general rule-of-thumb is that it takes three to six impressions before a consumer connects your store's products or service with your business name. One of those impressions might be a press release or some free publicity. One might be some very visible signage. When your business accomplishes something that is newsworthy, write a press release and send it to local media.

Think about the jewelry department in a department store or a discount store. It is almost always placed at a prime traffic spot so that customers can't miss it on a daily basis as they enter and leave the store over a period of time. The stores know you're not going to buy every time you walk past, but someday, when you are in the market for jewelry, you will remember something you saw in one of those counters or at least remember this was a good place to look for jewelry. That's when the location of the jewelry department (a higher margin department than most others, by the way) will pay off. For the same reason, you must be noticeable in the marketplace via radio, print or direct mail on a regular basis so that you will be remembered. So . . . can you afford to repeat your ads?

Be Consistent in Your Message.
It takes a while for prospects to trust you. Be sure that all your marketing efforts are saying the same thing and rowing your image and message in the same direction.

Competition & Advertising
When it comes to advertising, watch your competition closely (especially the competition you respect). When you look at your competitors and what they are doing with advertising, you must ask

yourself if what they're doing is working. What is their message and is this a message that would work for you? Don't advertise with no plan just because your competition is doing it.

Reponses Vary with What You're Selling.

Keep in mind what you are trying to sell. If you're selling $10 fashion watches, you will get a far more immediate response than if you are selling $2,000 grandfather clocks. If you're selling houses, it will take you much more advertising over a period of time than if you are trying to sell barbeque pits in the summertime.

Use a Professional, (Good) Copywriter/Designer.

Compromising on advertising just to advertise generally means throwing money down the drain. Consider spending the money on a professional copywriter. I'm not talking about someone that will put whatever you tell them to write in the ad. I'm talking about someone who is recommended, or whose work you know—someone who will tell you what needs to be done. Having a computer, camera and graphics software does not make you or anyone else an ad agency or good copywriter. Yes, there are some very creative people out there who can pull it off. But odds are you're not one of them. There's a lot to learn about writing advertising copy, and most people, including many in-house newspaper or magazine employees, don't cut it. In other words, do NOT tell me that advertising just doesn't pay "for your store" if you haven't put together a professional ad with the right message. Find a *real* professional, and listen to them!

Using the Right Media

What media is right for your business? Well, there isn't one "right" media. I will cop out on you here and just say that it entirely depends on the type of business you're in, and exactly what you're trying to accomplish with your advertising. For now, I'll only make a few comments about possible media choices.

> Newspapers: If someone is looking for tires today and you have a tire ad, you will most likely get their attention. Otherwise, your ad will be scanned over and then spread over the bottom of the birdcage.

Magazines: Magazines have a much longer life than newspapers, but they are pretty expensive and don't come out very often. They are much easier when targeting certain demographics (i.e., *Oprah* vs. *MacWorld*).

Yellow Pages: Carefully choose which yellow pages to be in. Do your customers come from a mile or two away or will customers drive across town or across the state to see your store? If you are going to be in the yellow pages with a small ad, be classy, be as informative as possible, have a strong headline and include an offer (a reason to call you). The yellow pages should be used as a communications tool, not as just some cold listing. Lastly, do NOT allow the yellow pages people to write your ad!

Radio: I love radio, but you generally cannot target a geographic area, other than a whole city or whole metro area. You might have a little control over customer demographics, depending on your station, but not much. If you have one location and your ad covers a whole metro area, you may be wasting your money, unless you sell a higher ticket item for which people will drive a distance. If you do advertise on radio, keep in mind that a third-party endorsement from a media personality who has great credibility can be golden.

Television: Expensive, and it has the same problems as radio. Consider buying "fringe" spots that air just before and just after prime time. You'll catch a lot more viewers than at other non-prime times, and the rates are much cheaper.

Direct Mail: Great way to target specific customers demographically, individually and geographically. As a small business owner, direct marketing should be the name of your game. Direct mail is very dependent on the quality of the mailing list, and it can be as expensive or inexpensive as you want. Here is where you can expect the highest of all response rates. Here is also where you can compete with the big boys. Want to be cheaper and effective? Try postcards. Potential customers don't get to decide whether to open them. Your information is right there in front of them. More to come on direct mail advertising in my next book.

Internet Advertising: A whole new generation of people use the internet overwhelmingly to find information. It is an inexpensive, easy way to target demographics, and it is growing in popularity over other media by the minute. It is easily the fastest growing of all categories represented here.

"Don't let your ads paint a picture your stores can't live up to."

Appearance, your inventory, your visual merchandising and even your sales help need to be primed to take advantage of any advertising investment you make! Also, do not create expectations and image via your ad that your store cannot support or back up. Arriving at your store after a great ad should not be a let down. In other words:

"Don't let your ads paint a picture your stores can't live up to."

In Conclusion:

Good advertising is an investment. If you can't make it produce money instead of losing money, DON'T DO IT!

Don't let coupon, radio, TV and newspaper people talk you into any advertising on which you are not 100% sold. Yes, you can't always be sure, and God knows I've wasted my share of money too. But you need to be sure of at least a few key things before you even attempt it:

- Be sure the media you use is right for your target market.
- Know what you are trying to accomplish and exactly to whom you're selling.
- Make sure your ad is professional and well written by someone who knows what they're doing. Don't be afraid to challenge them on their copy and placement.

- Know that you will be able to measure the effectiveness of your ad. Key your ads (an ad "key" is a way of letting your business know that the customer came in and bought because of the ad—it may be a special coupon, a "mention this offer" ad or a special phone number with a call to action such as "ask for offer number 555" or "ask for operator #9").
- If you're not making money after a reasonable effort, then kill it!

REMEMBER:
The Best & Cheapest Advertising Is *A Great Customer Experience.*

When you can create genuine enthusiasm for your store from customers who love the experience of shopping your store, you have advocates who sell your store on your behalf. To produce your own store's "word of mouth" advertising, you must consciously work on creating a positive, over-the-top experience for the customers who come through your door. This can become a memorable experience first and then real loyalty over time, comes from a customer connection that is much more powerful than good prices or even great merchandising. Again, this generally happens as a result of surpassing the customer expectations.

Creating a great experience will still cost you in payroll, fixtures, design, training, etc., but it is far superior to increasing your advertising budget.

"On the average, five times as many people read the headline as read the body copy. When you have written your headline, you have spent eighty cents out of your dollar."

David Ogilvy

 The Real Thing
(Emotion vs. Reality)

Have you ever heard the quote "perception is reality"? In other words, how you perceive something is what is real to you. Our perception of reality is what really matters in our lives. If your store is perceived by a given group of customers as the best place to shop in town, then to them, it IS the best place to shop in town. Things don't have to make sense or be logical. Reality is not what is important when it comes to things we want to buy. Perception and emotion take over where reality leaves off.

A company that knew and understood all of this for years forgot during the eighties and had to learn this lesson again in a very hard and expensive way. While you've probably heard this story before, you may not have really heard it with this much detail or really thought about what it all means.

For years, this company made a special product that had no real value at all, other than people seemed to like the way it tasted. It had no nutritional value. It was even artificially colored to change its appearance. There was even a movement to have it banned from store shelves because it was considered harmful to the people who drank it. Over the years, many competitors came on the market and tried to give them a run for their money. As it approached its 100th year of business, the company began to see a disturbing trend. The market share of this company had been dropping for the past twenty years. And, one of its many competitors had been gaining ground on their commanding market lead. Worse yet, in private and closely guarded company tests, its competitor's product was actually now preferred by the company's own loyal customers in blind taste tests. This was a fact that the company felt it could not ignore. Even though they had tinkered quietly with their recipe off and on for years, the #2 selling product was still preferred in taste tests by most customers. But now, the competition started performing their own blind taste tests in public to show the world that their product was actually preferred in taste to the old #1 selling product. Very embarrassing, to say the least!

With top-secrecy and after quietly searching and testing extensively for a new recipe that would test and taste better than the upward trending competitor, the company finally felt confident they had a product that could end the disturbing trend and solidify their market position as #1 in the marketplace for years into the future. In the largest and most significant marketing blitz ever undertaken, the news was announced to the whole world. The formula of the nearly 100-year-old American icon, Coca-Cola, was miraculously changed and improved! It was a new improved version of Coca-Cola. The company had decided that it was more important for the soda to continue to be the best tasting in the world rather than to stay with an outdated formula that studies had shown people no longer preferred. Research showed that consumers wanted a smoother and sweeter tasting drink. For marketing purposes, focus groups had also shown that the word "new" provoked an immediate and positive response. Coca-Cola spent approximately $4 million to research and create "New Coke." The research, taste tests and tons of rather sophisticated data revealed that customers would rate the leading sodas as follows:

#1 New Coke
#2 Pepsi
#3 Old Traditional Coke

The figures easily indicated that "New Coke" was preferred over both of the other drinks! A news conference was held in January 1985, and the company CEO announced to the world that "the best soft drink in the world, Coca-Cola, is now going to be even better."

The news made front-page headlines all over the country and topped the news around the world. On the same day as the announcement, Coke's major competitor, Pepsi, put out front page ads in the nations leading newspapers saying, "the other guys just blinked" and that Coke was reformulating their brand to be more like Pepsi because the fact has been, that "Pepsi tasted better than Coke."

A whole new look was adopted for "New Coke," while still keeping the traditional company logo and trademark that was the most recognized and valuable in the world. In spite of Coca-Cola's very expensive and very detailed planning, within days, 96% of all Americans knew about the change to Coca-Cola and the large majority of them were not happy! Coca-Cola, in it's efforts to be proven right in their decision, invited millions to taste the "New" Coca-Cola at grocery stores and other locations around the country. But it made no difference. Coca-Cola drinkers were not happy!

- 40,000 letters protesting the change came in to the company.

- Tens of thousands of unhappy calls reached the company switchboards.

- At the Houston Astrodome, audiences booed New Coke commercials on the giant video screens.

- A Washington Post columnist chided that "Next week they'll be chiseling Teddy Roosevelt off the side of Mount Rushmore."

- One customer wrote in, "Would it be right to rewrite the Constitution? The Bible? To me changing the Coke formula is of such a serious nature."

Coke held more public taste tests to prove their findings and to prove that all the criticism and hate mail was mistaken. The taste test again showed:

#1 New Coke

#2 Pepsi
#3 Old Coke

"New Coke's" taste continued to beat out both old Coke and Pepsi in blind taste tests. No contest! The management of Coca-Cola was ecstatic. They were sure they had made the right decision after all. However, considering the major backlash and it's public relations nightmare, Coca-Cola decided to keep the old Coke, calling it "Coca-Cola Classic," in an effort to placate its loyal customers. This too made front-page news in virtually all newspapers around the country. The idea was that, in time, the stubborn traditional Coke lovers would learn to love "New Coke" too. But, by the end of the same year, after all was said and done, the **sales figures** over the following months indicated the following:

#1 Old Coke (now called Coke Classic)
#2 Pepsi
#3 New Coke

The taste test proved conclusively—without a doubt—that "New Coke" tasted better than the others. How could they have possibly screwed up? Coca-Cola had just made the largest marketing mistake in history! The problem was that Coca-Cola researchers had missed one very critical factor. The researchers had never told their consumer/testers that the potential new formula would replace the old formula. Evidently Coke drinkers had thought it would be an alternative to their traditional Coke!

The facts of history will show that America loved the taste of "New Coke" better, but consumers would not even admit it to themselves, thus making things miserable and embarrassing for Coca-Cola. "New Coke" had become a dismal failure and amounted to no more than 3% of the market by April of 1986, a little over a year later.

Coca-Cola had done such a tremendous job of marketing over the decades at becoming interwoven into the American fabric that replacing Coca-Cola was indeed "like breaking the American dream or like not selling hot dogs at a ball game," as one loyal consumer put it. While everything else was changing in the world, consumers wanted their Coca-Cola to stay the same. They loved their Coca-Cola and all of the studies and all of the brains, marketers and analysts had never considered the most important emotion of all . . . LOVE. People loved their Coca-Cola! Yes, consumers buy based on emotion, not logic and the word "emotion" has been mentioned countless times throughout this book. For 100 years Coca-Cola had sold and built a brand based on marketing emotion. Even today, Coca-Cola far surpasses Pepsi in worldwide sales.

Guerilla Marketing
And Other Ideas

22

I'm sure you've heard of "guerilla marketing." Jay Conrad Levinson is generally credited as the father of guerrilla marketing because of all of his books on the subject. The idea was to make it easier and more effective for small businesses to compete in the marketing world with the big guns out there. He showed that by being innovative and sometimes extreme or over-the-top, you could get yourself noticed. Wild and crazy at times and yet effective, the concept of guerilla marketing has become very popular. Good guerilla marketing can be a lot of fun because of the unique and outlandish yet intelligent ways employed to get your business noticed.

There are hundreds of good guerilla marketing ideas out there, and more great ideas are created every day. I have compiled a list to give you some ideas to start, so be imaginative. Using your imagination here can be rewarding in many ways. Brainstorm with your people and find one or more of these that might work for you or use them to spark your own ideas. Regardless, this chapter is just a token offering of some low cost, good and great guerilla marketing tactics that are being used successfully by the little guys (and sometimes even the big guys).

Combine & Coordinate Your Efforts as some successful guerrillas marketers will tell you as these strategies often work better in coordination with other marketing ideas, so don't limit yourself to an idea without employing any other types of effort and then say, "Well, it didn't work!" Often, it's an assortment of marketing strategies used together over a consistent timeframe that entices and wins over customers.

Again, Be Prepared: If and when you use some of the concepts commonly referred to as guerilla marketing, you need to be able and ready to deliver the goods as promoted. In other words, you need to have your store merchandised well and your customer service needs to be at a high level if you're going to start making claims and overtures to bring customers in your store. Also remember that if you do get yourself some traffic, do not disappoint your customers, because a bad reputation can travel just as fast as an imaginative, eye-catching guerilla campaign!

While all of these ideas are not for every business or store, there's sure to be something in here for you to try.

Here They Are!

Press Releases Generate Some News
Do what the pros do. Write and distribute your own press releases, as long as they are truly newsworthy. Press releases are free. You can learn how to effectively write them yourself, and it's not all that hard. Get them out to newspapers, magazines and television and radio stations. Even if you fail to get attention from 75% of your distribution recipients, you will still get free publicity to thousands of people. Whenever **anything** somewhat newsworthy happens OR whenever you can create something newsworthy connected with your business, send a press release to the media. The idea is to grab any free coverage possible, so try and create some fun, crazy or wild promotional event to draw attention to your business.

Business Card & Books
I've seen this one used in my own local bookstore. In this case, the business takes their business cards and places them in every book that relates to their business. Obviously a computer repair business might put one in every book on the shelf in the library or bookstore about computers. Talk about target marketing. Wow! And it's cheap too.

Waiting Room Magazines
Same idea as above, but a more broad targeting approach. Put your business cards into magazines every time you go to these places. People are trying to kill a lot of time (especially if it's a doctor), so they'll see it!

Hold a Crazy Contest.
There's a double benefit. You get the publicity of the announcement to potential customers and the media. Then, if you have multiple winners, you can announce winners, one at a time, over a period of time to the media. Just as an example—if you were a computer repair business, you could announce a "most screwed-up computer" contest and then award the winner with a plaque and a free or discounted repair, and then make an announcement to the press.

Cross Marketing
What other businesses cater to the same customers you have but are NOT in your market? This is certainly nothing new, but many businesses underestimate the power of this idea when the right partner and promotion is found. Maybe it is because it's an old idea that it is often too easily dismissed. Find another business to partner with and promote each other. Put flyers or brochures at another store or business that does business with your type of customer and you do the same for them. Put a coupon for another business with your receipt. And have them do the same for you. For instance, a chiropractor might hook up with one of the new "healthy feet" type stores. The chiropractor offers a special discount at the foot store and maybe puts up a sign in his/her office. In return, the foot store offers a free initial exam at the chiropractor's office. These offers can really work if you find the right combination. A restaurant might offer a special discount at a particular retailer and the retailer might offer its customers a coupon for a free desert at the restaurant. Obviously the expense for such an effort is minimal, but this is cross promotion at a basic level. It can be much more sophisticated than this. Use your imagination!

Cross Marketing Variation

As an alternative to cutting prices, find another retailer that offers merchandise that coordinates or compliments your stores merchandise. For example, you sell men's clothing. If you were to find a shoe store or a sporting goods store with an owner who liked this marketing idea, you could then create gift cards and exchange your cards for his. You begin offering your customers a free gift card (with minimum purchase) good at the sporting goods or shoe store. As an alternative to offering a substantial promotional discount in your store of 25-50% off, you might offer your customers a $25.00 gift card to the other shop with a purchase of $50.00 or more in your own store. Obviously the amounts can differ. Maybe you require $100.00 in purchases depending on what your average sale might be. The great positive here is that your customer paid full price for your merchandise, but they also got a good value. The end result is that your $50.00 shirt is still being perceived and sold as a $50.00 shirt while you've just generated some additional sales without discounting your merchandise.

Find A News Story & Get Free Publicity.

Find a news story that relates to your business. Then issue a press release to the news media offering yourself as an expert commenting on the story. For example, a photographer might issue a price release commenting on the merits of the just announced photographic exhibit at the art museum. If you're a tree trimmer, you might issue a press release connected to a news story on storm damages to area trees. A security firm might issue a press release commenting on a major burglary story in the news. You never know what part of the media may pick up your press release and run with it, thus giving you some very good publicity.

Movie Theater Ads

You've seen them at the movies, so you know your customers will, unless they don't happen to go to the movies. The price is reasonable. Just be sure you use good photography and graphics and have an offer. Make sure you're able to approve the ad before it goes to the theaters.

Fly Flags

Flags can pay almost immediate dividends. Your flags can say "open" or special event", but it's really not that important. What's on the flag is really secondary here, but you can even have your own logo put on the flags. They obviously provide color and motion and attract instant attention. You just don't pass by flags without noticing. Flags automatically say something special is going on here. Consider buying two or three sets of different colors whether vertical or horizontal. This allows you to change them up without getting stale. (Check with your city about any sign ordinances that might be in effect.)

Book A Celebrity Guest At Your Store.

Invite a celebrity guest to an event at your store. It may be easier to find one if you can tie in their presence with a charitable cause or even a charitable event at your store. Also, consider using people connected with the market your store represents, a television news anchor or even a local author where there is an appropriate tie-in.

Offer A Radio Station Free Merchandise To Give Away.

Radio stations are always looking for prizes and gifts they can give to their listeners. The station will mention what business the gift came from, as well as a location. Offer free merchandise or gift certificates. Draw attention to your regular giveaways and to the station on your website to tie it all together. Try to make your free gift something interesting or exciting or tasty that would be fun for the station to give away on the air.

Have A Customer Of The Month.

This might not only encourage customers to give you their emails, addresses and phone numbers, it allows you an opportunity to submit a brief write-up to your local newspaper to name the customer, what they received and get your store's name out there once again. Also make sure your customer gets a copy of the article once it's published. You can also frame it and highlight it in your store or on your store's front window.

Make Use Of Promotional Products.
Market yourself where people are active on a day-in, day-out basis. You can market yourself on purses, golf balls, t-shirts, umbrellas. Find one that sets you apart and grabs attention in a big and appropriate way.

Become A Blogger And Promote Your Business.
Promote yourself as an expert on certain products or services you offer by writing a blog with articles and tips on subjects relating to your business. Or, if you're looking for cheap and effective feedback in a quick fashion, consider creating a blog for simple, effective communication with and from current and even potential customers. What a great way to research and possibly fine-tune an idea, a product or even a service.

Zero In On Serving Various Minority Groups Better.
Be aware of the growing cultural market in this country. The buying power of black Americans, Hispanics and Asians is growing rapidly, and you need to appeal to these groups as a part of your marketing efforts. Then there's the whole group of citizens with disabilities. How could you become the place to shop for them? Talk to some of these folks about their unique needs and wants, or call social workers to get their opinion. If you can serve one of these market groups more effectively, you can gain a real advantage and some serious loyalty over your competition from at least one of these groups.

Get Your Website On A "Top Website" List.
If you have a great website (and you probably should be working in that direction anyway) get some more attention by joining a top site list. Try to get an extra link back to your website. Obviously you'll want to go for sites that would be appropriate for your business.

Local Internet Advertising
Check out Google's program that links to its map service and allows businesses to drive Internet traffic to their brick and mortar locations.

Social Networking

Create a target group for your business on one of the social networking sites like MySpace and Facebook. These sites have millions of users online and can segment and target customers by age, geography and even personal interests. Go after these identifiable groups as they apply to your business. Also, try to include Twitter, Facebook and MySpace logos as a part of your advertising, right along with your own logo and name. Wouldn't it be good for your customers to know they can find out about store discounts, contests, new arrivals and clearance via this free media, especially when you consider the many that are online almost every given day?

Look at having a Twitter sign or a Facebook sign for your store. They should be on receipts, store windows, as well as all advertising. Those customers who value social networking will know what those logos mean, and they'll find you. You do want to be found, don't you?

Show Customer Appreciation.

Go after the top 20% of you customers. Send them personalized thank you notes or gifts. Let them know how special they are to you. Take a look at the website for M&M's. You'll find out that you can personalize your M&M's. Put "Thank You" on the candy, if appropriate, or better yet, put your business's logo on the candies and send them to your absolute best customers as a big Thank You! How often do you think a customer gets a thank you gift (much less one so unique) from a store?

Use Email Or Create A Newsletter (not necessarily a quick response, but cheap).

Collect and send out valuable or interesting information to your customers according to their interests and buying habits. Also send out one or two motivational quotes each day or each week to customers in your database. They could also be just notes of encouragement for those with whom you are a little more familiar. This obviously keeps your name and business front and center in their minds. Another common option is to create a newsletter containing specials, detailed information on products you sell, as well as other tips and timely information. Whether you use email or a mailed newsletter, give customers the option of opting out of your regular communications, as you don't want to aggravate them.

Contribute To A Charity Event.
Find out what charities your customers tend to support and contribute gifts in your businesses name to those charities, as a way to publicize. Your customers begin to look at your business as an active and supportive member of the community and will tend to have a bit more loyalty to your business. If you want to have a positive image, you need to be a positive force in your community. Donate products or services where you can to charitable auctions, and make sure your name is on everything you do.

Charity Night At YOUR Store
This is a great win/win promotion especially for gift oriented stores, jewelry, fashion, home accessories stores, etc. Take your slowest night of the week or a night you're not normally open and offer a specially selected charity 15–25% of your total sales for the evening. You or one of your people can man the checkout; however, any other sales help could be volunteers from the charity. Your store ends up with some great good-will created by your contribution, and you also end up with some exposure to friends and family of the volunteers who have never visited before. My experience has been that volunteers can be pretty pushy and persuasive salespeople in the name of charity. Host it on an annual basis and it will build each year, especially if it's well promoted.

Become A Regular Caller To A Radio
Show (Where Appropriate).
Yes, this is a long shot! If you are entertaining, funny or interesting, and you have something applicable to contribute, you may have a chance to briefly promote your business, if you can become a regular caller to a talk/radio show. Sometimes being an expert on a topic may get you more time as a caller. If your calls add something to the show and you become familiar to listeners, you have better a chance

at becoming a regular and a better-known expert. But it can't hurt and it's free!

Create Your Own Holiday.
If you are a garden nursery, you might create "Buy Your Wife a Rosebush Day." Or a hardware store might create "Buy Your Son a Tool Day." Why not? I believe the greeting card manufacturers have created a few of these days. You'll need to publicize it. Put out some temporary "real estate size" signs around town. Advertise. Be consistent and do it every year, and over a period of time people will get tuned in to it and even expect it.

Create An Annual Award And Publicize It.
Create an award for some special volunteer work or a special act of kindness or generosity on a citizen's part. Then make sure the newspapers and media get a photo and understand who is presenting the award—YOU!

Use Your Own Vehicle.
This is one idea that is certainly not genius. Get some professional decals made and put them on your vehicle. It's advertising and the more your vehicle is out, the more it will get read.

Another Variation On Cross Marketing (cross-printing?)
What if you were a gourmet chocolate store and you convinced a printer that he should include a coupon for your stores in the middle of the notepads he sold? I believe the value and popularity of his/her notepads would go up, as would your sales.

Go Offsite With Window Displays.
Look for possible locations to create window displays away from your store. Airports, theatres, malls, hospitals and large office buildings often have display areas they rent out to local retailers.

Distribute Your Own Promotional Coupon.
One of the least expensive promotions you can run is to insert a coupon or flyer into a customer's shopping bag or hand them a coupon

as they leave the store. You can't get a whole lot cheaper than printing something out on colored paper!

This type of promotion can be as simple as printing "Bring this coupon with you on your next visit and receive 10% off" at the bottom of the page. Remember that returning customers are the meat and potatoes of any retail business; with this, you've just given a recent customer a little incentive to return. Encourage them to come back soon by including a date or specified time frame in your promo, such as ". . . until June 15th, 2010."

Besides offering customers a certain percentage off their next purchase, you might use a coupon promotion to advertise particular items, either products or services that are currently coming up on sale or a "buy two, get one free" promotion.

If you wanted to focus your promo on bringing in new customers, you might try something such as a "bring-a-friend" discount. You could even offer the original customer who brought in the promo coupon a 10–20% off discount on products or services if they also brought a friend into the store, and a 30–40% discount if they brought two friends in.

The way you use your coupon or bag insert is limited only by your imagination. Anyone with a computer and printer can easily design a coupon or advertising sheet that can be used in this way.

Other Outdoor Signs
Ever notice the large amount of builder signs or realtor signs out on the weekends? Use a clever line or even just a website address (if it's descriptive). Just be careful of local signing laws. Weekends are best, as local authorities generally don't enforce signing ordinances on weekends. Just be sure the signs are down by Sunday night.

Host An After-Hours Gathering Or An Open House.
Promote a "Party & Purchase Night" or a "Sip & Shop Night". Wine, snacks or hors d'oeuvres could be served. Consider some special

music, a special guest or a demonstration of some kind. Do it for your employees and their friends/relatives. Get employees to hand out postcards or invitations to their friends, relatives and even area employees for a special event or sale. If you're a clothing store, your staff could wear what you sell. Your guests should get a small gift or at least a nice discount on purchases when they show their special invitation at the door. This creates a feeling of exclusivity for all who attend.

Also, consider inviting prominent local politicians and the press, along with anyone else appropriate for a special event. This event could also be used as a kick-off for a special promotion. An alternative might be to give out special discount passes for attendees or friends of attendees to use after the initial evening. Just try not to think of your open house as a way to boost sales immediately. Instead, view it as a way to win over and build future customers. Your in this for the long term.

Advertise In Unusual And Creative Locations.
Advertising on the websites of other businesses, on service station videos, in restrooms and even on park benches are all good possibilities. One business pays to fill city potholes and then has its logo painted on the potholes with the city's blessing. You can also advertise in the poster area or on the seats of bus stops. Don't forget that advertising on the outside of the bus will get your business viewed by a lot of potential customers on a daily basis, whether they take the bus or not. You don't even have to like buses! Just make sure these are your target customers.

As an Example:

In and around Louisville, KY (headquarters of KFC), Kentucky Fried Chicken is filling in potholes faster than you can say "Finger Licken' Good." As part of a new marketing campaign, KFC receives the right to brand and label potholes with a stencil that says "Re-freshed by KFC." This idea is working for them on a couple of fronts. (1) The city gets many of its potholes filled and paid for. (2) KFC is getting some great advertising on roads and highways every day. Talk about traffic! (3) KFC gets some great PR and goodwill by taking care of potholes for previously aggravated drivers. Imagine the mileage a special drink could get out of the term, "refreshed by."

**Pick The Slowest Day Of The Week To
Hold A Weekly One-Day Sale.**
You know what the slowest day of the week is, so why write it off? Why not turn it around and create a weekly tradition that will build as time passes and word spreads. Try promoting it on a banner or by putting flyers in shoppers' bags.

Become Known As A Desirable Radio Talk Show Guest.
Email a radio show host or producer with an accurate description of your business and an eye-catching subject line for your email. Make the message brief, outlining what you do and how or why you would make an interesting guest (with a link to your website). Be familiar with the radio show and its host to make sure you understand the personality and tone of the show. If you don't research this, you can't know if you'll fit in too well as a guest.

If you do plan on trying to get yourself some attention through radio, you need to be confident in your ability to speak, be interesting and entertaining. Radio shows are there to entertain, and if you're not there to be entertaining (as well as informative), forget it. Be more friendly, more talkative, more excited, more funny, more outrageous and more animated (yes, I realize it's radio, but it comes across in your personality). If you're not truly interesting or entertaining, you'll disappoint the producer or host and WILL NOT be invited back.

NOTE: Do NOT cold call the show's host or producer in an effort to get on the show. You will most likely be considered a pest or an annoyance. To get your business called by the stations, consider contacting "show prep" services such as radio411.com, interprep.com, tomslake.com with an email and link to your website. If they like what they see, they are capable of getting the information out to literally hundreds of radio stations in a few days with their own recommendations.

Monthly Workshop

Hold a workshop or seminar about a service or product you offer through your store. They could be monthly, quarterly or semi-annual, depending on the types of products or services you offer.

Get An 800 Number Or A Special Phone Number.

Get a very memorable, appropriate local or toll-free phone number for your store. If you're a retailer and you have a website, consider an 800 number, especially if you plan on doing business outside of your immediate geographic area. If you're a service, manufacturer or anyone else that hopes to do business by being listed in a regional yellow page book or on the internet, you most likely need an 800 number. At least give it some open-minded thought. If you were a prospective customer shopping the internet pages, wouldn't you be a bit more likely to call an 800 number?

Use A Voicemail System.

Use one only to record after-hour messages and inquiries. Also offer basic store information including business hours, website info and special promotions.

Trade Show Marketing (no booths)

If you're attending a trade show or even know of one where the attendees might be customers for your business, do some advance planning. Get yourself attention by handing out a special cloth or canvas bag with your business name, website and logo plastered on it. Maybe a special gift with your business info on it is given out as attendees arrive. Make it something they'll appreciate or use at the show (i.e. notepads, breath freshener, footpad inserts, etc.). You'll be noticed.

Host A Blood Drive.
Publicize your blood drive by contacting radio, newspapers, TV news stations, etc. This can be great for retailers or businesses where customers must come to your place to do business. Use a banner with your phone number and website info on it. Keep your business cards and literature out where it can be easily seen and picked up.

**Join A Trade Organization Associated
with Your Store's Products.**
Depending on the type of retail store you operate, join a trade or business organization related to your business.

SOME MORE IDEAS FOR INCREASING SALES

The following list represents a collection of brief ideas also aimed at increasing sales. While most of the items on this list are still marketing oriented, consider it as a second list of sales ideas to complement the many ideas we've just covered.

Remember, when things get slow or times get tough, marketing is NOT the first place to cut expenses. There are many places to cut back, but marketing should not be your first thought. When things slow down, there's still going to be the same number of retailers competing for even fewer sales dollars, so you must do something to increase or hold on to your share of the pie. Consider using more outdoor banners or signing, emails to your customer base, direct mail, specialty publications and other forms of advertising. Go through the guerilla marketing list again with a more open mind!

**Compare Your Business To The Competition
in All Areas of Your Business.**
What are they charging? What customers are they going after and how? What incentives are they offering? Find out what separates you from them to learn how you can be better, more noticeable, and more memorable. Who has the best customer service and why? Who has the best customer checkout process? Who has the nicest restrooms? If you only compare yourself to your primary competition, you can

only be as good or somewhat better than them. But what if your competition isn't that great? If you want to raise the bar in all areas of your business, you need to be comparing yourself to the best you can find in any number of areas. Your own customers will certainly be comparing you to any of the places where they do business in terms of service, people, atmosphere, comfort, etc.

Listen To Your Customers.
Seriously ask your customers "one-on-one" how they feel about your business and take the time to truly listen to their answers. Well thought out surveys (that can be anonymous) are a great way to assess how you're doing in taking care of them and addressing their true needs, as well as finding out how particular products are being received. As a retailer, call some of your better customers to get their feedback. Imagine how much more important you would feel if someone called you and expressed their interest in your opinion. When you do get feedback, take what they say seriously and try to implement ways to integrate their feedback into your service. If you want your business to become stronger and healthier, show customers you are listening and many of them will spread the word on your behalf.

Participate In Merchant Association Or Shopping Center Ad Space.
When the association or shopping center purchases a large ad, individual merchants are allowed to buy a piece of the overall ad. These ads can command a lot of attention that you wouldn't get on your own.

Join A Barter Organization.
Being a member of a barter organization means that other members will come to you because they can spend their trade credits with you (something they can't do with another business that doesn't accept trade). You will increase your sales as a result of barter sales, and then you can spend those extra trade dollars wherever you want on advertising, printing and other services your business needs. This gives you dollars to spend you didn't have before and might not have been able or even known yet that you wanted to be able to spend.

Use An Email Marketing Service.
Email marketing is being used more and more by small businesses in an effort to find lower cost ways to market themselves. One possible option is verticalresponse.com. They are a self-serve, email-marketing firm that will help create, manage, and even analyze your email. Emailbrain.com allows you to create, manage, distribute and even track newsletters and email campaigns. Also dotster.com offers a variety of lower cost email marketing solutions for small business.

Offer Samples Or Free Work.
Offer to do a free design for a business if you're a graphic designer. If you make dog treats, hand them out at a dog show or offer them at a vet's office. If you're in landscape design, offer to do a small landscaped area and keep it up at a park or at a local restaurant (equipped with a sign indicating that the space is provided by your business and a phone number, of course).

New Exterior Signs
Improve the exterior signage at your store. Get new letter fronts on neon channel lettering or light your sign in a different way. If it's a painted sign, go for a whole new look. See if you can find another offsite location for a sign that will tie in with your store sign.

Have A Drawing For A Prize Or Gift Certificate.
Use the entry forms to get customers mailing addresses and emails. You want the addresses of these people. They are the ones who you already know for sure that come into your store to shop.

Go After The Boomers.
Baby boomers are turning 50 every 7–8 seconds. Since they were born, this group has been a very important segment of the marketplace. This slice of the population will grow substantially over the next decade while the other segments remain relatively flat. This group is still a powerful buying group that is more open to new things and ideas than their predecessors were.

Make Better Use of Lighting.

Use lighting to draw attention to your store and to specific merchandise inside. Create more attractive window displays to make customers to take notice. Make more use of educational and marketing videos to better educate them.

Consider Using A Motto Or A Slogan.

While this won't do anything for sales today, over a period of time it helps people identify with your business and remember it. It really does work! Think of some from the past: "You're in Good Hands with _____" and "_____, when you care enough to send the very best." "Just Do It" from Nike. "Have It Your Way" from Burger King. On a local level, there used to be a slogan for a hardware store in St. Louis: "Everything from scoop to nuts." A local roofer in St. Louis uses the slogan, "For a hole in your roof, or a whole new roof, Frederick Roofing!"

Monitor The Marketing Of Those Who Have Impressed You The Most.

Are there a few companies out there that you feel understand customers and capture their emotions the way you feel your company should? Adopt some of their concepts and behaviors you can use and adapt them for your business where possible. Collect advertising and marketing ideas that you like on an ongoing basis. At the very least, it will help you convey what you want from some other advertising folks trying to help you.

Get Some Free Marketing Help.

Visit the business schools of local universities and talk to a professor about making your business a marketing project. In return, your business could become a case study for the professor and students. You get some great ideas and knowledgeable help, and the students get to learn from the real world.

Buy up old defunct phone numbers from competitors who have gone out of business. Depending on your business and who the ex-competitors are, it could pay off handsomely in new customer business.

Consider Do-It-Yourself Online Public Relations.
The internet has affected public relations for small businesses in a big time way. If and when you have legitimate news or announcements, you can write a press release that includes the normal contact information for your business as well as the all important link to your website. Yes, the pros will do it better, but you can have your press releases done by places like LowCostPressReleases.com. They will help write, edit and distribute your releases for very reasonable fees. To submit a press release, you can go through websites like www.PRWeb.com.

Get Free Local News Coverage.
Play up your business as much as possible with news releases. Pay a pro to right them or learn how to write them yourself. Looking at other news releases on a major company's website is a good way to learn what should be included and what should not be included.

Find a charity or a cause to support that may give you some publicity. Do something unusual or spectacular so that you can't be ignored. If you're an ice cream business, sponsor an ice cream eating contest for charity.

Go Where Your Best Potential Customers Are.
Have a display or be where your best customers will be. If you're selling gourmet dog treats, be at a dog show or at least have brochures there. If you're selling car care products, be at an antique car show with a booth. If you do kids parties, have an ad on the screen at your local movie theatres, especially if kids movies are shown there.

Pair Up Slow Items With Items in Demand.
This is one way to help move the merchandise that isn't moving like it should. Package it, or offer it with something "in demand" and mark it as a special buy or with a special price.

Host A Seminar.

Seminars can be cheap. A financial planner and a lawyer could conduct a free retirement seminar. Then split the costs. A dog trainer may hold a free class on basic discipline for dogs. As a result, some people will ask about his other services.

Public Speaking

Get yourself invited to a BNI (Business Networking International) meeting or a chamber meeting as a guest speaker. Become a guest speaker at a local trade show.

Get Referrals.

Encourage your customers to come in and get their friends to sign up for the mailing list or customer loyalty program. Offer them discounts for each referral they provide.

Have Some Class Or Style About
Everything You Do—Be Aware!

How would you rate your store for class on a scale of 1–10? What do your employees or your answering system sound like when customers call? Again, the way you answer your phone communicates the very first impression about your store as a class act. How do you and your employees dress on the sales floor? Do you look professional? Are you dressed worse than the people your meeting with? What is the image you want your store to convey? Does its appearance inside and out match the clientele you're trying to reach and the image you're trying to convey? What does your checkout area look like? What do your restrooms look like? Are the light bulbs in your lighted sign burnt out? You get the idea.

In Conclusion:

Becoming a guerilla marketer or any kind of marketer these days also means having the tools, equipment, software, etc. necessary to win the war. This means using technology (i.e. computers, internet, emails, blogs, cell phones and scanners) as a part of your efforts. If you're behind the times, take some classes or get some help from a good friend.

Also, remember, any of these ideas are much more effective if done in combination and coordination with other marketing efforts. Whatever ideas you choose here should be targeted and appropriate for YOUR target customer. Certain ideas will most likely never be appropriate for certain target groups. Once you decide which strategies to use, arrange for them to work in conjunction with more traditional marketing efforts, such as newspaper, radio, better signage, etc. Also remember that whatever you do may not get results right out of the box. Maybe certain targeted customers don't make a purchase on their first visit or even second visit. But at least you can capture their information for your database out of that first visit. And secondly, if they each end up spending $500–$1500 over the course of a year, then wasn't it all worth it?

"What, exactly, is the Internet? Basically it is a global network exchanging digitized data in such a way that any computer, anywhere, that is equipped with a device called a "modem" can make a noise like a duck choking on a kazoo."

Dave Barry

"The message for business people contemplating their place in cyberspace is simple and direct: get linked or get lost."

Vic Sussman and Kenan Pollack

"The Internet will help achieve "friction free capitalism" by putting buyer and seller in direct contact and providing more information to both about each other."

Bill Gates

"I feel I'm able to serve my customer by knowing what she or he wants. One of the ways I'm able to do this is through my website and email: people give me great ideas, tell me what they want, what they don't want. It's really instrumental, and helps me stay in touch with people."

Kathy Ireland

Internet Tips:

23

There are plenty of good books on websites out there, and the medium seems to change almost by the day, so I am not going to get into the finer points of websites (nor am I qualified to). But I will make a few key observations and recommendations.

My first and major recommendation is this: IF YOU ARE NOT MAKING GOOD USE OF THE INTERNET—YOU NEED TO START NOW! Start with a Good Website! Every business should have a good website. (I'm a real genius here, wouldn't you say?)

You don't necessarily need to make it your primary goal to sell merchandise on the internet. As a brick and mortar retailer, your first and foremost goal with a website should be to get your customers to your store by communicating who you are and what you're all about, as well as working to create more and more reasons for customers to visit. You may never even want to sell online, but at a minimum, your website should start out by including basic information on what your business is all about. A brochure page that provides simple, relevant information such as store hours, a map, address, phone number and brands carried is better than nothing. Also, promotional information or event information that you want your customers to know is important.

It should have a look and feel that reflects your store's atmosphere, values and overall image. The key is to make it easy for your customers to reach you and receive information about you. A good website isn't necessarily there to generate internet sales dollars or make you the next "amazon.com." It really can be a very efficient communications and PR tool that helps your business connect with your customers. Include your website address on all printed marketing materials, as today people look for services and products online and this is one good place to offer pertinent information, stories and special offers.

Think of your website as one more weapon or tool in your quiver of arrows (so to speak) to fight the marketing and retailing wars. Not necessarily for internet sales, but <u>for the minds and hearts</u> of your customers.

Since the internet is a two-way communications tool, it's not really being fully utilized until it can help you excite and engage your customer in some way. Try to communicate a feeling and create an emotional connection through the images and words on your site. It could also actively connect with your customers by getting a customer response of some kind or providing motivation to act in some way. Yes, a sale preferably, but if not, how about a signing up for newsletter, a blog, comment area or a contest? (Get visitors to do something they might not have done if they hadn't visited your site.)

Anything and everything you do on your website should be done with YOUR customers in mind. Think of content, appearance, tone or attitude, language, vocabulary, benefits, and interests. Make it your objective to increase the average time visitors spend on your site via the content, appearance and interactivity and consistently work to give them more reasons to return to it.

At the same time, you also need to be building your own customer email list so that you can send promotional and interesting information to your customers. **<u>Remember the greatest website in the world is useless if you don't get people to it.</u>** Review your current website and determine how it compares to the following suggestions and questions below. The answers to these questions will help determine some of the features or functions for your website as well as what you want out of your web designer.

Before you begin:

♦ Know what you want to accomplish on the web.

♦ What image do you want to present to your visitors or potential customers?

♦ What do you want people do be able to accomplish when they visit your website?

Other suggestions in brief are as follows:

Make sure you're marketing and promoting your site both offline and online.

Build your site with the features and capabilities of the average computer user in mind (nothing too sophisticated, or you can lose potential visitors).

Do not require you website visitors to download software in order to use or look at your website, and make sure every page downloads as rapidly as possible.

Try to include related content and articles that relate to your store's products and services for users to reference.

Use your website as an efficient way to offer coupons or encourage customers to sign up for email offers.

Consider the appropriateness of a news section on your site.

Consider highlighting a different product each week or each month if you're going to try to generate sales.

Do NOT launch your website until you have a decent amount of content. Why disappoint your first visitors?

Keep interest in your site up. Your home page should be updated regularly so it doesn't become stale. You want people to keep coming back because they want to see what's new, and you must give it to them. Develop some calendar or system for keeping things fresh and exciting.

Consider registering variations of your company website address, so that if a potential visitor remembers it incorrectly, spells it incorrectly or adds the wrong punctuation, they will still be able to bring you up on the computer.

Questions
The goal for any website homepage should be to get visitors to click past it and get further into the rest of your site. Use the following questions to determine if you're on the right track.

♦   Is the copy on the site clear, concise, understandable and grammatically correct?

♦   Is your site attractive and interesting?

♦   Does it reflect the image and culture of your business?

♦   Do the pages load quickly?

♦   Are the contact page and site map easily found? Keep your customer service number visible on all pages.

♦   Is your content fresh, current and updated regularly?

♦   Do any photographs you're using look appropriate and professional?

- Is there plenty of relevant information on the site, (i.e., details about your business, policies, phone numbers, mailing address)?

- Is the audio or video on your site relevant and clear?

- How are you getting visitors to your site? Is it working?

IMPORTANT NOTE:

There are times when the internet MAY be a more cost effective alternative over a direct mail campaign. Before you begin working on any direct mailing campaign, ask yourself if this could be better accomplished via the internet. The answer may be NO, but response time for email is much quicker (often days instead of weeks), and postage alone will usually cost more than an entire email advertising campaign. When you add up paper, printing costs, postage, etc., direct mail can cost 10–15 times more than email marketing. Either way, the key is getting the customer to open up the e-mail or direct mail piece and read it! At least ask yourself, "Is there a good reason why I should be using one over the other?"

Social Networking (and Why You Need to Be There)
The good news is that retailing has gained a whole new weapon that helps to level the playing field for the little guy. Social networking. Yes, it is important, and YES, I do recommend making use of this tool for your store. Even if you already agree with me, I realize the challenge is to somehow find the time to handle this on top of everything else.

What is "Social Networking"?
It's really millions of people broken down into specific groups who have something in common online, like auto enthusiasts, fashion followers, movie watchers or even political groups. These people are

looking to meet other people, to communicate about something they have in common and share first-hand information and experiences about any number of topics. . . from product reviews and company service complaints to golfing, gardening, and professional alliances. Once someone joins a social networking site and begins reading comments, they usually want to respond to what they've read (it's only human). Younger customers are using all of these networking sites, which include YouTube, Facebook, Twitter, MySpace, LinkedIn, Citysearch and Yelp in amazingly increasing numbers.

Now Sears, Walmart and Starbucks are just a few of a growing number of retailers that "tweet." In fact, by the time you read this information, there will probably be a whole new vehicle and opportunity in this rapidly changing technology. Social networking has taken the whole customer research/comparison-shopping element of the buying decision and turned it on its head by giving shoppers more power and information than ever. The end result for us retailers is to keep in mind that shoppers will promote the stores and products they love as well as those they love to hate! Human beings have always had the need to voice their two cents. Now the talk (whether critical or complimentary) reaches a much, much larger audience through this medium!

Social Networking Really Is a Very Powerful Tool.
Again, you really need to be a part of this technology! Think about it this way: When a product, brand or retail business is recommended to you from a friend rather than some paid advertisement, it gives the product, brand or retail business a completely different level of credibility. After all, which will influence you more? An ad that says "our customer service is #1" or a customer comment posted online that says "The customer service at Joe's Clothing was better than anywhere else I've ever been?" But keep in mind, the reverse is also true: If you're doing a bad job of something, the word can spread faster than the flu at kindergarten.

A Gordon Guideline

Remember, when a customer goes to your website, it means the potential customer had to make a decision to visit you. On the other hand, social networking allows you to expand your visibility and reach shoppers where they were already congregating. It is the equivalent of going out to the street corner in another neighborhood where customers are standing, and talking to them about your store or your products instead of just talking to those inside your store who already made the decision to be there.

A Research Tool

When you consider you can announce new products, promotions, or provide answers or explanations that can put your store in a more positive light, it makes sense to be a part of social networking. If you think about it, advertising, research, public relations, customer service and even sales to some extent, are now only a mouse click away. Now through social media, instead of just wishing we all had the same customer research budget of the big boys to set up surveys and focus groups, you can just tap into what consumers are passionate about or what's on their minds. You can use this new medium to learn just how you can provide better customer service and to arm yourself with information that will turn your target shoppers into better customers. If you are truly interested in improving customer service, this is one good way to find out what you need to correct or adjust.

A Marketing Tool

Facebook has well over 200 million users and is now larger than most radio and television networks, so more major advertising and marketing efforts are changing course and pouring more money into social networking (at the expense of television and especially newspapers). When you add the traditional online advertising and websites that you can use for viral marketing to the various social networks out there, it all becomes even more important and powerful.

Ok, what is viral marketing you say? It's really a form of advertising and/or marketing that uses the social media or networks to help "spread" (like a virus, from consumer to consumer) a message that was created (in part) to produce "word of mouth" marketing, usually on the internet or by email. This can be for marketing, humor or even political purposes. If you want the word to spread about something new in your stores, try talking about it with consumers on blogs and chat rooms. Just don't come across like you are pushing product or purposely promoting yourself.

The important role that social networking now plays in retail can no longer be ignored.

Still Have Doubts About Using Social Media?
Wouldn't you like to know what your customers are saying or thinking about your market, or your competition or maybe even your store? Even if you think your store is too insignificant to get talked about online, the more you listen to your customers—and your competition's customers—the more information and opportunity you'll have to respond and improve your business. Remember the old saying "knowledge is power"? More and more sites allow users to rate businesses and their experiences. Use them. These could include services, restaurants and even your very own retail store.

A Gordon Guideline

I'm going to emphasize the word "connect" again. In the business world, Twitter and other social media are not about constantly talking about your business and how wonderful your business is. Social media is about "connecting" with customers and people by listening to them and interacting with them. You also connect with people by becoming a person that people want to listen to. It is about how you can help your followers/customers, and it's about the information you can provide them. People aren't looking to follow another advertiser spewing more propaganda! People will follow you because you provide extra value, not because of your self-serving agenda! Your activities should be about 90–95% information and help for the people who are following you. The other 5–10% can be about what your company can offer.

In Conclusion:
Do not neglect or treat this media lightly!
You will read elsewhere in this book that you MUST listen to your customers. This is one important way to do just that. You need to interact with customers and explain anything that needs explaining or emphasis. But remember, when you consider the size of the audience, communication via social networking needs to be honest and professional.

"The primary skill of a manager consists of knowing how to make assignments and picking the right people to carry out those assignments."

Lee Iacocca

"When the grass looks greener on the other side of the fence, it may be that they take better care of it there."

Cecil Selig

"Nearly all men can stand adversity, but you if want to test a man's character, give him power."

Abraham Lincoln

Do You Have A "People Plan"?

24

We all know that every business should have a business plan and a marketing plan, but very few business owners understand the need for a "people plan." Many retail owners work on earning customer loyalty, but they hope or pray for employee loyalty. The fact is you must earn employee loyalty as well, because employees are feeling less of a sense of loyalty to their employers than ever.

While loyalty from employees is on the line there are more college graduates than ever and the average businessman will tell you that there's an increased shortage of talented and hardworking people available in the labor pool. The best employees that are left have lots of options, and many want more challenging, fulfilling work with better pay and benefits. Truly good people tend to know they're in demand.

For all of us, our American economy and its standing in the world does not seem to be what it used to be. Capitalism even seems to be under attack. Taxes increase as life becomes more stressful. Workers are worried about healthcare while they see jobs moving offshore, and they feel as though they have little ability to make things work out for themselves. Add to this the fact that in retail, things are changing faster and faster and business must react more rapidly than ever to the market place. Many retail operations are dropping like flies, as what worked yesterday does not necessarily work today. Taking all of this into account, it's easy to understand how all of this might be a challenge for the average retail store operator or manager.

#*!t Rolls Downhill.

Considering the stress all of this places on the average retail store operator, think about the impact these issues can also have on the attitude, security and productivity of the average employee. This is where something called "Strategic HR (Human Resources)" has become an important management tool. Now, please don't let your eyes glaze over because I mentioned the words "Human Resources" . . . the idea here is for a given business to become more productive and more profitable through a more broad, high performance approach to "human resources." But I also realize that a small business owner can't afford his or her own HR department, and often does not even have the interest in understanding, so called "high performance" HR.

I think at least we can all agree that hiring the right people and making sure they get a certain amount of training and supervision is important. However, while some owners know how to train and supervise their people adequately, most business owners and management drop the ball with anything beyond this.

Studies from Harvard and companies like Administaff have shown there's a distinct advantage for companies that link this people approach with their goals. If you at least agree with me that you'd like to increase sales and become more profitable through your own people, then pay attention.

If you can also agree that your people are your business's most important asset, then consider giving a bit more attention to a new approach in the way you handle and manage this all-important asset.

Owners spend all kinds of time and money to make sure their technology is well maintained, and they often make sure their people are trained to operate it well. They calculate their ROI (return on investment) for a new piece of equipment and usually make sure their valuable equipment is well taken care of . . . **but often they drop the ball when it comes to the employee side of things**! What if that employee is under stress because he's not happy, not being treated well, feels unchallenged or unappreciated? What if he's sick but avoided going to the doctor because his health plan stinks? What if he, or a family member, has a drug or alcohol problem or a serious family issue that is taking away his focus? What if one day your employee does something stupid with some machinery or your computer because he's fed up, or maybe he's been functioning poorly and the quality of your product or service hasn't been up to par for months? Then what is your return on investment? How valuable is a good P.O.S. system, or a computer or even a good service department without a well-adjusted human being to operate it all?

If you don't have an effective way of treating your people well, developing your them, motivating them, challenging them, treating them fairly, ethically and legally, you increase your odds of joining the thousands of other businesses out there that may have had a great retail concept, product or service, but never lived up to their true potential. Why? Even if your vision was sound and you had the greatest idea out there since sliced bread, poor handling of the "people part" of your business can stop you from being able to properly and fairly test or carry out your concept as envisioned. That would be a really sad and forever regrettable tragedy! So what if:

You are making poor hiring decisions.

You haven't been motivating or managing your people well.

Your people are stealing you blind.

You haven't had much of a plan for retaining your good employees.

Government regulations, legal bills or an employee lawsuit suddenly begin to drain you financially.

When people think of human resources, they think hiring, firing, payroll and managing employees. But superior HR practices or "best practices" in HR says that the key to having and attracting the best people and operating at peak levels means having a great company culture that includes developing, training, motivating and providing a positive, comfortable environment for ALL of your people.

The bottom line is this—if you want to improve your company and you want to improve your customer service, you MUST improve your people. In order to do that, I have outlined some key areas that you need to think about if you want to take your business in the right direction for the long term. Keep in mind that the points below are just scratching the surface in terms of truly developing a great people plan.

1. Create and maintain a strong company culture. Every business has its own unique culture—positive or negative—whether it was planned or happened by accident. Creating a positive one makes the difference by being a place that attracts good people and makes good people want to stay.

2. Hire the right people. Duuuh! But this means having the right people doing the right job in the right way. It also means having an effective way for your business to find and bring on the right people. In retailing your people become an extension of you.

3. Have a well thought out reward system. Do you reward your employees for a job well done? Do you believe that this might affect their performance over the long haul? Almost all human beings like being told they're special and they're valuable. People receive a certain amount of satisfaction from making a positive difference in business, but this has to be part of an ongoing effort. Have you tried to define exactly what type of performance or behavior you want to reward or recognize from your people?

4. Retaining the best people. Most employees will actively look for a new job, especially if a down economy starts to improve and they begin to feel more secure. If you want to hold on to your best people,

you need a well thought out strategy for keeping employees. Think about the high cost of training, bringing new employees up to speed and lost sales or major customer gaffs. With a declining pool of good and skilled labor, holding on to *good* people is becoming more important then ever.

5. Have a training and development program. Special employees (the kind I believe you want to keep around) want more than a job and a paycheck—they want to know they can grow in their jobs and become more valuable to their company and others. You may have an idea who your special people are, and which ones are leaders, but what are you doing with them and for them? You need some kind of training and development program, as well as some sort of feedback from a mystery shopper who comes into your store as a customer and tests the habits and capabilities of your people. Again, if your people don't get better, your company won't get better!

6. Develop fair, legal, quality policies and practices. Do you have a well-written set of policies, procedures and systems in place? Having a comprehensive set of written policies and procedures in place protects you and your people, and it helps your employees understand exactly what is expected of them. Stability, predictability, fairness and ethical practices are key in creating the right company culture. Government regulations are becoming increasingly complex, and insufficient or inadequate policies and practices can be very costly to any business, especially a small one. Do you have a job description that won't come back and be used against you in a court of law? Do you have an employee manual that won't violate federal and state laws? These are other areas you need to consider.

A Gordon Guideline

Remember that if and when you must have employees, your employees are the most critical resource you have, and they can walk out the door and leave you hanging at any time. Your employees can make or break your business. They are the ones who help create and improve your products and services. They are <u>your</u> representatives at the front lines with your customers. They are in a position to protect you or steal you blind. You can't be everywhere all of the time, and you can't do it without them, no matter how good you think you are!

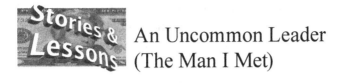

An Uncommon Leader
(The Man I Met)

During my days with Venture, I was aware that top management of our company left the ivory towers of the corporate office every so often to take a tour of the stores in another city. They always seemed to let the stores know a couple of weeks in advance of their planned visit. We always knew what day they would arrive, even if we didn't know what time. The stores would spend quite a bit more on payroll in anticipation to get things into shape, to create an illusion that things looked wonderful all of the time. The stores were also better staffed on the appointed day. So, management just got a totally inaccurate picture of how the store actually looked and functioned. I never totally understood that. Yes, they may have let us know so that the extra effort would be put forth to get things ship-shape, but they never seemed to get a REAL picture of day-to-day operations.

When they did arrive, they walked around with an entourage of management people, stopping only to grill a particular department manager. If you weren't part of the grilling, they bypassed and often totally ignored you. You kept your distance and kept your place, never to say anything unless you were spoken to. If you weren't part of the grilling and conversation, then you'd be lucky if one of them gave you a nod as they walked by. Part of you wanted to be ignored, while part of you wanted to be important enough to actually talk to the big boys!

One day I was working at the front of my experimental pet department, making sure that the front of my department was looking as inviting and attractive as possible. I had been working pretty hard and hadn't really been paying much attention to anything that was going on around me. All of a sudden I looked down the main aisle of the store and saw two men walking towards me, dressed in suits. As I zeroed in, I couldn't believe my eyes. One of the men was the chairman of the company; the other I didn't recognize. As far as I knew, this visit was unannounced! Hurriedly, and in a panic, I got some boxes I was working with out of the aisle and into the stockroom so that things looked as good as possible. Upon returning I noticed they were much closer, but the chairman was now standing at a column and was on one of the store phones, talking to someone. The other nicely dressed man continued to walk in my direction. He walked up to me, put out his hand to shake mine and said, "Hi, I'm Sam Walton."

At that time, I'd heard of Walmart. To me, they were that chain of stores that operated in the country and small towns. As this was in the mid 1970s, they weren't that big yet and certainly did not have the respect of the retail world at that point. I'd heard the name Sam Walton before, so I knew who he was and was somewhat impressed. To this day, what has stayed in my mind was that this man went out of his way to walk up to me and shake my hand and talk to me like I was an equal. I don't remember what we talked about. All I knew was that I had never seen upper management act like that before. It was refreshing, and it restored my faith that senior management could be real people too. This guy didn't consider himself a god or someone to look down on the little people. He treated me with respect.

Interviewing New People

25

No managers or owners ever seem to be trained on how to interview prospective employees, yet all of corporate America does it anyway. And they don't necessarily interview any better than the average small business owner. The only difference may be that corporate America has an HR department to do background checks and give the screening process more time.

The good news is that I honestly believe that having someone who is personable and passionate about what they're doing is the key factor when it comes to retail employees. I don't care what kind of training they get or don't get, if they can be genuine and learn customers names and preferences and then work to satisfy those preferences they are miles ahead of almost anyone else. This is good news for those who can't afford sophisticated sales training programs or owners who really can't train someone in sales techniques. This means that you need to focus on having the right personalities to begin with and you are a good part of the way there. The bad news is that you can't just throw bodies at the situation when it comes to covering your sales-floor.

Just remember, an interview is not a time for you to talk and just breeze it. Give it the time and forethought that it deserves with some good questions that get at the heart of what type of person you want working for you. Following are some guidelines that have served me well over the years in uncovering some interesting facts and character traits. In addition, try to look for the obvious questions and background behind what is stated on the resume:

1. If they're late for the interview, move on. If they can't be on time for the interview, what will happen on a day to day basis?

2. If your business is small and you're interviewing hourly employees, spend at least 20–30 minutes with them. If they are going to be even more significant to your business, leave at least one hour for each interview. It's important for you and the prospective employee to have a little time to become more relaxed.

3. Make sure you ask each person the same basic questions so you can compare responses. To do this well, prepare your questions in advance (see point #6 for good interview questions).

4. Most interviewers end up doing most of the talking and don't really learn what they need to know. Give your "interviewee" 70–80% of the time to do the talking. Remember, you're not learning anything while *you're* talking.

5. Write down your thoughts right after the interview so that you can keep people straight and have appropriate follow up conversations or points to address later.

6. Ask open-ended questions similar to the following. They have always served me well, no matter what the position was.

Why did you leave your last job?

What did you like about it? What did you really dislike about it?

If I were to ask your boss about your biggest weakness, what would he or she tell me?

If I were to ask your boss about your biggest strength, what would he or she tell me?

If you get this job, what is your single biggest concern?

Where do you see yourself in 5 or maybe 10 years?

What do you like to do in your spare time . . . for fun?

Tell me about a challenge or problem you overcame in your work life. What was the outcome and what did you learn from the situation?

Fill in the blank:

I have no patience for _____.

I am at my best when _____.

I hate it when someone tells me _____.

I am almost always _____.

Important Questions for Retail Store Operators
How long will it take you to get to work? *(You really want people who are no more than 15–20 minutes away, max. If they're working part time and only working 3–4 hours at a time, it is hardly worth it for them to travel or try to get in if they're needed at the spur of the moment.)*

Do you have any dependents? *(If they have small children, who still stay with them?)*

How many hours a week do you want to work? *(If they say 40 hours, they will most likely be looking elsewhere if you give them less.)*

What hours are you available to work? *(You're probably going to need weekend people.)*

How does your spouse/parent feel about you working? *(If you're talking to a wife and her husband is not happy about this, he may make her life and yours a real hassle. The same can hold true for a student who might feel the pressure from a parent who isn't thrilled about him working while still in school. They could also end up quitting on you abruptly because of pressure from their parent.)*

What obligations (family or otherwise) do you have that will conflict with your job? Club meetings? Upcoming vacations?

Other conflicts (like a second job)?

Why do you want to work for us? *(If they just say they are looking for a job, they may not be your person. If they say they love _____ about the proposed job, or they like working with people, that makes me a little more comfortable.)*

Do you have any physical limitations that would prevent you from doing the job or are there things you can't or won't do? (It is against the law to ask about an individual's possible handicaps. Employers are generally required to make special accommodations for physically challenged applicants.) You MAY ask the candidate whether he/she is capable of performing all the job duties of a written job description.

Do you have a problem with locking up your cell phone in a locker while you're working? (Tempting distractions must be avoided, or your people will be text messaging instead of working.)

Customer Service and Sales
(Separating the Men from the Boys!)
(If you're hiring a salesperson, have them briefly sell you about something with which they're familiar.)

While it gets uncomfortable for any of us when dealing with a really upset customer, can you describe an instance when you've handled one?

Has there ever been a time when a customer asked you for something unreasonable? How did you handle it?

What is the one big situation in the past when you learned a lesson about dealing with a customer?

Can you give an instance in the past when you went above and beyond the call of duty to take care of a customer?

Where have you shopped where you believe they do an exceptional job at taking care of customers? Why?

What do you like most about working with customers?

What do you like least about working with customers?

Dealing with the public can at times get stressful and tiring. How do you keep yourself enthusiastic and fresh?

This last question has proven many times over to provide me with some critical information about a prospective employee. Sometimes it has salvaged someone good that I was ready to write off. Often it has totally changed my impression of someone, for better or for worse. It always amazes me how revealing the answers can be and how indifferent some people are about what they disclose! Sometimes it reveals a severe character flaw. Sometimes it reveals something as simple as a serious lack of common sense, but it has been a magical question for me.

If there were one thing you would like to drill into my head today about yourself (whether we've talked about it or not), what would you like to make sure I understand about you, before you leave here today?

To avoid facing a shortage of good candidates for your business, carry your business card with you at all times. Anytime you run into someone who provides you with great service and has a great personality, leave them your card and tell them that if they are ever looking for a job, just give you a call.

Last but not least. . . Check references!

"It's ironic that retailers and restaurants live or die on customer service, yet their employees have some of the lowest pay and worst benefits of any industry. That's one reason so many retail experiences are mediocre for the public."

—Howard Schultz
Chairman & CEO of Starbucks

 Managing By Fear and Intimidation

Our mission statement about treating people with respect and dignity is not just words but a creed we live by every day. You can't expect your employees to exceed the expectations of your customers if you don't exceed the employees' expectations of management.
　　—Howard Schultz, Chairman and CEO Starbucks

"Too often at May Company, they wanted a head on a platter when things didn't work out. Wal-Mart on the other hand, created an atmosphere where employees were willing to stick their necks out and try new ways of doing things."

Over the years, one of the main things I always carefully observed was the way managers treated their employees. In my career I've had some bosses who were jealous, insecure and scared. There were also workaholics who had gone through multiple marriages and wanted to take you with them. Many of the poor managers out there can eventually snuff out the glimmer of creativity in good people, not to mention the spark of optimism or enthusiasm that motivates them. Their employees end up burned out, feeling more and more insecure until they move on to something better if they aren't terminated first. In some large corporations as well as small businesses, you can almost cut the fear with a knife! In a larger business with multiple levels of management, you'll often see that, after forcing out what might have been a great employee, the bad boss remains behind to screw up the next employee!

In our increasingly fast-paced world, it is becoming even easier to lose track of the importance of human relations and direct human interaction. Human interaction these days seems to depend on cell phones, email, text messaging, twittering, blog sites and the very heavy use of a Blackberry or iPhone. The very use of text message and cell phones makes any of us less likely to truly sense and feel how our management and communication habits personally affect each other. You can't see facial expressions, fear, tears, worry, relief, general body language, etc. And you can't hear voice inflections and tones. I'm not aware yet of any great leaders who have effectively motivated and inspired their people through just a combination of text messages, email and cell phones. While I'm not saying it can't be done, I believe inspiring employees becomes much more challenging for most managers when using only virtual interaction.

One of the major reasons I feel that Walmart has grown into the 800 lb. gorilla is the positive way that their corporate culture has affected and inspired their 2 million plus associates. Over the years, Walmart (starting with Sam Walton himself) worked to create a company-wide culture that inspires creativity and motivates its employees to achieve excellence. As a retailer, they are in a league of their own when it comes to encouraging their people at all levels to come up with ideas to make Walmart even better.

At May Company and its various divisions, the company culture was often to find fault and punish failure. In addition, blame generally traveled down the management structure (almost never upwards). May Company, with a relatively "poor" corporate culture regarding the human element could be repressive and often unforgiving of employee errors. On the other hand, Walmart inspired its people by offering positive reinforcement and treating employees with dignity (I know that every company has its exceptions). May Company executives (certainly not all) created an environment where management ruled by creating fear and offering veiled threats of termination or the demise of a career. At May Company, praise was just too infrequent and, in some circles, almost frowned upon. There was actually an ingrained belief among many managers that by creating an atmosphere of fear, you would get more out of your employees.

On the other hand, Sam Walton said, "Outstanding leaders go out of their way to boost the self-esteem of their personnel. If people believe in themselves, it's amazing what they can accomplish."

> *"People want to know deep down that they're doing a good job. They want to be able to go home and say, 'Guess what? The manager came by today and recognized that I did something well, and he told the other people in the store meeting about it.' People don't realize the value of that. You have to catch people when they're doing something right, not always when they're doing something wrong."*
> —*David Glass, former President and CEO Walmart)*

Sam Walton often said that "If you take care of your people, they will take care of you," and he's been proven right. Just look at how Walmart's sales have passed every retailer in the country like they were standing still. Even 100-year-old companies like May Company, Sears, Montgomery Wards and J.C. Penney have either been left in the dust or their names have turned to dust.

Mark Twain once said, "I can live for two months on a good compliment." More and more companies are learning that personal recognition is a powerful tool in building morale and motivation. A pat on the back such as a personal note from a co-worker or a supervisor can make all the difference in the world. Administaff is another company that practices what it preaches by motivating and rewarding the small accomplishments as well as the big ones. Smaller, informal celebrations are held often throughout the company and they have been proven to be many times more effective than just a once a quarter or once a year formal event.

The fact is that employees spend most of their lives in the workplace, and well-run businesses fully recognize the negative side of using fear to motivate their employees.

Effects of a "Fear & Intimidation" Atmosphere:

1. It encourages people to protect themselves and "cover their rears." It all becomes about self-interest.
2. It encourages people to hide the truth and to avoid bringing news, especially bad news, to the boss, which can cause companies to operate in somewhat of a disillusioned state, never fully understanding what is really going on.
3. Good people will not put up with it over the long haul, so that there is a constant drain on talent, while those that preach the company line and become "yes" people stay on.
4. It can cause low self-esteem in employees, which affects how people treat each other and hurts the overall atmosphere and culture of the company.

There is little place for fear in corporate America or your business. When fear is part of the management pattern, respect and integrity gradually disappear and creativity becomes more of a rarity. Company morale declines and loyalty goes out the window. If you think about it; why should or would it turn out any other way? It is also very expensive including the increased likelihood of lawsuits, increased turnover, loss of productivity and even depression.

"Make up your mind today that your business will be different."

Setting Firm Expectations For Hourly Employees

26

(Or, Staying Ahead of the Game)

There are many sharp and hard-working people in retail—thank goodness. In general however, hourly retail help cannot be paid the kind of money that many other jobs command, and as a result, the small shop owner finds himself working with a younger or less well-trained pool of talent. For this reason, it becomes even more important for you to stay ahead of the game by knowing what troubles and worries young or less skilled workers may have in store for you. Are we communicating here?

You must set clear rules and expectations for younger workers and clearly spell the rules out for them. **<u>And then enforce those rules!</u>** I'm talking about common sense basics here. . . like showing up for work (and showing up on time). The more you can anticipate what younger or less responsible workers might do to you, the better. Part of the solution is also developing good systems and procedures for handling everything, and then assure employees are trained to follow the systems without fail. If you can reinforce and remind them of your expectations, then you'll have fewer unpleasant fires to put out and life will be easier for you! Do I make myself clear here? Following is some specific and valuable advice from someone who has weathered the storms of lower-wage workers . . . ME!

> If you accept unacceptable performance or behavior from time to time, it is only a matter of time before you'll be routinely accepting a more routine poor performance or behavior.

Occasional tardiness will become frequent tardiness---then consistent tardiness.

Occasional shortages in the cash drawer can go from occasional to either larger shortages or regular shortages.

Sloppy or unkempt appearance often goes from rare to occasional to routine sloppy appearance.

A poor cleaning job goes from rarely to occasional to regular.

NIP IT IN THE BUD! Poor performance or unacceptable behavior cannot become acceptable! (If at all possible, purchase a video system that allows monitoring of your store from your notebook computer at anytime. Let your employees know they will be monitored.)

> "Trust, but verify."
>
> Ronald Reagan

From the first interview and first day of hiring onward, attendance and punctuality must be emphasized as a critical factor in each and every employee's performance. This needs to be stressed numerous times (not once or twice). Clearly explain that any absence without notification will be considered cause for dismissal. Assuming YOU value and understand the importance of your discipline in this policy, then YOU must let your people know that you mean it. Anyone who has to be absent for any reason must notify their manager at least two hours prior to their scheduled time on the job. Inform your people that more notice is highly preferable and expected if at all possible. Here are some additional important expectations that should become written policies and should be acknowledged in writing/signed off by any new employee.

1. Repeated tardiness may result in loss of hours or dismissal.

2. Any employee may be fired immediately and without advance notice for any of the following reasons:

a.   Theft or proven dishonesty

b.   Violation of company cash handling procedures, including under-ringing

c.   Falsifying company reports or records

d.   Deliberate destruction or damage of personal or company property

e.   Embezzlement

f.   Possessing firearms on company property or on company hours

g.   Knowingly and willfully completing or clocking in another employee's timecard or allowing another employee to do the same to yours

3.   Disciplinary action or termination may result from any of the following:

a.   Insubordination

b.   Rudeness or any action while on company time that might discredit or result in loss of goodwill toward the company

c.   Failure to report a sale or refund at the time of the transaction

d.   Falsely claiming sick leave

e.   Any negligent or intentional action that results in injury to yourself or to others, or action that may result in damage to the company's or others' personal property

f. Undependable attendance

g. Failure to abide by company dress code

h. Failure to treat all customers and individuals on company property equally and with respect, regardless of race, sex or color

i. Trading hours with another employee when it results in the absence of either employee

j. Willful violation of company safety and loss prevention procedures

k. Allowing friends to linger or hang out around the store

VERY IMPORTANT!

There is one more very important concept to explain to your people (as nicely as possible). If you can get this into your head as well as theirs, the better you will all be in the long run. In fact, I have raised my children to clearly understand this concept, and as a result, I believe they have a real advantage in life over those who do not understand it.

It is not the employer's responsibility to pay every worker enough to support family, lifestyle, nice car, big screen TV, or anything else. Raises should not be automatic. This is one reason why so many raises in this world are mediocre. Raises are for people who make themselves more valuable and hard to replace in your store. If an employee doesn't become more valuable to your store then they become relatively easy to replace or exchange for anyone else out on the street at the going wage. Giving someone a raise is not in the constitution or the bill of rights, as some probably believe. The more valuable any given employee becomes to you and your business, the more profitable they become to have as employees, and as a result, the more they are worth to you.

> "Being liked by your employees is nice. Being profitable is more important and MANDATORY!"
>
> Rich Gordon

The above policies are not meant to be complete but only to give an idea as to what expectations and policies should apply to all employees.

"The Offer"

Even after carefully interviewing a new employee, doing background checks and making careful decisions, Zappos. com (an online e-tailer) does one more remarkable thing to assure they have the right people. In the employees first month it provides a training period at normal salary that emphasizes the company's mission, strategy, and company culture. Most importantly, during this time it stresses the company's focus and obsession with customer service.

The surprise: After a week or so during the month-long training period, Zappos makes what it calls "The Offer." They offer their employees a rather impressive $1,000 bonus if they will quit today. Believe it or not, they actually bribe new employees to quit. As a result about 10% of their new call-center employees take the money and run.

Zappos understands that people who are willing to take the company up on "The Offer" are not really all that committed to having THIS job. If there is a contradiction between what the company is looking for vs. what the individual employee values, Zappos wants to know right away. The thinking is, why go through the training expense, the learning curve expense and more importantly, the possible loss of customers due to a lack of the right customer attitude. Over time, CEO Tony Hsieh and management have raised the size of "The Offer" bonus. It started at $100, went to $500, and may even go higher than $1,000 as the company gets larger.

The Lesson: Zappos totally understands that companies don't connect emotionally with their customers—people do. If you want to increase the odds of creating memorable experiences, you need the people who have the commitment, attitude and personality to do the job. The sooner you find out, the better!

"You've got to kiss a little ass to kick a lot of ass."

—Unknown

"People often say that motivation doesn't last. Well, neither does bathing—that's why we recommend it daily."

—American author, salesperson, & motivational speaker

 30 Ideas For Motivating
Your Most Important Assets

27

If you can't interact with your people and manage them right, everything becomes much more difficult and more likely to fail. You don't need to be a genius at retailing, but if you can surround yourself with the right people, motivate them and then keep them happy, it will make up for a lot of your own shortcomings. Yes, I realize that just about everyone understands the importance of motivating employees and keeping good people. The real problem is how we do it. Is it accomplished giving out ultimatums and making people fear for their jobs? Does it require constant supervision and micro-management? Or, should it be done by creating a positive atmosphere and setting a positive example? I'd say go for the positives. This is in addition to basics like valuing your people, paying them a decent wage and keeping them in a positive corporate culture.

Let's just agree on some basics then. All managers have different management styles, backgrounds and experiences to draw on. Some are good, and some not so good. There isn't one way to handle every employee, because employees are all unique, with different personalities, skills, weaknesses and strengths. In all cases however, there are some common do's and don'ts when it comes to motivating and keeping people that will serve you well. These are in no particular order. Just remember the more "motivational" ideas here won't be of much help if you ignore too many of the other guidelines.

General Guidelines and Ideas

1.   Show your people that you value them. Value them, as well as the talents, ideas and contributions they bring to your business. I mentioned earlier, your people are your most

important asset. I will now add to that sentence, *Your* people and the relationship you all have with your customers is your most valuable asset by far. Employees as well as customers want to feel appreciated and valued, and neither will feel valued if you don't set the tone and the example.

I once believed that it was important for me to show my employees that I knew how to do things better then they. I was the first one on the job, the fastest at getting a job done and I strived to show that I was the best at the job. Employees begin to resent a boss that tries to always be better at everything and seems to hold him or herself up as better. Employees need to be complimented and made to feel good about what they try to do. Trying to prove to them that they are inferior or substandard to what you can accomplish will work against you in a big way. The turn-around for me was telling a rather quiet female employee for the first time that I could never be as good as she was at the job she was performing at that particular time. I don't remember what it was, but you could see the change in her face and her body language. That's when the light bulb went off in my head!

"Tell me, and I forget. Show me, and I remember. Involve me, and I understand."

Author unknown

2. Putting policies before people. Remember, procedures can be wrong and can also be improved upon. Yes, I know rules are there for a reason. They're especially important when it comes to safety, security, treating customers right and treating people fairly, but after that, they may not always be critical. When you always put policies and rules ahead of people, you ignore the fact that a experienced human being is there in part to know when exceptions need to be made for customers as well as employees. Flexibility, particularly with employees in

a small business, is very important and at times you may need to judge and adjust the importance of your policy on a case-by-case basis. If you can't be flexible when necessary, you run the risk of losing good people. Maybe not immediately, but perhaps over the long haul, after you've forgotten all about your inflexible decision. As each situation would come up, I would ask myself, "Does this person care and have my best interest in mind?" The answer to this question would usually guide me as to when to make exceptions to the rules.

3. Train your employees. Training and opportunities to improve themselves or their skills are important, both for them and you. **If you want your small business to improve, you need your people to improve**. Most employees recognize that they need to continue to add to their skills. **If you won't help them and another business will, your business will be a much less attractive place to stay**.

4. Give employees challenges. Jobs that are more challenging show you have confidence in them. People get bored and almost everyone I know likes to be challenged at times, especially if they know they have your confidence.

5. Do you have ALL the answers? I don't . . . and I don't believe you do either. And if you think you have all the answers, you're probably not a very popular boss. It's ok to admit that you don't know everything. **Too often managers confuse confidence with always being right**. They are NOT the same thing. A good manager cannot solve every problem on his own. Seeking help is not a sign of weakness, and there are other people who know more than you about many subjects that are important for your business's success. Since no one has all the best ideas and answers, one of the best ways to show your people you value them is by asking your people for their input (and not just your inner circle). Asking people for their opinion can be magical, even more than a compliment. Just be sure you are sincere. Have an open mind. You just

might learn something, and you may help your employees gain some confidence and learn something too.

6. Spend regular one-on-one time with each employee. Try for once a month if possible. It doesn't need to be a formal meeting. A friendly conversation about their lives or asking about their interests on or off the job is highly valued by anyone, including employees.

7. Recognize that everyone is not motivated by the same things. We all have different stimuli that spur us on to better performance. We're not all motivated by getting a trophy or a ribbon. Some people want money. Some just want to feel appreciated. Some are embarrassed when singled out for an honor or reward in front of others. A designer or an artistic person may be much more motivated by the opportunity to work on a special creative new project, while many sales people are more likely to be motivated by money. But even here, you can't put all salespeople in the same basket. Some of the areas that can differ from person to person are as follows:

- New challenges and opportunities to prove oneself
- Recognition, awards, being singled out for a job well done in front of your peers
- Flexibility with schedules
- Promotion and a chance to move upward on the ladder
- Feeling a part of something important and groundbreaking
- Clear objectives and a chance to take the ball and run with it
- Special privileges
- Feeling involved and feeling a part of something important.
- Job security & peace of mind
- Being able to use one's gifts, talents and potential

We've all seen the person that just comes to work and goes through the motions with minimal effort. It may not all be the employee's fault. Take the time and effort to figure out what will make the difference for this person. No, I'm not talking about coddling, I'm talking about treating someone with respect and in a way that you would want to be treated if you had some issues. I don't want to hear about how tough your bosses of the past were on you. That doesn't solve a thing. Move on!

8.   Communication. This relates closely to many of the points in this chapter, but it is critical in managing people. Too many managers do a very poor job of communicating their intentions, reasoning, wishes, purpose and specific needs or expectations. Employees need and want to know what is expected of them and you didn't hire your people because they were mind readers. Be specific about what you want from your people. How do you train your people or ask them to carry out an assignment? Does it usually work? Have you ever seen a boss who has some vague vision or idea of how they want something to look? It might be a particular wall display. It might have been a special written presentation or project. Sometimes, the boss is pretty lousy at explaining what he or she wants, or his or her patience for explaining anything stinks. The boss may have even had a clear idea of what he wanted and couldn't communicate it, or maybe he didn't know what he wanted at all, but he couldn't or wouldn't admit it. The bottom line is that communication isn't succeeding. A lesser manager might blurt out in frustration, "I don't KNOW, just get it done!" or, "Isn't that what I'm paying you to do?" Do not become one of those bosses. I think we all know that it is demoralizing for employees to come back to the boss, proud of the job they've done, only to be told by the boss it's all wrong or have to watch the boss re-do the work in question. I've seen a lot of managers who don't get what they want out of their employees at times because

they assume the employee knows or understands what they know.

If an employee gets a request wrong in a large company, the wasted time, effort and materials may be insignificant; however, when it's your business, the wasted time and money hurts a lot more. Owners and managers who get the best out of their people are good at getting their expectations across clearly. A good manager who wants to get things right with their people with little or no waste of time will work to improve their skills in this area. My idea for this starts and stands for the word R.E.T.A.I.L.

Recognize exactly what it is you want done before you make the request of anyone else. Too many managers finally realize and decide what they want after they see the first results come back from the employee's efforts. Be specific about the actual results you want. Rather than expecting your employee(s) to simply work blindly on tasks they don't totally understand, a good manager takes the time to explain what the project is all about and how it will all work into a final result.

Employ the right employee for the task you want done. Is this something they can achieve with the skills and talents they have? Is there some other employee who really should be doing this job? Are you sending a pup to do a dog's job?

Time Specific tasks are preferable. Set a clear time or deadline for getting the job done.

Actionable and achievable requests are a much better starting point. Do you just want something done NOW, whether you know what that is or not? It needs to be an actionable situation that can be solved or accomplished by someone else.

Information is key. Does the employee have the information or a way to know how they are doing, especially if the job will take some period of time? Is there some point of reference for you to find out if they're on track? Part of being sure they have the right information is to check on their progress when possible. Let the employee do the work without standing over their shoulder, but checking on their progress can prevent a lot of wasted time for both of you.

Look Like What, Exactly? Know what the result should look like. Can you describe to your people exactly what you want to see when they are done? How will they know they've accomplished the mission? You need to describe the result you want when the job is done rather than the job or activity you want them to do. There is a big difference between these two!

Keeping these six points in mind when giving any employee an assignment will give you a much better shot at getting the results you want, when you want them. If you hear yourself saying, "What I meant was," or, "I thought we had shown you how to do this?" after good time has been spent on a project, you still need some work. Try keeping R.E.T.A.I.L. in the back of your mind.

9.   Consider using visual aids and articles. Place these in easily seen locations to affect how employees see the real world and your business world. Yes, we've all seen and laughed at certain motivational posters and articles out there from our past, but these can be more beneficial than you might think. The use of attractive and eye-catching notices or bulletin boards that cover attitudes, motivation, creativity, leadership and goals are subjects that eventually do sink in with some employees.

10.   Consider each employee's age and over all phase in his or her life. Employees nearing the end of their careers are often

less motivated by a chance at promotion than others who are just starting out. This does not mean the older workers are less important. It just means that there may be other things they value more. New and younger employees may also be less patient and more demanding for change and new opportunities then older employees.

11.   Corrections, and compliments too. If you continually correct and chastise your people, you've got to understand that while they may be learning how to do the job, they may also be learning to dislike you and the job (and maybe even themselves). You can't continually focus on the negatives without recognizing some positives. As a matter of fact, some motivational experts will tell you it takes about 8–10 compliments and positive acknowledgements to offset one major correction or scolding. If you don't practice the more positive side of teaching and correcting with (sincerity), you WILL end up with people who are less than motivated and probably looking elsewhere for a different position. After that happens, where have all your corrections gotten you?

12.   Listening, REALLY listening. Yes, I know I just mentioned communication, but too many bosses will say that they communicate just fine—and many do, but communication is a two way street, so I am breaking out listening as a skill all by itself. We all can hear, but often we don't listen to what is said, what is meant and what is being said between the lines. Part of listening is looking into people's eyes and noting their body language. If you are going to be an effective boss and a boss for whom your people want to perform well, you must listen to them and understand their needs and concerns. And remember, you can't **ever** do this over a cell phone, text message or email.

13.   Celebrate together & remember birthdays and employment anniversaries. Look for good reasons to celebrate, and recognize your people whenever possible. When your

store achieves certain objectives or surpasses some major milestone, everyone on the staff needs to celebrate that fact. A little special attention and recognition for a birthday or time served is also appreciated. For example, try celebrating with a special lunch or evening gathering and recognition for everyone who's been with you two years or longer. All of this contributes to building a team atmosphere. I once had a boss who went out himself and picked a unique, personal gift for each and every employee each year for Christmas. He even did his own wrapping. Do you think his people thought he was special? He also had 42 employees.

14. Be aware of religious and cultural diversity. No boss should assume his employee is Christian, Jewish or any other faith. Christians must understand that Yom Kippur is an important date for the Jewish (with no questions asked). You cannot assume that your employees have the same cultural background or religious background as you do. You must respect their traditions, especially when making up schedules.

15. Be a turtle when it comes to whining. Let it run off your back. Some people do it as a matter of habit no matter what is going on. Just be sure that the whiners and complainers feel appreciated too, and you may find that there is nothing more that needs to be addressed. Some people will always be whiners. You're best bet here is to have a private conversation over the general effect they have on everyone else when they do carry on too much.

16. There must be consequences, but punishing people is not usually the answer. You can't expect morale to be great when poor performers are allowed to become "slackers" in front of everyone else. You've got to deal with it. But you can't discipline employees in front of their peers or treat them poorly. Taking away privileges, making working conditions worse or ruining the entire working atmosphere out of anger, are not good solutions. In fact, this approach will more likely

backfire for you. I'm sure we all agree there should be some consequences over the long haul for those that don't do the job or deliver, when needed, but it should come more in the form of conducting a corrective interview and adding a signed notice to their file.

17. Money isn't always the answer. Again, money does not motivate everyone. If your people are being paid a fair wage and still seem uninterested in taking things up a notch, money may not be the answer, and offering more money to them will probably not do the trick. While too little income will always make most workers feel undervalued and unappreciated, some people will never be motivated to do their best simply for more money. In addition, the same person may be less affected by money at different times, depending on their current personal issues.

18. Flexible work hours, within reason. Make clear to your staff you'll work with them in terms of schedule flexibility if they will let you know in advance what days they need off. Consider offering a surprise bonus day (especially on a unusually slow day) to someone who has worked especially hard without reward. Little touches like these add up when it comes to earning employee loyalty over the long haul.

19. Get the facts, Jack. I've certainly been guilty here. You come back to the business after being gone for an afternoon or a weekend and the assignment you gave was not carried out or finished. You're ready for someone to pay (sometimes it's taken out on whoever is closest). But you've got to get the facts. Someone could have called in sick. Maybe something was missing to get the job done. Maybe your store actually got too busy with customers. You can't always imagine the reasons that things didn't happen, but you've got to find out. If you make it a habit of not getting the facts before taking it out on the person or the staff too often, you will create a dark cloud over your store's atmosphere.

20.   Favoritism raising its ugly head. Have you ever noticed a boss who has his or her favorites? There is nothing wrong with having favorites. That is human. What is wrong is managing and treating people in a way that obviously displays your favorites. If you've ever been one of the employees who watches your boss treat one employee like his pal, you know how it can affect your attitude, especially when it comes to different work expectations from the boss. I had a boss who would spend hours behind closed doors with someone heavily favored. I had another who would regularly take one or two employees who should have been working on a Sunday to a professional football game instead, while everyone else was expected to work. Once you show you have obvious favorites, you will lose credibility with your people, along with their respect. Often, besides the obvious problems that arise directly from such treatment, your favoritism will also hurt you in many ways that you may never be aware of or even notice. This is not a problem for your employees to deal with. This is YOUR problem, especially since you are creating it.

21.   Watch your supervisors and their relationships with their employees. Many employees will leave a business—not because they're unhappy with the job itself —but because of a poor supervisor who doesn't know how to train or how to treat his or her people (especially in your absence). Often, when good employees or even good salespeople are promoted into management jobs, they go on little power trips and turn out to be terrible managers. I have seen some great employees who just can't manage. Many good employees have been screwed up by promoting them beyond where they should be. Whether you have one manager or multiple stores, watch your store managers for higher turnover, even if you've always known them as a great employee in the past. Maybe they need to read this book.

> *"We have a belief that our guests will only receive the kind of treatment we want them to receive if the cast members receive that same kind of treatment from their managers."*
>
> **Walt Disney World, Handbook**

22. Reward ideas and deeds. Try to think about rewards you have been given and how you felt when you received them. You can also think about rewards you've seen others get and which ones of those that you might have liked to receive. Try to work on a list of possible rewards for each of your people (possibly customized where appropriate). Look for reasons to give some type of reward each week if possible, regardless of how insignificant it might be to you. It may only be a $10.00 gift card, but people in general really do like working for bosses that reward and recognize.

23. Respect personal limitations. Everyone has limitations in their talents and abilities. Don't always assume your people can do what you can do. Often an employee's personal limitations can prevent him or her from doing what you would consider a top-notch job. Remember, in retailing as well as other fields, there are those that are capable of becoming stars as well as those that are in this job because they will never be artists or rocket scientists. Remember that not everyone is manager or supervisor material. Often, even those who are, don't always want the responsibility. But they're still good people to have on your staff.

Regardless, you must try to recognize and weed out the type of people you don't want on your team during the interview process. Then you must reward the people who can deliver with the talent they have. Desire and work ethic should also be rewarded as well. Some people will never be the best, but they may be trying harder than anyone on your staff.

Remember, the rest of your staff notices how you treat your people, and they will respect *or disrespect* you based on the way you treat *all* employees.

24.   Use performance appraisals wisely. Do not focus only on the areas of poor or inadequate performance. Concentrating only on shortcomings and not talking about the positives of an employee does not motivate. If an employee feels like you only see the bad things in them, then their attitude becomes "why bother?" A performance review should be more of a balance between suggestions for improvement and positive remarks.

25.   Look at "pay for performance." Pay for performance can be quite successful, especially as opposed to giving mediocre raises based on seniority or time on the job. A great employee who is new and excited may need to be rewarded sooner for doing a great job. On the other hand, an employee who has been around for years and is bored to death may have once been a great performer, but now feels stifled by his or her work. Just remember that some employees value security so much that being paid by performance *only* can feel like too much pressure for some people. (This is one reason why everyone isn't a salesperson.)

26.   Surveys can be good for employees, too. Consider doing your own informal survey to gauge the morale of your workforce. Ask your staff as a group to let you know in writing or in person what motivates them. If you have a close relationship with your people, you may already know.

27.   Hiding your lack of people skills behind technology. More and more managers are relying on emails, cell phones, text messages and voice mails to deal with people because many of them do not know how to relate one-on-one to real people, especially in person. Don't hide your lack of people skills by continually dealing with your people through technology.

Technology is important in today's business world, but not at the expense of developing a relationship with your people.

28.   Don't reprimand your people for what you mistakenly assumed they should know. Have you ever found yourself saying, "How could you not know _____?" or, "You should have known_____." As owners/managers we often assume that our people think and reason as we would do or that they know much more than they actually know. Maybe you've been in retailing forever and many of the things that come almost naturally to you, are not so obvious to your employees. Regardless, things can look very different through less experienced eyes! Chastising someone for your mistaken assumptions can lead to a disgruntled or even less confident employee the next time around. Before long, some or all of your people are afraid to act or do anything. I don't think you want to develop employees who are just trying to stay out of the way, avoid decisions, or taking action. Remember the benefits of an empowered employee?

29.   Be open to change, even if it comes from your people. If you have a hard time with change, you don't belong in business. Not being open to change can be a major mistake. Everything is not supposed to be done the way it's always been done. There aren't too many things that can't be improved upon, especially in the business world. Do not cling to your supposed tried-and-true methods in all cases. Take a look at things with an open mind and truly and fairly evaluate new ideas.

"When two men in business always agree, one of them is unnecessary."
—William Wrigley, Jr.

30.   Take responsibility. Being the boss means taking responsibility. I've known a few too many management people who were masters at delegating blame as well as everything else. Everyone knows you're the boss and you can blame

whomever you want, but deep down inside everyone knows who's really calling the shots. If something goes wrong under your supervision, be a leader instead of a weenie. Eventually, avoiding your share of blame or responsibility will catch up with you in one way or the other. Even if you are the owner and there is no one above you to know the truth, there is still a price to pay through the loss of respect and morale from your people.

> Give each person the encouragement or motivation to grow and excel in their own areas of responsibility. Some employees may never have the talent to be the best at anything they try to do for you. Consequently some of your people should compete against they're own record, not other employees. The idea is to constantly work to improve their personal best.

In Conclusion:

Keep in mind that more motivation isn't always the ticket to a better and happier employee. My own experience has been that a sincere, personal one-on-one conversation can go a long way toward resolving many situations. Those people who have almost always performed better for me have done it because they liked me as opposed to fearing me. There is **nothing** wrong with creating a friendship with your people.

If you haven't gotten anywhere with your efforts, it may have nothing to do with your management. If an employee is not happy doing what he or she was hired to do, or they would much rather be somewhere else, there may be nothing you can do other than encourage them to find some greener more suitable grass elsewhere.

One last thing that I always asked myself about an employee before dealing with a negative situation:

Does this person care about me or this company?

Do they have my/our best interest at heart?

Or, do they not care about this company, this job or me at all?

It was always much easier for me to overlook mistakes and try harder to find a way to save a person if I felt that the answer was that they cared.

 Some Last Words Of Advice . . .

The following little bits of advice have no relationship to each other. If I had the chance to sit down one-on-one with my own daughter or son to give a few pieces of advice prior to opening a business, the following might be what I would say:

Set Up an Advisory Group
Some people call it a Master Mind group or Power Circle. Businesses have benefited for years from groups like this. Ideally, your group should include people such as a CPA, other managers or owners of businesses, an attorney, retired executives and other civic movers and shakers. Many of these people may serve because they are friends or they are interested or just honored to help. GKIC or Glazer-Kennedy Insiders Circle is an excellent organization with business groups all over the country. This is a great place to begin or become a part an advisory group. (GlazerKennedyInsidersCircle.com or dankennedy.com)

A good goal would be to meet about four times a year to cover issues and decisions important to your business. The idea, obviously, is to draw on the experience and different perspectives that come from each of these people, who will hopefully be very objective about their advice and suggested alternatives. While you are not obligated to listen and the final decision is yours, the idea is to get insight and perspective from some professional or experienced outsiders. It would also be helpful if some of them were part of your target market.

Raise the Bar to Be in Your Business or
Find a Competitive Advantage

Again, many businesses fail because they really haven't differentiated themselves in the marketplace. Everyone seems to think that if they put a sign up and do the same thing the guy down the street is doing, people will come to them. You can't survive and thrive any longer by just doing a good job or by doing it almost as well as the next guy. Something must make you unique and special. Some people call it a USP or Unique Selling Proposition, but find **something** and hold on to it. The good news for you is that most small retailers try to find the cheapest common denominator to enter their marketplace. If they were going to be a little jeweler, they'd get some lighted, lockable counters and maybe some nice lighting and then they'd buy the jewelry that they thought would sell the best. But, if you did the same, what will be different or special about your jewelry business over anyone else's? Why will throngs of people beat your door down? The idea here is it to create something that few retailers can't or never will even attempt to copy. If you can do that, then you might have something! And, once you do that, you will probably even be able to charge more for it. The harder it is to copy, and the more expensive it becomes to try it, the more other businesses will resist attempting to do what you do. But find something. When you figure out how to do it, guard that special knowledge or secret with your life.

AGAIN—Pay Great Attention to Customer Service

You can survive when you offer the most expensive product or service available if you also have outstanding customer service or provide a unique one-of-a-kind consumer experience. You will always have business. Have you ever heard a business owner say that customer service is NOT important to them? I doubt it, but if it's so important to everyone that my question is laughable, then why is customer service worse in this country than ever? Why is good customer service such a rare find?

I will guarantee you that many businesses have failed and that many are failing right now due to poor customer service and a boss who is clueless about this fact. The boss either has no idea what good customer service is or he/she is living in another world apart from the reality of what goes on every day in his or her business. Think about this again . . . your customer service policies can make or break you. Yes, not all customers are going to choose service over price, and it may not pay or be appreciated in every case, but you're in this business for the long haul, not for one transaction. And most customers will appreciate it and love you for it. By offering truly exceptional customer service, you can and will win business away from retailers who don't seem to care.

Work On Your Business as Well as In Your Business

Michael Gerber, the famous E-Myth author, says most business owners spend way too much time working in their business rather than on their business. That maybe true for some, but my viewpoint is that too many retailers don't spend enough time in their business at all! Don't find too many excuses to be out of your store. If you dislike your business so much or you feel you have better things to be doing all of the time, you need to sell it or shut it down. Your own people can tell if you're really not into your business and it shows up everywhere, especially with customers. There's nothing wrong with working "on" your business so that you don't get bogged down with mundane day-to-day tasks that anyone could do. Just be sure that your not fooling yourself into believing that your time on the golf course or at home means your mind is working on the big picture.

Join at Least One or Two Trade Associations

Aside from the usual benefits of networking connections, these organizations can also offer a variety of information that you should be able to use. This can include sales figures, applicable services as well as new products and industry trends. Generally these associations provide certificates or wall plaques that show your membership or some kind of approval by your association with the organization. If you're given a membership certificate or wall plaque, you should display it conspicuously on a store wall. Displaying these at your business site in full view of customers gives them the warm fuzzies and assures them that you're for real.

Pay Your Employees and Pay Your Taxes When Due

A wise lawyer once told me, if you pay anyone, pay your employees and your taxes. Don't jack around with people's paychecks. Pay them the day they're due and even the hour you usually pay and no later. Make your payroll taxes on time, especially the portion that you withhold from your employee's paychecks. And come hell or high water, PAY THE IRS. Again . . . PAY THE IRS. They can and will come after you. They can and will hold you personally liable, including for any penalties due. Even with a corporation or LLC, you WILL be personally liable to pay all back payroll taxes. *Can I make myself any more clear here?*

Have a Passion and Extend That Passion

You really can make a difference in your business and the lives of your employees if you can show your people how what they do matters to you, their families, your customers and your company. A little thank-you speech or a note on the bulletin board once in a while doesn't cut it. It has to be done in your conversations and actions every day in the stockroom, the parking lot, the sales floor, an email, a card or even a handwritten note. It also has to be done through honest, well planned and thought out employee evaluations, incentives, rewards and, yes, benefits when possible. And if you tell me benefits aren't realistic right now, that's fine, but everything else IS possible and do-able.

Consider Drafting Your Spouse into the Business

If you can get your spouse to work at least once in a while with you in your business, the situation can be invaluable to both of you in the long run. No one else probably cares more about the success of your business then your spouse. He or she is a person you can trust and they can bring another perspective to the business. Another plus is that if your spouse works somewhere else and has little or nothing to do with your business, you may wish he or she had been more involved some day in the future. Besides giving your spouse a taste of your life at work, you really need him or her somewhat familiar with certain aspects of your business just in case something happens to you. Your spouse should at least know key people you're working with, including your accountant, attorney, key suppliers, and also know about ongoing issues that concern him/her. It's probably not a bad idea for him/her to know which key employees can be trusted too. Yes, it may be inconvenient and a pain in the neck now; however, the long-term benefits are there.

Understand That Employees Will Never Think About Your Business Like You Do

They do not own your business! **<u>You</u>** do! Your employees don't worry or think like you do. They're worried about what they're doing tonight. You're worried about where that shipment is. They think, "Thank Goodness it's Friday." You're thinking, "Where did the week go? I didn't get enough done." Your employees think, "When will that last customer get out of here so I can go on my date?" You're thinking, "Why aren't my evening sales better?" They're wondering why they can't get a raise sooner. You're concerned about getting your utility bill down. The bottom line is not to ever expect your people to think about your store or worry about it like you do--and should! In fact, their agenda will often clash with yours, even if it's not apparent.

Put Agreements in Writing

Even when you think it may not be necessary, it's really a good idea to put almost everything in writing. Verbal agreements seem to have a tendency to be remembered differently depending on whose ox is getting gored when you have no proof of anything. Obviously leases, rental agreements and storage agreements are usually in writing and should be. Anything worth more than a couple of hundred dollars should probably be handled in writing. All services should be handled with written receipts, deposits and purchase orders given and received as much as possible. If you're in doubt, or if there is a small chance of something coming up at a later date as an issue, put it in writing.

Get Signed Mechanics Liens

It is very easy to get burned by this one. I did even though I was fully aware of the potential exposure. First of all a mechanics lien is a legally enforceable claim which a contractor or person can make against the title to a property. In my case, I had hired a contractor whom I had already worked with before to do remodeling work in leased retail space I was preparing to move into. As the work was performed by the plumber and electrician, I asked for and received lien waivers indicating that each contractor had been paid for their work and they waived any right to a claim on the property. So far so good. Even though the property was not mine, I was aware of the fact that a contractor could lay claim to the title on this property if they were not paid for their work. This would mean that my landlord would have a lien placed on his property. Unfortunately, the landlord can then come after their tenant (me) for the money according to their lease. I thought I was covered, but later on down the line, I found out that my contractor had bought a lot of materials for my remodel for which he had never paid. I had paid the contractor, but had missed asking the contractor for a lien waiver on the materials. The contractor declared bankruptcy about a year after my job and the materials were never paid for, so the supplier went after my landlord to protect themselves and make sure they were paid. The end result was the supplier filed a mechanics lien on the landlord's property and the landlord came after me. I got burned for a total of $5,000, not to mention having the embarrassment of my landlord coming after me for a lien caused by my remodel.

Remember: While You're Building a Business You're Building a Reputation
Pay your bills when they're due and conduct yourself and your business ethically. The goodwill and benefits you will gain via reputation, trust and credit outweigh any downsides of doing anything else. Again, pay your bills and your taxes on time and keep your word.

Employ Your Children
Your children should be more reliable and trustworthy than others you might hire (if they're not, you have other issues). It's also one way for you to be sure they learn some important concepts. Aside from spending a bit more time around mom or dad, children under 18 don't have to pay Social Security taxes or unemployment taxes if they

make under a specified amount. With this and the IRS in mind, you can employ your underage children to work for you, whether you're a sole proprietor, partnership or a corporation. For more details, check out IRS.gov.

Work on Building Your Credit

Very few business owners ever really think about credit or consciously building their credit rating with area bankers, even though it's a smart practice that can pay off down the line when you really need it. The time to actually work on building your credit is when you don't need it, which is why it gets shoved down the priority list to never-never addressed. One way to do this is to consider borrowing from your bank every six months or so, while things are going well and your cash flow is decent. When you do borrow, you can place the funds in an interest bearing account and then repay it a little before it's due. While you may pay a small price for doing this now, you are increasing your odds and potential to borrow when you really need it down the line.

When Estimating Your Financial Needs, Plan Carefully . . . Then Add More Money

You may think you've carefully planned for your business's money needs, but you really can't know. Add some cushion to the cushion you already think you have. If you've estimated incorrectly and inadequately, you'll most likely have a very tough time going back to investors or the bank for more later, not to mention the fact you'll already look like a schmuck early in the game. You won't believe the costs that you never anticipated. It might be freight costs or shipping costs you didn't count on. It might be for a piece of equipment you never anticipated needing. It might be something in your lease that bit you in the rear. Take any of these issues and then multiply them 2-3 times or more and you'll probably be getting closer to the amount you should plan to have.

If You Have a Great Business Concept That
Meets the Challenges Outlined in This Book,
Don't Worry about the Economy

If you're going to be innovative or provide a real benefit to people, doing it during a downturn can actually provide some advantages, including an oversupply of cheaper retail space for lease. Talented and qualified labor becomes easier to find. Another special benefit if you can start a company during a recession is that you'll already know how to operate with minimal capital and your conservative business plans will be based on being very efficient and frugal. You're not spoiled on large, bloated budgets that need to be cut. As the recession ends and business increases, you may find yourself looking at the extra business as gravy, rather than being so needy of the funds.

Have Some Ethics as an Employer

Ethical behavior is about your own personal integrity, and it has everything to do with what you know deep down in your heart to be right or wrong. If you don't demonstrate ethics in your own daily decisions and activities, who will?

Ethics has to start with you (the owner). Your own unethical behavior is noticed and becomes contagious at times as your employees look to you as the leader. Employees who have ethical concerns after noticing your questionable behavior or dishonesty do pass it on to other employees (whether your business is large or small) either by word or by action. If or when this type of conduct becomes closer to the norm, employee morale and respect goes downhill, along with respect for personal possessions and store property. On top of that, employee loyalty is lost. However, the big problem is more likely to be flat out resentment and distrust as trust between boss and employee, or even between employees, is severely harmed. As I've already discussed, showing favoritism through preferential treatment is another big ethical mistake and happens all too often with bosses who actually believe they are fair owners or managers.

"The most important persuasion tool you have in your entire arsenal is integrity."

—Zig Ziglar

CONCLUSION . . . . .

At the beginning of the book, we talked about the challenges of retailing today as well as the importance of learning from other retailers. Make yourself a student of all things "retail." Again, no one has all of the best ideas and you never know when one idea from one retailer and one idea from another, coupled with your own imagination will turn into something really exciting and profitable.

If you had been the creator and first retailer of ice cream 20 or 30 years ago, and you had no ideas or vision for taking the business somewhere, all might have been lost. If your invention of the ice cream had been limited by your own laziness, or if you expected everyone to be excited about your product without your own enthusiasm and passion, you probably wouldn't have gotten too far. What if your idea for ice cream was limited to licorice flavored ice cream only, and that was as far as your imagination went? What if you hadn't been out in the world observing how pies, cookies, and candy were retailed, or if your idea was limited by the fact that you had never observed another retailer using sprinkles or chocolate on their products? Your odds for success would have been further reduced.

You see, your imagination and wisdom are directly linked to your own observations and experiences. If you aren't aware of trends or what else is going on in the world of retailing, you are at great disadvantage. What if you were in a small town somewhere, and you had never seen or heard of shopping malls or shopping centers? Wouldn't your knowledge of good traffic and great locations have held your potential back?

Taking this a step further, what if you had done most of these things right, but your retail idea for ice cream had been coupled with a lack of respect for your employees or customers? You would have failed! Most significantly, if someone else out there had seen your ice cream idea and had incorporated the missing elements above, it all would have been taken away from you and been made a success by someone else!

We also talked about the importance of building your business on your strengths and leaving the low hanging fruit to the likes of Wal-Mart. You must concern yourself with doing the best possible job with YOUR business. There is nothing you can do about anyone else's business. The best retailers locate themselves right smack in the middle of heavy competition, because they want to be where the customers are and they are confident in their ability to get their share and more of the pie.

Inventive, eye-catching merchandising that is capable of generating very profitable sales for your store will always be a challenge. This why you must constantly, AND I MEAN CONSTANTLY, give your merchandise presentation serious attention. It truly is trial and error. And if it is NOT your forte, then you MUST find someone who can do it for you. There is NO excuse for just another "me-too" store out there!

Customer service was emphasized throughout this book and with good reason. Customer service in this country stinks. And that is great news for you and anyone that wants to have "a line out the front of their *own* store." It makes it all that much easier for you to begin to distinguish yourself. Just keep in mind, you will not build a following of advocates on your stores behalf by just improving a return policy or handling some customers a little better. You need to take it as far as possible to be really noticed! You need to think constantly about what your people and your store can do to "create the experience."

I believe if you've learned anything from this book, it is that people matter. Regardless of what else you can or can't do in your business, you *can* have good people. Good people who are treated well, coupled with good policies, make for good customer service. It is within your control and it is critical. Part of having good people and good customers means that good ethics become a part of your daily habits and mission. No matter what type of business or retail shop you are trying to build, if you don't have a solid foundation built on ethics, you might as well be building on quick sand. Your lack of ethics will catch up with you at some point. There is an old quote, "When you've got them by the balls, their hearts and minds will follow." I would say, "While their hearts and minds may follow, *they* will not truly *be* with you, and when you no longer have *them* by the balls, everything and everyone will turn on you like a pack of wild dogs."

Remember, whether you're getting ready to open a store or if you've been in business for a while and you don't feel like your getting anywhere, you must understand that there must be a compelling reason for your store to exist. This is aside from the fact that you decided to open a store in order to make a living. Customers these days have ZERO tolerance for the ordinary. What will you do to make your store a "must" for customers in your market and product category? Again I ask, "Why would anyone in this day and age, pay the high rent and deal with all of the grief a retailer must deal with, and then just open another mediocre "me too" store?" If you believe your store is currently the best place for the consumer to shop now, my question is twofold.

1. Does everyone else agree with your assessment?

2. If it's true, then what are you doing to let everyone know about it?

If you can't tell me right now what your store is doing better than anyone, then chances are your customers don't have any idea what you do best also. Find that one thing that you do better than anyone in your market area and begin building a list. Then create another "best" and add to that list.

327

First and foremost in any successful business, you've got to have a vision for what you want. If you can't see it, feel it and put it into words so that others understand what you want and what you are trying to do, you're wasting your time. And once you have that vision, if you are not wildly passionate about it, you will most likely not do what it takes to put forth the extreme effort necessary to get the job done. If you've had a retail shop for years and this book has inspired you to try some new ideas and tactics, you will still need to have that passion and belief in order to make the changes necessary. A half-hearted toe in the water won't cut it. You've got to jump in all the way and commit.

Remember, there is no one formula or special secret for building a successful retail business. Your success is dependent on many important areas that all require your attention, but if you can improve or succeed with the ideas and concepts in this book, you can be a first rate retailer with a lot to be proud of. With everything we did cover in the book, we did not cover the important management of your expenses. You cannot spend yourself into oblivion and survive, but that topic will have to wait for another book. One thing that should be noted, those who have survived and excelled as a group, practice the following:

They take responsibility for their stores and are actively involved in their management.

They look outside the box and often ask why something can't be done better or differently.

They are totally committed to carrying out their vision, no matter the cost or what it entails. They don't give up. Never, Never Never. . . !

They accept failures as part of the business, especially with regard to merchandising and product selection. They learn from each mistake and move on.

They love what they were doing!

Don't let your store become a downer. Find a way to keep the fun in what you're doing and re-energize yourself from time to time to insure that your love for what you're doing is contagious to your employees and your customers! Good Luck! And as any good retailer would say, "Thanks and we appreciated your patronage! Come back again."

"Always do right—this will gratify some and astonish the rest."

—Mark Twain

Rich would be delighted to speak at your next meeting, convention or conference. For more information on consultations or events, you can contact Rich at Retail Redefined, 636-928-2336 or richlgordon@ retailrichez.com, or visit his website at retailrichez.com.

SOURCE MATERIAL

Clark, Maxine. *The Bear Necessities of Business: Building a Company with Heart*. John Wiley & Sons, 2006. Print.

"Consumer Reports National Research Center." *Consumer Reports: Expert Product Reviews and Product Ratings from Our Test Labs*. 2007. Web. 11 Aug. 2010. <http://www.consumerreports.org/cro/how-we-test/consumer-reports-national-research-center/overview/index.htm>.

"Corporate History." *Sears Holdings Corporation*. Web. 11 May 2010. <http://www.searsholdings.com/>.

CSM eMagazine -http://www.customerservicemanager.com

Gershman, Michael. "Tupper Ware Party Line." *Getting It Right the Second Time: How American Ingenuity Transformed Forty-nine Marketing Failures into Some of Our Most Successful Products*. Reading, MA: Addison-Wesley Pub., 1990. Print.

Milliman, R.E. "Using Background Music to Affect the Behavior of Supermarket Shoppers", Milliman, R.E. *Journal of Marketing*, 46 (1982): 86-92.

Muzak Study, 1991 "Business Music: a merchandising tool for the retail industry" Muzak LLC "Congruency of scent and music as a driver of in-store evaluations and behavior" Matilla, A. and Wirtz, J., *Journal of Retailing*, 77 (2001), 273-289

"Online Catalogue." *Williams-Sonoma, Inc. - Welcome*. Web. 11 Feb. 2010. <http://www.williams-sonomainc.com/>.

Pendergrast, Mark. *For God, Country, and Coca-Cola: the Definitive History of the Great American Soft Drink and the Company That Makes It*. New York: Basic, 2000. Print.

Schonfeld, Eric. *TechCrunch*. Forrester Research, 8 Mar. 2010. Web. 11 Aug. 2010. <http://www.techcrunch.com/>.

Schwartz, Barry. *The Paradox of Choice: Why More Is Less.* New York: Ecco, 2004. Print.

Silverstein, Michael J. and Fiske, Neil. Trading Up, Portfolio, a member of the Penguin Group (USA) Inc. Copyright, The Boston Consulting group, Inc. 2003, 3005

Stern, Neil and Ander, Willard. Greentailing and Other Revolutions in Retail. John Wiley & Sons Sept 2008

"TARP Worldwide Inc. | Arlington, VA | Company Profile, Research, News, Information, Contacts." *Goliath: Business Knowledge On Demand.* White House Office of Consumer Affairs. Web. 18 Apr. 2010.

Young, Jeffrey, and William Simon. *ICon, Steve Jobs, The Greatest Second Act in the History of Business.* John Wiley & Sons, 2005. *Wiley::Home.* Web. 12 Oct. 2009. <http://www.wiley.com/WileyCDA/WileyTitle/productCd-0471720836.html>.

USEFUL LINKS

◆ allbusiness.com critically acclaimed business information site on any number of topics including retail
◆ entrepreneur.com variety of tips and information for small business from the people who bring you Entrepreneur Magazine
◆ hrdailyadvisor.blr.com Practical Human Resource Tips, News Advice
◆ marketvolt.com e-mail marketing firm offers easy to use software at an affordable price that allows retailers to create branded, scheduled and auto-response emails with tracking capabilities
◆ National Retail Federation nrf.com
◆ sba.gov/smallbusinessplanner/index.html US. Small Business Administration, programs and services to help start, grow and succeed
◆ Tradeshow information tradeshowweek.com/directory/index.asp
◆ retail.about.com Very helpful site aimed strictly at retailers
◆ successmagazine.com Entrepreneurial website covering a variety of topics